ZHU YUANZHANG
AND EARLY MING LEGISLATION

SINICA LEIDENSIA

VOLUME XXXIV

TUTA SUB AEGIDE PALLAS · 1683 ·

ZHU YUANZHANG AND EARLY MING LEGISLATION

THE REORDERING OF CHINESE SOCIETY FOLLOWING THE ERA OF MONGOL RULE

BY

EDWARD L. FARMER

E.J. BRILL
LEIDEN · NEW YORK · KÖLN
1995

The paper in this book meets the guidelines for permanence and durability of the Committee on Production Guidelines for Book Longevity of the Council on Library Resources.

Library of Congress Cataloging-in-Publication Data

Die Deutsche Bibliothek – CIP-Einheitsaufnahme

The CIP data has been applied for.

ISSN 0169-9563
ISBN 90 04 10391 0

PRINTED IN THE NETHERLANDS

For Judy

CONTENTS

PREFACE

In the preface to my first book I noted that it took a decade to complete the journey from dissertation to monograph. This book has taken twice as long. The early career challenges I then confronted—learning to teach, gaining tenure, raising children, and repairing a late Guangxu-era house—gave way to other distractions. The children are grown and writing manuscripts of their own; the house has been remodeled by professionals. Editing a journal, chairing a department, advising graduate students, and expanding my horizons to comparative early modern and world history have all slowed the progress of the second monograph.

This study began as an effort to understand how the founding of the Ming dynasty influenced the course of modern Chinese history. I assumed that the creation of a strong imperial state must have had a profound impact on social and cultural life. I was also curious about how the imperial state's role might have changed as its vigor declined and other forces asserted themselves. My goal was to move forward from study of the dynastic founding to investigate the largely-ignored fifteenth century. The first step was to be a study of the social legislation of the early Ming dynasty, the founder's blueprint for the new social order. I hoped the inquiry would provide a baseline for exploration of the "black hole" of the middle Ming. Since the mid-1970s I have worked on translating and analyzing a number of Zhu Yuanzhang's codifications and pronouncements on social order. Preliminary thoughts on the problems discussed here have been explored in conference papers and articles, the most important of which are cited in the text. This study, and the translations appended to it, sum up what I have done so far. I am not optimistic about my ability to complete the task. The first monograph took ten years, and the second, twenty years. According to this curve, the third monograph might be projected to take thirty years (by adding one more decade) or even forty years (by doubling each time). In either case I doubt that I will make it.

My approach to the Ming founder's social legislation makes little effort to place the codes in the context of Chinese legal history. Nevertheless, I hope that the translations will be of some utility to students of the law. I also regret to report that Yang Yifan's studies of Chinese codes and of the *Grand Pronouncement* came to my attention only after most of the writing was done. I have put some citations in the text to alert readers to their existence but have not fully expoited all they have to offer. Mention should also be made of William C. Jones' new translation, *The Great Qing Code* (Oxford: Clarendon Press, 1994). It will greatly advance the study of

Chinese law. Unfortunately it arrived too late to be consulted in the preparation of this manuscript .

The bulk of the work was carried out during a sabbatical leave in 1984-85 when I was fortunate enough to hold a fellowship from the Wang Institute of Graduate Studies. I would like to take this opportunity to express my profound gratitude to the Wang Institute for their generous support. I also wish to acknowledge support received upon a number of occasions from the Graduate School of the University of Minnesota.

The intellectual debts I have accrued in the course of this study cannot be adequately expressed in the spare citations of scholarly publications. I have benefited enormously from discussing and arguing with my closest colleagues, Ann Waltner and Romeyn Taylor. Professor Taylor was kind enough to read and comment on an earlier version of this study. I am also grateful for the constructive, encouraging, and sometimes detailed, comments of several anonymous readers. I have learned a great deal from graduate students, particularly Chang Jerlang, Ho Yun-yi, Lin Tai-yung, Anita Andrew, John Ness, Hsu Pi-ching, Jennifer Downs, Yao Yusheng and Jiang Yonglin. My greatest debt is to Jiang Yonglin who arrived as a visiting scholar at the Law School just as I was struggling to revise the translations which are appended to the text.

Over the years I got support and encouragement from many quarters. Brian McKnight, Kwang-Ching Liu, the late Robert Somers, and James D. Tracy invited me to give conference papers and Denis Twitchett asked me to submit a contribution to a symposium on Chinese law. Portions of this latter article, which appeared in *Asia Major*, are encorporated into the text as are some tables and bits of language from my other articles. Encouragement and help of various kinds was received from Stephen Young, Wallace Johnson, Fu-mei Chang Chen, William C. Jones, Jack Langlois, Wan Ming, and Audrey Eyler. The staff of the East Asian Library of the University of Minnesota, particularly Richard T. Wang, Yuan Zhou, Emiko Weeks, and Wang Yuh-shiow provided assistance with sources over the years. Peter Bol suggested that I submit the manuscript to E.J. Brill where my inquiries met efficient and positive replies from Dr. F. Th. Dijkema, Patricia Radder, Gert Jager and Gera van Bedaf. I am obliged to Andrew Miller for editorial help and Rick McKinney for assistance in preparing the manuscript for publication. All of the above can take some share of credit for whatever is worthwhile in this book; responsibility for the errors and shortcomings is mine alone.

Minneapolis, June 1995 Edward L. Farmer

CHAPTER ONE

RECREATING CHINA

When the Qing dynasty came to an end in the fall of 1911 the great majority of Chinese, the Han people, regained control over their affairs after nearly three centuries of Manchu rule. Resentment against the Manchus had been growing since the 1890s when Sun Yat-sen organized the Revive China Society (Xingzhonghui) and Huang Xing the Society to Revive China (Huaxinghui). In the last years of the dynasty ardent young men were sometimes moved to demonstrate patriotic feelings by cutting off their queues, hated symbols of submission to Manchu rule, even though such an act was punishable by execution. Of the many who raised their voices to blame China's weakness on the Manchus, none was more forceful than Zou Rong, whose inflammatory essay, "The Revolutionary Army" (*Gemingjun*), urged his countrymen to overthrow the imperial system through revolutionary action. Even as he condemned traditional autocracy he called for racial salvation from the Manchu invaders who had defiled China's land, its people and its ancient culture:

> The autocracy of the last few thousand years must be swept away, the slavery of thousands of years abolished. The 5,000,000 barbarian Manchus adorned in their furs, lances, and horns must be destroyed, and the great shame they have inflicted in their 260 years of cruel and harsh treatment expunged, that the Chinese mainland may be purified (Hsüeh 1971, 164).

Han Chinese resentment against alien rule was not a new phenomenon in the Qing dynasty. More than five centuries before, a similar note was sounded by Chinese insurgents denouncing the Mongol Yuan dynasty. In the mid-fourteenth century patriotic Han Chinese sought to rescue their homeland from the baleful influence of foreign conquest. As he was about to drive out the Mongol remnants Zhu Yuanzhang issued a proclamation to the people of north China. It began with an account of how Yuan rule had undermined the proper hierarchy of Chinese society:

> Since ancient times rulers have governed the empire. China resided in the center and brought order to the barbarians. The barbarians resided outside and submitted to China. It was never the case that barbarians resided in China and governed the empire. After the Song throne was overthrown the Yuan northern barbarians entered and ruled China. All within and without the four seas

> submitted to them. This was not a matter of human force; it was conferred upon them by Heaven. At the outset there were able rulers and enlightened ministers, capable of ruling the empire. But, lamentably, intelligent men and determined officials were still relegated to inferior positions. From that time on the Yuan officials ceased to heed the ancestral instruction and ruined the moral norms. For example, in the Dade period [1279–1307] a senior was dethroned in favor of a junior. In the Taiding period [1324–27] a minister killed his ruler. In the Tianli period [1329] a younger brother poisoned his older brother. Younger brothers even took their older brothers' wives, and sons committed incest with their fathers' concubines. Superior and inferior were interchanged without regarding it as unnatural. They deeply profaned and disrupted the proper relations between father and son, ruler and minister, husband and wife, older and younger (MSLHW, 401–2).

As this passage reveals, Zhu was not contesting the legitimacy of Mongol rule; they had won the mandate of heaven. What Zhu Yuanzhang chose to emphasize was the moral laxity that set in after the Yuan founding and the threat their practices posed to the natural hierarchy of Chinese social relations. Zhu's task was not just to rid China of foreign rule; it was to restore social order to the empire. His effort to create, or recreate, that order is the subject of this book.

The Social Construction of China

The revolutionaries who formed an alliance in Tokyo in 1905 chose Sun Yat-sen to be their leader despite his modest origins and foreign education. Thus it was that Sun Yat-sen became the first president of the republic proclaimed on January 1, 1912. Instinctively, the revolutionaries made (lit., the "Southern Capital") the base of their operations, for it was there that the last Han Chinese dynasty, the Ming, was established in 1368 following an era of Mongol rule. Sun Yat-sen capitalized on this symbolism by visiting the tomb of the Ming founder, Zhu Yuanzhang, on the outskirts of Nanjing. Sun's brief term as provisional president ended in February when the dynasty formally abdicated to Yuan Shikai in Beijing and China began its descent into warlordism. Undeterred, Sun Yat-sen set about rebuilding his revolutionary movement with aid from the Soviets, but he died in 1925 without regaining power. The symbolic link to the Ming founding was reaffirmed by the Nationalists when they formally inaugurated their Republic of China government at Nanjing in 1928. Sun Yat-sen's remains were installed in a mausoleum near the tomb of the Ming founder, underscoring the parallel in their historical roles.

Unlike the first emperor of the Ming, Sun Yat-sen was denied the opportunity to reshape China according to his own ideals. One of his most memorable observations was the complaint that China lacked cohesion like a "plate of loose sand." The blueprints he sketched out for a three-stage revolutionary process, a five-power constitution, and economic development were enshrined by the Nationalists as an official ideology, the Three People's Principles (*Sanmin zhuyi*). His vision was a mixture of traditional and modern, Western elements. It was authoritarian and elitist, privileging experts and the political leadership, while remaining suspicious of the more egalitarian elements in Western democracy and rejecting Marxism outright as inappropriate to China. Sun was most important as a symbol of the new China, the Father of the Country (*guofu*), free from taint, not just by the Manchus but by the whole imperial past. His suit of jacket with upright collar and trousers (*Zhongshanzhuang*) became a distinctive style of national dress for Chinese men.

Chiang Kai-shek, who succeeded to the mantle of Sun Yat-sen's leadership, made more explicit use of the imperial past in his effort to redefine China. Confucian sacrifices were reinstated and classical texts such as the *Four Books* became staples in the national curriculum. The New Life Movement of the early 1930s tried to revive traditional Confucian values as social cement for the struggling young republic. Chiang blamed China's ills on the twin evils of Manchu domination and foreign imperialism. His vision for a Chinese revival, spelled out during the Second World War in *China's Destiny*, was also never realized. In 1949 Chiang fled with his forces to Taiwan while Mao Zedong established the People's Republic of China on the mainland. Mao made Beijing his capital, signalling continuity with the imperial past, even as he attacked feudalism, imperialism, and the bureaucrat-capitalism of the Nationalists. Mao was stridently hostile to both the Confucianism that Chiang Kai-shek promoted and the liberalism of Western-educated elements within the Nationalist movement.

Yet, despite his overt hostility to the Confucian past, it was Mao whose career most closely resembled that of Zhu Yuanzhang, the peasant who rose to become the Ming founder in 1368 (Rapp and Andrew 1991). Mao studied Zhu's life and borrowed freely from his record. Like Zhu, Mao believed that he had a historic mission to transform China, claimed a special link to the people, and harbored a deep animosity toward bureaucrats and the educated elite. Like Zhu, he had decades in which to shape the new order to his will. And, like Zhu, he did not shrink from using savage force to carry out his mission. Yet, much as he may have resembled a founding emperor in political style, Mao was at heart a revolutionary. He espoused a Marxist world view, headed a Leninist political party, and enjoyed the support of a Stalinist governmental apparatus. He sought to reclaim China's greatness by creating a new socialist China, not by reviving the old order. In this respect his redefinition of China contrasted with that of Zhu Yuanzhang, who cloaked even his innovations under the mantle of a return to the Chinese essence. Institutionally, Mao's heritage was most unlike Zhu's. Mao disdained the use of law, revised state and party constitutions on expedient grounds, devastated the very party structure which had brought him to power, and left no viable blueprint for social order after his death.

As the millennium approaches it is apparent that the redefinition of China begun at the turn of the century is still underway. When Mao died in 1976 his vision and his actions were at once questioned. His career was re-evaluated and his policies largely abandoned. Some have tried to redefine socialism while others have given up on Marxism in any form. Still others have called for a revival of Confucianism. Mao's successor, Deng Xiaoping, sent China down an uncertain road of economic development and rapid social change. While the edifice of party dictatorship remained in place throughout the decade of the 1980s it is arresting to note that Deng and other senior leaders controlled China from positions of technical retirement above and outside the formal structure of party and government. That aged men could do this reveals the fact that Chinese society continues to operate on unwritten rules of hierarchy that have nothing whatsoever to do with the Leninist model imported from the Soviet Union. The dominance of senior male revolutionaries is testimony to the survival of traditional norms from the imperial era.

From the perspective of the late twentieth century this book looks back to the fourteenth century, to the last time Han Chinese redefined their community. That revival followed centuries of division and the first period when all of Han China had been subjected to foreign rule. The Ming founder, Zhu Yuanzhang, created a new order that lasted for centuries. It featured enhanced imperial power, limited autonomy for private groups and institutions, a generally defensive foreign policy, and vigorous promotion of orthodox Confucian norms of thought and conduct. A prominent feature of the Ming order as Zhu Yuanzhang fashioned it was the use of rituals, regulations, and codified law to shape and define Chinese society and culture. The purpose of this constitutional edifice of guidelines and codes was to realize, perfect, and preserve a kind of social hierarchy that had been ignored and damaged under Mongol rule.

Zhu Yuanzhang and the Ming Revival

The opportunity to redefine China in the fourteenth century came about with the downfall of the Yuan dynasty. The Han Chinese elements opposed to the continuation of Mongol rule included both educated advocates of Confucian orthodoxy and partisans of millenarian sects inspired by Buddhist and Manichaean doctrines. Zhu Yuanzhang's career provided a link between the radical religious movements and the elite proponents of the traditional orthodoxy. He came from the lower stratum of Chinese society and referred to himself as a commoner from the right bank of the Huai River (*Huai you buyi*) (Wu Han 1965, 129). Orphaned before his sixteenth birthday, he became a monk and wandered through the war torn countryside begging before joining a millenarian insurgency (DMB, 381–82). Despite the fact that he apparently never subscribed wholeheartedly to its doctrines, Zhu soon assumed leadership of the movement. The state he proclaimed in Nanjing in 1368 preserved in its name, Ming, a reference to the Manichaean notion of light or radiance, but the new ruler was not a champion of the millenarian beliefs. As far as we can tell from the sanitized records handed down to us Zhu was anxious to alter the ideological coloration of the movement he inherited. Early on he turned to Confucian scholars for guidance on ideological matters.

The linkage between the Chinese elite tradition and the Ming founding is touched upon by F. W. Mote in an important review essay. Mote's point is that the Ming founder's ideological outlook was generally in agreement with that of the Confucian scholars and, further, that by late Yuan times the Confucian ideology was the only one that could be used to found an imperial state. The salient passage reads as follows:

> He was himself no philosopher, and he was quite ready to accept the philosophical superiority of the literate tradition in his civilization, without necessarily having examined and understood it all by himself. His move up the social scale had not made an intellectual of him, but it had made him accept the "great tradition" as proper and normal. And on the level of the great tradition, there was no competing force, no room for choice. Whereas in the immediate post-Han centuries an aspiring dynast could have promulgated a great variety of ideologies, by the 14th century Chinese civilization had become culturally unified to a degree that no longer permitted such freedom of choice. By reason of his becoming the emperor (or aspiring to become one) he automatically had to conform to the only set of standards for rulership that existed—i.e. those forms and practices, and their underlying philosophy that we call (and they called) Confucian (Mote 1961, 23–24).

Mote is probably right that the ideological spectrum was narrower in late Yuan times than in the post-Han era, that Confucianism was the obvious ideology which would have to be used to legitimize any new political order, and that Zhu Yuanzhang generally subscribed to Confucian beliefs. Certainly this is how things worked out. Nevertheless, it is possible to challenge his assumptions on a number of points. It is not true that Zhu Yuanzhang was "no philosopher." In fact, he interested himself in a number of philosophical questions from astronomy to ritual to jurisprudencc and displayed a high degree of intellectual independence from his scholarly advisors. He spent as much time lecturing them as he did listening to their instructions.

It is also not the case that there was "no room for choice" in the matter of the great tradition. Even if we accept that the Chinese educated elite were predominantly wedded to the Confucian tradition, this does not mean that there was no possibility of a radical alternative. Could a state have been founded on the White Lotus-Maitreya doctrine? Not easily, certainly, for that would have involved a massive educational effort and the transformation or replacement of the educated elite. This was the problem faced by the Taipings in the nineteenth century and the Communist Party in the twentieth century (Gates and Weller 1987, 15). It would have been a long shot, but such a possibility existed in the mid-fourteenth century. There were many, some of them among Zhu's followers, who anticipated millenarian change.

Even if we accept that there was no viable alternative to the great tradition it does not follow that there was no room for choice. How "culturally unified" was China by the fourteenth century? How widely were Mongol cultural values and customary practices adhered to among the Han Chinese population? What was the relative strength of Buddhist, Daoist, and Confucian ideologies at the elite and popular levels? To what extent, and in what ways, did these doctrines coexist, intersect, or intermingle in people's thinking? How uniform was the Confucian outlook shared by members of the literati and how deeply did its acceptance extend among the Chinese population? The degree to which Confucian norms had won acceptance in Chinese society prior to receiving prolonged state patronage in the Ming dynasty is a question worth keeping open for further investigation.

Saying that Zhu Yuanzhang had to conform to Confucian standards is akin to saying that Mao Zedong had to conform to the standards of Marxism. It still leaves considerable room for maneuver. In Zhu's case there were a range of competing Confucian perspectives from which to pick and choose. As it happened, the advisors with whom he surrounded himself were linked to the Jinhua tradition of Neo-Confucianism. Their tutoring gave his view of the great tradition a particular coloration. There is, too, the matter of Zhu Yuanzhang's aptitude, inclination, and personality. He was by no means a pliant pupil. A child of poverty, he never forgot his humble origins or the plight of the common people. His statecraft was suffused with an element of populism that set him apart from other dynastic founders. He disdained luxury and excessive displays of wealth. A passionate and vengeful man, he harbored a deep distrust of officials and nobles. He was sure enough of his opinions to challenge and pass judgement on scholars whose learning greatly exceeded his own.

By Ming times Neo-Confucian thinkers were of several minds on how morality and law were to be combined. The classical goal of a close minister-ruler relationship in which the Confucian scholar-tutor would guide the ruler to a virtuous course of action through instruction on the classics persisted. However, under Mongol rule ethnic Chinese, especially those in areas that had been under the Southern Song dynasty, were assigned to a lower social position than Mongols and their Semu collaborators (Yanai 1963). Confucian scholars were in a separate tax category, exempted from labor service, but were by no means part of the ruling elite (Huang 1977, 202). The chance to instruct an emperor and save the world from the top down must have seemed a remote dream (Weggel 1980, 86; de Bary 1981, 18). In those circumstances Neo-Confucian thinkers interested themselves in the implementation of their vision from the bottom up. The special place of law in Jinhua Neo-Confucianism was a reflection of such a strategy. They called for law to be employed as a means to transform public attitudes and behavior. It was an instrumental use of law divorced from the earlier reliance on religious belief (Raeff 1983, 41).

In late Yuan China the rise of Zhu Yuanzhang provided a vehicle for the implementation of the ideas of the frustrated Jinhua thinkers (Langlois 1981b; Dardess 1983, 131–81). The Jinhua scholars assumed the need for a ruler who could save the world through the operation of a bureaucracy that would impose a system of laws upon an ignorant populace in a world suffused with evil. While Liu Ji, Wang Wei, Song Lian and Hu Han generally shared with Zhu Yuanzhang a belief in the need for a strong state and active emperor, their attitudes toward law were by no means uniform. Liu Ji, for instance, denied that heaven could purposively intervene in human affairs and advocated a manipulative and coercive form of government based on Han and Tang models which could destroy evil. The ruler would rely more on expertise than virtue and would impose brutal restraints on his closest advisers (Dardess 1983, 133-47). A contrasting view may be found in the writings of Wang Wei who stressed the importance of the ruler's mind in knowing and a general body of principle that was both universal and unchanging. Relying on this knowledge the sage ruler would use only benevolence, righteousness, rites, and music to order the world (Dardess 1983, 147–56).

The guiding intelligence that sorted through these views and gave shape to the Ming synthesis was that of Zhu Yuanzhang. Zhu began building a regional state at Nanjing in 1356 and presided over the new Ming empire during the thirty years of the Hongwu reign period from 1368 to 1398. Such was the impact of his reign that he has come to be viewed as one of the most forceful and influential rulers ever to govern China (Teng 1967; Wu Han [1965] 1979). Like Mao Zedong in more recent times Zhu was a figure of heroic proportions. And, like Mao, the record of his rule was mixed. He was celebrated as a champion of the common people and a sage dynastic founder, and he was feared and reviled as a demented and ruthless tyrant.

Had some other person ruled instead of Zhu Yuanzhang we must suppose that different decisions would have been made, and that the Ming government would have taken on a different character. For this reason Zhu Yuanzhang's personal qualities are of considerable interest. It was his cunning and ambition that enabled him to build a viable state, his ruthlessness and paranoia that drove him to destroy his enemies and subordinates in great numbers, and his compulsion to realize his moral vision that prompted him to constantly reorganize the government and codify the laws. Scholars have been perplexed by the seemingly contradictory aspects of Zhu's personality and career: demonic use of terror and conscientious attention to institution building. Some have focused on the terror while others have emphasized the constructive side of Zhu's reign. In the middle are more balanced accounts that contrast the early years of his reign with the later years or which see in Zhu a range of qualities from sage to tyrant (Mote 1961, 19).

The scars of Zhu Yuanzhang's early career are easy to see. His pronouncements from the throne were full of statements of sympathy for the plight of the common people and hostility and suspicion for wealthy landowners and clever scholar-officials. Years spent in military campaigns and political intrigues produced an obsession with personal security. He was pragmatic and cautious in military affairs and extremely sensitive to the loyalty of his subordinates. He ruthlessly prosecuted and butchered thousands whom he suspected of plotting against him or disobeying his orders. The degree to which his suspicions were the product of paranoia and the degree to which they were founded in reality is a matter for psychohistorical judgement. Likewise his penchant for personal cruelty, torture of officials in court, and extreme sensitivity to criticisms, real or imagined, are all matters open to scholarly investigation based on theoretical speculation and surviving historical evidence. The documented record of his reign is sufficient to support a number of conjectures about his actions and motives but is probably not detailed enough to permit a deep or nuanced psychological portrait of the inner man.

Accounts of Zhu's early rise as a regional power holder stress the discipline of his army and the care he took to minimize harm to the civilian population. How is this picture to be reconciled with the image of a bloody despot that characterized Zhu on the throne? F. W. Mote speculated that the rise to power may have affected Zhu's personality:

> But after 1367 when the whole world suddenly came into his hands, Chu Yuan-chang lost his pliability and his humility. He must have been overwhelmed by the size of the prize that had befallen him, and beset by fears that he would lose it just as easily. His character changed under the weight, and his life came to be dominated by an ever-deepening suspicion which may in fact have made a mad-man of him. Without losing his shrewdness, he none the less appears to have become a victim of obsession that deprived him of reason and balance (Mote 1961, 23).

Zhu Yuanzhang's thirty-year reign was marked by an extraordinary amount of bloodshed but also by considerable institutional innovation and a substantial outpouring of edicts, essays, codes, and other documents. The picture of Zhu that emerges from these events shows us two faces of the man that are not always easy to resolve. One face is that of an insecure and tormented despot, a tyrannical ruler who saw evil and conspiracy on every side, who trusted no one and methodically killed or drove to suicide most of his old comrades in arms, his nobles, his highest officials, and thousands of others who were condemned, often in a wholesale manner. In 1390, Zhu Yuanzhang estimated that he had already killed fifty to seventy thousand people and in 1393 alone another fifteen thousand were put to death (Massey 1983, 4). He feared conspiracies against his person and saw satirical intent even in the use of innocent words and phrases, although careful research has demonstrated that stories of a literary persecution by Zhu Yuanzhang, provoked by his misreading of documents, is largely the product of fabrications by later writers (Chan Hok-lam 1977).

So harsh was Zhu's rule that terror pervaded his government. A rich lore has survived, much of it descriptive of his demonic side. He was capable of towering anger. He delighted in cruel and unusual punishments. He demeaned his subordinates and elevated himself, raising his throne above the audience hall and forcing even the highest officials to stand in his presence when conducting court business. He developed a jaundiced, almost despairing view of the immorality of his officials. He came to assume that they were driven primarily by greed and that in the face of the harshest warnings, threats, and sanctions they would still do the wrong thing when the opportunity presented itself. Nevertheless, Zhu expended boundless energy in trying to dissuade them from doing wrong. At court he used eunuchs as agents to carry out beating, torture, and imprisonment of his officials. The imperial bodyguard, the Embroidered Uniform Guard (*jinyiwei*) was also employed in spying and security work. Both the debased atmosphere of the court and the secret police apparatus of the imperial house long outlived the Ming founder.

Zhu Yuanzhang was the central agent in the recreation of China. His shortcomings—his suspicious nature, his sensitivity to criticism, his penchant for cruelty, and the widespread killing and terror that he inspired—all contributed to the personal side of Ming despotism. Beyond the atmospheric elements of Ming government that were tied to Zhu's personality and style of rule were the institutional arrangements he put in place (see Dreyer 1982, 152-56). This more enduring side of Zhu's achievement was the constitutional edifice of Ming despotism.

The Ming Constitution

In his monumental work *Ideology and Organization in Communist China* (1968), Franz Schurmann characterized the modern revolutionary situation as one in which the social order was destroyed and had to be replaced by organization. While the word organization might not fit comfortably on the institutions and methods used in the early Ming, the point is still relevant.

In the face of a profound social upheaval conscious efforts were required to recreate a social order.

Following the collapse of the Yuan and the defeat of his rivals the Ming founder enjoyed an extraordinary historical opportunity to redefine and reorganize China. In the broadest sense the work of the Ming founding can be thought of as the process of composing and promulgating a constitution or grand design for the establishment and maintenance of the social order. The constitution of the August Ming dynasty of fourteenth-century China was of the diffused type: rather than a single labelled document, it consisted of the whole edifice of declarations, regulations, practices, and precedents created by the imperial government.

Whatever his psychological state and personal style of rule, Zhu Yuanzhang was a shrewd and far-sighted legislator, a constitutional architect who looked beyond the exigencies of the moment to the creation of institutions that could last for many generations. Despite his concern with opposition and evil Zhu had a comprehensive vision of China, the dynasty, and his role as a founding emperor. He was careful to legislate for all sectors of the society—the imperial family, the eunuchs, officials, nobles, and commoners. Elaborate codes spelled out how the bureaucracy was to be organized and how village life was to be regulated. Law codes and the *Grand Pronouncements* provided guidance for the population at large. Religious activities were reformed as were rituals for dealing with heaven and the spirits. In all of these legislative activities Zhu showed himself to be energetic, persistent, and creative. Codes were proposed, reviewed, modified, and reissued over a period of three decades. Even though Zhu lacked a formal education, he obviously made serious efforts to inform himself about classical precedents and the details of complex legislative issues. Over time he developed enough confidence in his own views to set aside both historical precedents and the advice of learned advisers. By the time his reign was over Zhu had compiled a body of works which qualify him as one of the great legislators of Chinese history (Hucker 1978).

Like the Roman constitution, the Chinese constitution derived from the ordinances and enactments of the emperor. In theory it was flexible, subject to modification by subsequent imperial rulings. In some respects it was rigid, with specific written provisions that were to remain in force, immutable for all future generations. Unlike modern democratic constitutions the regulations of the Ming government were aimed at protecting the privileges of the rulers and imposing obligations upon the subjects, not at conferring rights on a body of citizens. Another immediately apparent aspect of the Ming constitution is the preponderance of specific statutes covering every facet of imperial concerns.

Understanding of Chinese social legislation can be facilitated by introducing some distinctions. In their introduction to an edited volume on *Law and Social Control* Eugene Kamenka and Alice Erh-Soon Tay put forward a three-part classification of types of law: *Gemeinschaft*, *Gesellschaft*, and bureaucratic-administrative (1980, 7). The *Gemeinschaft* (community) and *Gesellschaft* (association) dichotomy they draw from the well-known work of Ferdinand Tonnies. *Gemeinschaft* represents the ideal type of the agricultural community, an organic community in which the individual is subsumed within a social family. In the *Gemeinschaft* order there is no formal distinction between public and private, civil and criminal offenses, justice and administration, law and morality. People are judged not impartially as equal individuals but particularistically on the basis of their occupation, social standing, family and the like. The *Gesellschaft* ideal type, by contrast, is associated with the rise of commerce and the bourgeoisie. Its emphasis is on the private rights and interests of equal individuals. It stresses rationality, predictability, formal procedures, precise legal definitions, and adjudicative justice (1980, 15–17).

To these two types, which can be thought of as deriving historically from the premodern agricultural and the modern commercial orders, or to some extent the non-Western and Western European orders, Kamenka and Tay add the notion of a bureaucratic-administrative type of law. Within a bureaucratic-administrative system individuals are the objects of regulation, not important as persons with rights and duties, but agents for carrying out roles in a hierarchy. The bureaucratic-administrative ideal type entails vertical integration by means of supraordination and subordination.

This tripartite distinction of ideal types does not describe actual social systems but rather paradigms against which real systems can be measured. Applying these distinctions to the Ming Chinese case yields immediate benefits. The social legislation of Ming China was closer to the *Gemeinschaft* type than to the *Gesellschaft* type. The addition of the bureaucratic-administrative ideal helps to clarify another dimension of the picture. Kamenka and Tay suggest that bureaucratic-administrative elements operated in the Chinese legal system as an external force to bring social practice into line with a set of *Gemeinschaft* values which were not being observed:

> The state-imposed laws of imperial, traditional China, where they are not primarily rules of bureaucratic organization, as they so largely were, may be seen in either of two ways. They presuppose and seek to maintain the social life of the *Gemeinschaft* and even the emperor's seemingly arbitrary exercise of judicial and punitive powers is taken to be part of his parental function. In this sense, they are the laws of a *Gemeinschaft* concerned with a whole man and an organic society. At the same time, the dominant Confucian tradition with its strong internalization of *Gemeinschaft* values had to insist that rigorous punitive intervention by the state and its magistrates was a sign that social harmony had been breached, that the *Gemeinschaft* had been broken. It thus presents state law, not as a product of the *Gemeinschaft* but as an attempt to restore the *Gemeinschaft* through a basically external intervention, through

> the iron-fisted exercise of power relations, of domination and submission. The external intervention was justified or ideologized in so far as its aim was to restore the *Gemeinschaft* and in so far as it was based on the emperor's recognition of his duties as *parens patriae*, but the punitive laws themselves could be seen, in this context, as terroristic interventions, as resting immediately if not ultimately on bare domination and submission (Kamenka and Tay 1980, 23).

Legislation in Ming China took the form of pronouncements by the ruler. Weight was added to the emperor's statements by his invocation of religious and historical sanctions. Time and again he would emphasize the fact that he was the recipient of heaven's mandate and the legitimate successor to the rulers of the preceding Yuan dynasty. His formal rulings were thus more than the decisions of an individual or group, they were to be understood as divinely sanctioned standards for all of society for all of time. The required or forbidden behavior was clearly stated in an objective manner to facilitate enforcement by appropriate agents, usually government officials but sometimes the people or even the gods and spirits.

Imperial codes are excellent sources for the study of the Ming constitution for several reasons. They were issued by the emperor and thus provide rather direct evidence of imperial intent. Often they contained or were accompanied by imperial edicts making the emperor's intentions explicit. Second, because they were publicly proclaimed and widely circulated they have been well preserved and are accessible to us. Because they were designed to guide the conduct of members of the society and to be enforced by members of the government they tend to be clearly stated, logically organized, and comprehensive in scope.

Taken together the codes and imperial rulings constitute a body of constitutional law. The term law when applied to Ming China designates a different range of elements than law in European or American society. As the distinction between *Gemeinschaft* and *Gesellschaft* makes clear, Ming law was not concerned with civil matters, particularly the rights and property, that are at the heart of Anglo-American law. Ming law was by nature different from Western law: its functions, parameters and concerns all grew out of a Chinese historical and cultural context. Vandermeersch has observed that there is really no separation of the legislative, executive and judicial functions in traditional Chinese government. The judicial functions were carried out by officials who were at the same time the instruments of executive action. Legislation, such as it was, took the form of rulings by the emperor and thus were not clearly set apart from executive action. The purpose of Chinese law was to create and uphold a social hierarchy in terms of kinds of activities and classes of people. The result is a form of law Vandermeersch calls ritualism (Vandermeersch 1985, 3-14).

Vandermeersch's analysis underscoring the ritual aspect of Chinese law is helpful. Law in Ming China was really a combination of elements that included penal law but shaded off in one direction toward administrative regulations and in the other direction toward ritual. In fact one can draw no firm line between these elements. When we speak of Ming law we should keep the ritual elements in mind and not divorce them from our definition. The relationship between ritual (*li*) and law (*fa* or *xing*) was formulated in classical antiquity. Ritual was to prevent things which were going to happen while law attempted to prevent what had already happened (Ch'ü T'ung-tsu 1961, 249). Another way of putting it was that what was excluded by ritual was taken up by the law so that when ritual failed punishment was employed (Ch'ü 1967, 255).

The father of Neo-Confucianism, the great Song philosopher Zhu Xi, assumed that the legal and moral orders were intimately connected if not identical. He saw virtue and rules of propriety, laws and punishments on a kind of continuum. Such a view is suggested by Zhu Xi as quoted by Langlois:

> In my humble view, laws are the tool of government, and punishments the methods for assisting government. Virtue and the rules of propriety are those things which issue from the root of government, while virtue is the root of propriety. Thus they exist in a relationship of end and beginning. While it is not permissible to discard the one, laws and punishments can do no more than cause the people to remain far away from crime. The efficacy of virtue and the rules of propriety is such as to cause the people constantly to move closer to the good without being aware of the fact. Therefore he who governs the people must not merely depend upon the branch; he must also deeply seek out the root (1981b, 156–57).

Ordering the World

When the Ming Dynasty was proclaimed in 1368 the Han people had not been politically united under a single Chinese ruler for more than three centuries. The unity of Chinese society, such as it was, was imbedded in customary practices, cultural values, and historical memories. Zhu Yuanzhang considered himself to be the instrument chosen by heaven to save the world, to restore order to the empire. Mongol rule, in which barbarians were superior to Han Chinese, was clearly a historical aberration. Mongol customs that violated the hierarchical logic of traditional Chinese institutions were likewise offensive. Zhu's task was to understand the great order of the Chinese world, and, as emperor, to bring social practice into conformity with the ideal.

Romeyn Taylor has characterized traditional Chinese society as a hierarchical system unified by belief in the homogeneous integration of the cosmic, religious and human orders:

> Chinese society in its entirety came to be hierarchically organized in an empire, and this empire-society was understood by its members to be universal (*tianxia*, "all under heaven"). No autonomous political domain, no body politic, no state was acknowledged to exist in contradistinction to society. But the social whole itself was encompassed by the pantheon of the official religion to integrate these three domains, all of which were hierarchical in form, nested one within another to constitute a hierarchy of hierarchies (Taylor 1989, 493).

Assuming that Zhu Yuanzhang sincerely believed in the unity of the cosmic and human orders and in his own role as the agent of their reconciliation or alignment it is not clear how he was to carry out his task. Heaven may have chosen him, but it did not issue him tablets engraved with the laws nor did it speak to him directly detailing a course of action. He was caught between a lofty and unattainable ideal and the chaotic uncertainty of an ignorant and confused humanity. There were problems of knowledge and problems of action. As heaven's instrument he faced the problem of knowing heaven's will and correctly fathoming the cosmic pattern. As a ruler of China he was mired in the realities and compromises of politics. He had to consider what was possible and how to attain it.

William Blackstone, author of the famous *Commentaries on the Laws of England*, wrote that all human law was based upon divine law (revealed in scripture) and the law of nature:

> This law of nature, being co-eval with mankind and dictated by God himself, is of course superior in obligation to any other. It is binding over all the globe, in all countries, and at all times: no human laws are of any validity, if contrary to this; and such of them as are valid derive all their force, and all their authority, mediately or immediately, from this original (Blackstone [1765] 1979, 1:41).

Natural law was a Western, not a Chinese, notion and we are cautioned not to think of Chinese law in terms of Western conceptions of divine intent knowable through the exercise of reason (MacCormack 1990, 40–41). But, like Blackstone, Zhu Yuanzhang and his advisers believed that human law derived from the divine order which could be known. Knowledge of the cosmic order was obtained primarily from the past. The ancient sages had understood the ways of heaven and had transmitted their knowledge to mankind. But the line of true teachers had long since died out. The teachings of the ancient sages were embodied in the classics which had been passed down from generation to generation. Thus the knowledge provided by the classics was an imperfect reflection of the teachings of the ancient sages. The guidance available to Zhu Yuanzhang from the scholarly community was indirect and distorted at best. It was relayed to the present through the mediation of generations of students, teachers, and scholars who themselves all fell short of the sages in the profundity of their learning. Moreover, they tended to be organized into sectarian schools of thought incapable of providing the whole picture. An alternative to dependence on mortal teachers was to seek direct knowledge of the heavenly pattern. If he did this the emperor made the claim to superior knowledge, in effect, to sagehood, and thereby opened up an area of potential conflict between the throne and the community of scholarly experts.

Zhu's problem was not just a matter of knowledge, of correctly divining heaven's will: it was also the problem of reconciling the human world with the cosmic ideal. This was the meeting of heavenly principle (*tianli*) and human feeling (*renqing*). Some elements of Chinese society were simply incompatible with the hierarchical character of the great tradition. The market system, for instance, operated on different principles and thus presented a threat to the social hierarchy (Taylor 1989, 500-501). Heterodox religious sects and ethnic minorities represented other pockets of diversity which challenged the power of the dominant system to transform, encompass, isolate, expel, or destroy them.

Within the Han Chinese society, government was an imperfect process. Historical precedent was the primary guide for those spheres of human activity that could not be brought into conformity with classical ideals. Thus knowledge of the past, or historical citations, provided the idiom in which political decisions were discussed. Restoring antiquity (*fugu*) was an acknowledged if unattainable goal. Alternative policies were often cast in terms of precedents from earlier dynasties. Even where contemporary conditions required innovation the terminology used often added a veneer of antiquity.

Taken as a whole Zhu Yuanzhang's social legislation encompasses four main themes. The first is the broadest, the desire for world salvation through comprehensive moral reform. In this guise Zhu was the agent of heaven and earth, invoking sacred principles and appealing to the ghosts and spirits, and of mankind in the citation of historical precedent and canonical authority. Even before the founding the heroic scale of his vision was evident in the statements Zhu made about his mission to restore order. Shortly after the founding it was given concrete form in a vigorous and comprehensive program of codification, including the compilation of the *Commandment*, the *Code* and any number of regulations to govern ritual and other matters. The combination in the *Commandment* of articles on governmental offices and articles concerning society at large make it a good source of illustrations of these first two themes. The emperor stated his views on legislation when he issued the *Commandment* in the first month of his reign (see appendix 2). Codified law was a basic tool of government which could provide guidance to the people. Legislation needed to be clearly and simply stated so that the people could understand it and obey it.

The second theme was the much narrower interest in the disciplining of followers and management of the affairs of government. This was a more mundane role: the ruler as law giver. Pragmatic utterances on the importance of administrative discipline and social cohesion were present in Zhu's earliest statements about legislation. However, when he set out to guide Ming society to the ideal state of social order the founding emperor became entangled in an insoluble conundrum. Human nature and human behavior required the regulation of law. The application of law to society required the operation of bureaucracy. The bureaucracy, however, was staffed by officials whose loyalty and honesty could not always be trusted. Thus the bureaucracy became a target for regulation. The contents of the *Commandment* were directed first and foremost at the officials and functionaries who staffed the government offices and carried out the routine work of administration. Regulation of the bureaucracy, in turn, exposed the shortcomings of the ruler himself. As the performance of his administration fell short of the goals he had set Zhu looked for scapegoats. He found fault with himself and with the people at large, but he placed the primary responsibility on the officials who were supposed to be his surrogates and agents.

A third theme, related to the second, but maturing later, is the vengeful desire to root out and destroy evil, particularly among the officials. This was Zhu Yuanzhang as the prosecutor, judge and executioner, the wrathful, perhaps unbalanced, instrument righteous punishment. This theme became most pronounced after the first decade of Ming rule when the founder had encountered difficulties in managing his officials. The Hu Weiyong affair of 1380, in which his chief minister was accused of plotting to overthrow the throne, was the most dramatic point in his loss of confidence in officialdom. The legislation that best exemplifies the Ming founder's disillusionment with officialdom are the *Grand Pronouncements* that began appearing in 1385 (Langlois 1988, 152). In these texts one can sense the heat of Zhu Yuanzhang's passion, his suspicion of the motives of officials, his hatred for lying and cheating, and the savagery of his determination to eliminate misbehavior.

A fourth theme in the Ming founder's legislation is the determination to resist the ravages of time. This was Zhu Yuanzhang as patriarch, speaking to his descendants and villagers alike with the sage voice of an elder of the clan and the community. This theme is most in evidence toward the end of the Hongwu reign period as the emperor contemplated the problem of succession. The *Ancestral Instruction* and the *Code*, both issued in revised forms in 1397, and the *Placard of People's Instructions*, issued in 1398, all reflect this interest in legislation as a bulwark against social change, as a device to preserve the dynasty. In the preface to the *Ancestral Instruction* the Ming founder speaks directly to those who will succeed him to perpetuate the "laws which I have fixed forever" (appendix 1). In the first two articles they are instructed to enforce the *Code* and the *Grand Pronouncements* and to execute anyone who might so much as propose reestablishing the position of prime minister.

The Ming Dynasty had neither the expansive power of the great Han and Tang unifications nor the cultural brilliance or economic dynamism of the smaller Song Dynasty which is justly celebrated as a high point in China's cultural history. The Ming was a lesser China in contrast to the geographically more extensive empires that preceded and followed it, both of which politically integrated the steppe and the sown. The long evolutionary process of joining together China proper, Han China, with the northern lands of Inner Asia found its fullest expression in the Qing Dynasty of the Manchus (1644-1911). In this context the Ming period was a prolonged but ultimately unsuccessful resistance to the integration the Manchus eventually achieved.

As the last period of Han rule before the twentieth century the Ming founding was not simply a return to what had existed in the Song Dynasty before the Mongol conquest. It was in some respects a conscious restoration of the past, but it was also a time of change and redefinition. The legal and institutional enactments of the early Ming rulers strongly influenced the development of Chinese government and society for the next six centuries. The tendency toward political unification under a strongly centralized state headed by an all-powerful emperor was the culmination of a form of rule first realized in the Qin and Han dynasties. The imperial government's embrace of Zhu Xi's Neo-Confucianism helped to promote those doctrines in education and social practice generally. Explicit codification of norms was clearly designed to encourage moral conformity to orthodox standards. The goal was to create a proper China, where people behaved the way true Chinese should behave. This was the early modern recreation of traditional China.

CHAPTER TWO

SAVING THE WORLD

When Zhu Yuanzhang was born to a poor peasant family in Anhui in 1328 all of China had been under foreign rule for five decades. Parts of the north had been controlled by Khitans, Tanguts, Jurchen, and Mongols for more than three and a half centuries. During the Yuan dynasty (1279–1368) China was reduced to the status of the easternmost khanate within the Mongol world empire. The Mongol ruler of China was simultaneously grand khan of this great Eurasian empire and the son of heaven within its Chinese subdivision. Under the Yuan, as under the Liao (907–1125) and Jin (1122–1234) dynasties, a variety of governmental arrangements were worked out through the merger and modification of Chinese and Inner Asian political and social institutions. For generations some educated Chinese participated in these regimes, simultaneously accommodating themselves to the practices of the northern conquerors and seeking to win the foreigners over to the superiority of Chinese language, culture and statecraft. Despite considerable accommodation between Chinese and their Mongol rulers there remained an acute awareness of the alien character of the Yuan regime and a nostalgia, shared by Han Chinese of different social strata, for the glory of earlier dynasties and the independence of self-rule unknown for generations.

Within ten years of Zhu Yuanzhang's birth, revolts with religious trappings were springing up here and there. In 1344, when Zhu was sixteen, famine and sickness claimed the lives of his father, mother, and an elder brother. Zhu sought refuge in a local Buddhist monastary, the Huangjue *si*, which could not afford to feed him. He spent three years as a mendicant begging daily for his food until late 1348, when he returned to the Huangjue Temple. He studied there for four years, learning how to read and write and gaining a basic knowledge of Buddhist doctrine. By the 1350s popular insurgency became widespread and Yuan rule weakened markedly. In 1352, at the age of twenty-four, Zhu enlisted as a soldier in the forces of the minor insurgent commander Guo Zixing. Within five years he rose to command his own force, moved south of the Yangtze, took Jinling (Nanjing), and started to build his own state (DMB, 381–84; Wu Han, 214).

Nothing in Zhu Yuanzhang's background as a poor peasant, a Buddhist monk, or a common soldier made him an obvious candidate to overthrow Mongol rule and found a new dynasty. Nor was it obvious what kind of a regime would replace the Yuan if it were to fall. Even a cursory inventory of the contestants for power in the middle of the fourteenth century must convince us that there could have been no consensus on the question of the outcome of the struggle. Zhu Yuanzhang's regime was only one of a number of contending forces struggling to gain power in mid-fourteenth century China. Clearly, any number of outcomes were possible, including Yuan survival, division of China among regional warlords, the triumph of a messianic movement, or unification and founding of a new dynasty under a Han Chinese leader such as Zhang Shicheng.

Rivals for Power

In the two decades after 1350, factional struggles tore at the fabric of the court and Yuan rule weakened. China proper was ripped apart by regional insurrections (Mote 1962, 8–37; Dardess 1970; Mote 1988b, 11–57). Prominent among these popular rebellions was an uprising aimed at the restoration of the native Song dynasty. Even more widespread than Song loyalism was the popular religious ideology of the Red Sashes, a millenarian doctrine with strong Buddhist and Manichaean elements that promised an end to the troubles of the world with the appearance of a Prince of Radiance (Ming Wang). It was a time of great disorder and uncertainty.

After centuries of foreign rule and decades of civil war there were many visions of what the world should be like. The Mongols and their allies had enjoyed wealth, power and legal privilege under a system that explicitly placed the non-Chinese ruling groups in a superior position. Merchants and religious missionaries of many stripes benefitted from the trans-Eurasian mobility made possible by the Mongol world empire. Literate Chinese, some of whom offered their administrative skills to the Yuan, kept alive the scholar-centric Neo-Confucian ideology and the memory of the great Song bureaucratic order under which the scholar-official class and their ideology had reached full flower (de Bary 1981; 1982). Throughout the countryside landlords, small holders and tenants—peasants of all kinds—struggled to survive and perhaps enrich their families and clans. Along the coast and in the major river basins of central and western China regional states were formed by adventurers of every type, some of whom strove to expand their holdings and unify the empire, some of whom aimed only at self-defense and survival as local warlords. Among the common people insurgency was energized by the messianic doctrines promising a radical transformation of the world through divine intervention and the onset of a new age.

One possible outcome of the time of troubles was continued domination of the Mongols themselves. The Mongols had proved themselves to be the most potent conquerors in all of world history. In view of the fact that parts of north China had been under the rule of a series of non-Han groups for as much as four centuries it hardly seems unreasonable to suppose that elements of the Yuan court might have hung on for a while longer. The last Yuan emperor, known by the posthumous temple name of Shundi (reigned 1333–70), occupied the throne for thirty-five years before being driven out of his capital at Dadu (Beijing) in 1368 (DMB, 1290–93). Shundi was a weak figurehead ruler, but he was viewed as the legitimate son of heaven by those who wielded power at the Yuan court. The Chancellor of the Right, Toghto, was the best hope for a Yuan rally (Dardess 1970, 550) but, as it turned out, the most powerful figure was Kökö Temür (d. 1375), an able general from a landowning family in Henan who rallied a large force to counter the rebel Red Sashes, whom he drove from their capital at Bianliang (Kaifeng) in 1358 (DMB, 724–28). He was designated Prince of Han and given broad powers to establish a regional government staffed with more than two thousand officials of his own choosing. Kökö's relations with the Yuan court had deteriorated into open warfare by 1368 when Zhu Yuanzhang's armies took north China. In the face of the southern threat Kökö made peace with the Yuan court, continuing to support it in Mongolia where he saved Karakorum from Ming attack in 1372.

Kökö Temür's initial military success and ultimate loyalty to the exiled Yuan court indicate that even at the eleventh hour able and effective commanders still considered the Mongol ruling house a worthy cause. For the Mongol nobility and their closest Chinese associates the Mongol khanate, not the Chinese imperial throne, remained the prize. Had they prevailed, the whole question of a return to Han rule might have been delayed. Zhu Yuanzhang's high praise for Kökö Temür's ability and his recognition of the legitimacy of Yuan rule are also indicators of the credibility the Yuan cause enjoyed in the eyes of its opponents.

Many times in Chinese history the decline or collapse of central power produced conditions favoring the emergence of a class of regional power holders who exploited the possibilities of a hospitable geographic niche to assert a degree of independence. An example from the late Yuan era was Fang Guozhen (ca. 1319–74), a pirate who controlled the coastal area of Zhejiang (DMB, 433–35). An illiterate man with a family background in the salt trade and fishing, Fang's familiarity with the sea served him well in a career of coastal piracy that began around 1348. The source of his strength was a fleet of ships that allowed him to prey upon the supply lines along which grain was moved by sea to the Yuan capital in the north. Under pressure from the Yuan forces Fang repeatedly surrendered to the Mongol court only to rebel again when conditions changed. Each surrender brought him a higher rank, eventually a dukedom, and increased responsibility for protecting the grain shipments he had once harassed. In this manner Fang Guozhen won Yuan tolerance of his regional independence but also made it clear that he had no higher political ambitions. By 1367 the encroachment of Zhu Yuanzhang's forces compelled Fang to surrender to Zhu. Given a nominal office, he lived out his life in Nanjing under the watchful eye of the Ming ruler.

The fact that Fang Guozhen's sons were given military ranks and granted permission to build a monument to their father's memory suggests that the Ming regime did not regard him as a symbolic threat to the cause of the new dynasty. Such was not the case with leaders of the more pretentious rival regimes. From either an ideological or an institutional point of view regional warlords like Fang Guozhen, while their existence was symptomatic of central government weakness, did not represent an alternative direction for the evolution of the Chinese polity. There was little precedent since the Sui unification for long-term survival of regional states in China proper. Ideologically, regional identities had less appeal than the concept of a unified empire. None of these states attempted to rationalize a permanent partition of Chinese territory.

The first great wave of anti-Yuan rebellion was inspired by the messianic religious ideology of the White Lotus-Maitreya cult, a popular fusion of Buddhist and Manichaean elements. Manichaeanism contributed the notion of a struggle between the forces of light and darkness (good and evil) while Buddhism supplied the idea of a future Buddha or Maitreya whose appearance would deliver the world from its troubled cycle of karmic rebirth and suffering. Believers in the doctrine looked forward to a Prince of Radiance (Ming Wang) whose arrival would signal the deliverance of the world from its troubles.

The movement in the name of the Maitreya, which was active even before 1330, matured into a full-scale rebellion in north China after 1350. The rebels, known for their dress and ritual use of incense as the Red Sashes, the Red Army, or the Incense Army, were headed by Han Shantong (d. 1355) and his son Han Liner (d. 1367) who were White Lotus sect leaders (DMB, 485–88). In addition to the belief in the Maitreya and a Prince of Radiance, their doctrines included a claim of descent from the fallen house of Song. Although Han Shantong was captured and executed, Han Liner was installed as the first emperor of a Great Song dynasty with the reign title Longfeng (Dragon and Phoenix) and the additional Manichaean designation as the Lesser Prince of Radiance (Xiao Ming Wang). Liu Futong, a White Lotus organizer, was prime minister and active leader of the movement. The Song regime reached the peak of its vigor in 1358 when the old Northern Song capital at Bianliang was taken and an assault was attempted against the Yuan capital. Conditions quickly worsened, however; Bianliang was lost in 1359 and by 1363 Han Liner was under the protection of his southern subordinate Zhu Yuanzhang. Since the fate of the Song state was in Zhu Yuanzhang's hands, we will return to it later.

A second branch of the Maitreya-worshipping radical insurrection was that headed by Xu Shouhui (d. 1360) in the middle Yangtze region. Xu was emperor of the Tianwan state that moved its capital to Hanyang in 1356 and soon acquired a vast territory. Within that realm the Sichuan basin was under the command of a Red Turban leader, Ming Yuzhen (DMB, 1069–73). In 1360 Xu Shouhui was assassinated by an opportunistic subordinate named Chen Youliang, a leader who has been compared to Zhu Yuanzhang in the sense that they both represented offshoots of the millenarian movements who turned toward the gentry elements and attempted to establish traditional dynastic orders (Dardess 1970, 550–52). By moderating their ideological positions and appealing to the landed and educated elite elements in the society both leaders were seeking to broaden the base of their followers and foster social stability.

At this juncture Ming Yuzhen broke away and in 1362 he proclaimed the Xia Dynasty, named after the earliest state known to Chinese history. Ming Yuzhen died four years later in 1366, leaving the throne to his son Ming Sheng, then just a boy. What is most interesting about the Xia regime is its ideological orientation. Ming Yuzhen changed his name from Min, a surname, to Ming (Brightness) to indicate his adherence to the Manichaean cause. His son took the throne under the reign title Kaixi (Beginning of Brilliance) and was also known as the Lesser Lord of Radiance (Xiao Ming Zhu). Except for the worship of the Maitreya Buddha, Buddhism and Daoism were suppressed in Xia territory while Confucian ceremonial and rituals were observed, schools were opened, civil service examinations were held, and some use was made of ancient Zhou dynasty terminology in naming government offices. What we see in the Xia state, then, is an effort to combine appeals to the Confucian traditions of the Han elite culture at the same time that lip service was paid to the symbols of the radical millenarian movement. It was a combination of elements bearing many resemblances to the Ming regime.

Zhu Yuanzhang's treatment of the Xia regime is worth noting. The Xia ruler, Ming Sheng, was not taken until 1371. He was given an honorary title and held in Nanjing for a year before being exiled to Korea in 1372 at the age of seventeen. The Korean King was asked to grant him permanent residence under suitable conditions for an ex-ruler. Ming Sheng's family enjoyed exemption from corvee service and taxation on the lands granted them until the middle of the seventeenth century. Apparently Zhu Yuanzhang felt that Ming Sheng was too potent a symbol of the millenarian movement to risk either putting him to death or keeping him in China. As late as 1475 a rebel leader among the Miao in Guizhou claimed descent from Ming Yuzhen.

Zhu Yuanzhang contested control of the Yangtze region with two major rival states: that of Chen Youliang on the west and Zhang Shicheng on the east. Chen Youliang's Han state was large and militarily powerful but apparently loosely organized. Chen ruled for only three years from the time he had Xu Shouhui assassinated until he was killed in the great naval battle on Boyang Lake. Even though Zhang Shicheng was less dynamic than Chen

Youliang, his state may have represented a more formidable alternative to the new order Zhu Yuanzhang wanted to create.

Zhang Shicheng (1321–67) made the transition from salt smuggling to rebellion in 1353 (DMB, 99–103). By 1354 he controlled a piece of territory around Yangzhou where the Grand Canal met the Yangtze River and started to call himself Prince Cheng. In 1356 he took Suzhou and made it the capital of a regime organized along the lines of the Yuan government but that made use of some traditional terminology. In the following year Zhang accepted a title from the Yuan court and agreed to supply grain to the Yuan capital in the north. In addition to being a rich grain producing area Zhang's territory accounted for more than half of the salt in China. The area under his control continued to expand until 1363, at which time he took the title Prince of Wu. After ten years of fighting Zhu Yuanzhang finally succeeded in capturing Zhang and removing him to Nanjing where he was beaten to death.

Zhang Shicheng's regime is difficult to assess through the surviving accounts that are often colored by partisanship to the winning cause of Zhu Yuanzhang. Nevertheless, a few elements suggest that Zhang's state of Wu may have posed a formidable challenge for Zhu. First, there is the curious fact that both Zhu Yuanzhang and Zhang Shicheng used the regional title Wu. Zhu Yuanzhang became Duke of Wu in 1361, but Dardess notes that the *Veritable Record* incorrectly says that Zhu became Duke of Wu in 1356 instead of 1361 (1970, 557; MSLHW, 45). In 1363 Zhang Shicheng took the title Prince of Wu, and Zhu did the same in the following year (MSLHW, 175). In 1367, after allegedly arranging to have Han Liner die in a boating accident and eliminating all references to the state of Song, Zhu elevated himself by formally converting the calendar to the Wu reign. Second, Zhang was generous in the treatment of his subordinates and succeeded in winning scholars over to his cause. In the long rivalry between the two leaders there were more defections from Zhu to Zhang than the reverse. Third, the core area of Zhang's state was the richest in China with many of the wealthiest and most educated families. When Zhu conquered the region he imposed unusually heavy taxes and forced many of the rich families to move to depopulated areas in Anhui. He remained suspicious of the loyalty of the Jiangnan elite.

These four cases represent some of the alternatives to the Ming regime that ultimately prevailed in 1368. At the one extreme lay the possibility of continued Mongol rule that would have frustrated the efforts of all the regional power holders to establish a new order. No doubt there was considerable sympathy for the Yuan cause among the privileged classes. Defection of Yuan officials to the rebel cause were few and the cases of loyalty to the Yuan court common. Scarcity of educated and experienced administrators was a marked feature of the rebel ranks, and the leaders of the insurrections were almost uniformly from modest backgrounds. This fact as much as any colored the opposite extreme, the possibility that China could fragment into a latticework of small parochial states headed by unsophisticated leaders of limited ambition and perspective. Such interregnums had occurred before in Chinese history, lasting more than three centuries between the Han and Sui, but a mere five decades from the Tang to the Song.

Ming Yuzhen and Zhang Shicheng represent two intermediate possibilities of Han-led imperial states that would have marked a clear break with Mongol rule and a reassertion of the political power of the Chinese heartland. The two regimes differed markedly in their ideological and social orientations. Ming Yuzhen tried to integrate elements of the radical Manichaean movement with enough of the Chinese elite tradition to legitimize the Xia in the eyes of both the upper and lower strata of society. Had the Han state triumphed, the White Lotus–Maitreya doctrine might have been built into the ideology of the new state. Zhang Shicheng, by contrast and despite his own modest beginnings, was located in the most developed center of Chinese elite culture among the educated and wealthy families who had fallen from a favored position in the Southern Song to the lower end of the social spectrum in the Yuan. Had Zhang Shicheng prevailed, China might have witnessed a revival of the civil and commercial culture of the Southern Song. Geographically, and to some extent ideologically, Zhu Yuanzhang was caught between these two alternatives. The formula he developed for rule lay somewhere in between.

Ideological Orientation

Zhu Yuanzhang was twenty-nine years old when he established himself as a regional power holder with the capture of Nanjing in 1356. At that time he was technically a subordinate of the Red Turban Song regime nominally headed by the Lesser Prince of Radiance, Han Liner. As he rose in station and began to define his own regime and style of rule, Zhu dissociated himself from the doctrines of the radical millenarians and embraced traditional Confucian views of statecraft and social order (Dardess 1970, 555). Zhu was not a revolutionary. Despite the fact that he had been a Buddhist monk, Zhu was not drawn to the Manichaean or Maitreyan visions. His ideal society was cast in traditional terms, closer to the views of orthodox Confucian scholars than to the visions of radical insurgents. His goal was to overthrow the Mongols and restore or recreate a proper Han Chinese social order. In ideological terms his path was simpler and more conservative than that of his millenarian associates. He was saving the world from disorder, not ending it to start a new age.

As he moved from insurgency to state foundation Zhu Yuanzhang embraced the cultural conventions that had evolved over the centuries. The alternative, creating a new order that violated the logic of the great tradition, would have been next to impossible. Sangren seems to suggest something of the sort when he says that order was possible only in terms of a hierarchy in which hegemonic order (*yang*) encompasses disorder (*yin*). For this reason a "heterodox" movement such as Zhu Yuanzhang's would be compelled by "the structure of orthodox Chinese epistemology" to become orthodox in the process of building a secular order:

> Otherwise there is no possibility of conceiving social stability or legitimizing social institutions and authority. That heterodox movements like Zhu Yuanzhang's seem to move toward orthodoxy as they achieve political and military control suggests that this Durkheimian conjuncture of the social and the cosmic was a necessary condition for the building of secular order in China. The totality of Chinese cultural orthodoxies and the heterodoxies they implied were incapable of legitimizing radically new political structures; the cultural alternatives were limited to two, valorized social hierarchy or world renunciation (1987a, 84).

The marriage of Neo-Confucianism to the Chinese state was one of the most important aspects of the Ming founding. The term Neo-Confucianism is an awkward English shorthand for a multifaceted body of thought that evolved within the Confucian tradition from Song times on. The term is a liability because it suggests a greater uniformity of classification than probably existed and because it does not correspond precisely to any term in Chinese. Sometimes Neo-Confucianism is used to translate the term *lixue*, or school of principle, associated with the great Song synthesizer Zhu Xi (1130–1200). At other times it has been used to include both *lixue* and the rival *xinxue*, school of mind, that reached maturity in the work of the late Ming thinker Wang Yangming (1472–1529). The term survives because it is useful. It is a convenient label for the thought of the Confucian scholars (*ru*) of all stripes from the Song dynasty on, distinguishing them from Buddhists and Daoists. When greater precision is needed, however, one must either qualify the meaning of Neo-Confucianism or use other terms.

Professor Wm. Theodore de Bary adopted the usage of "Neo-Confucianism" to include all the tendencies in later Confucian thought and "Neo-Confucian orthodoxy" to designate the stream of thought descending from Zhu Xi (de Bary 1981, xvi). De Bary and others have shown that there was considerable dynamism within Neo-Confucian thought from the Song to the early Ming. Strangely enough it was during the Yuan dynasty, under the rule of the Mongols, that Neo-Confucianism achieved the status of full-fledged orthodoxy (de Bary 1982). Orthodoxy in this context must be understood in two senses: as an ideology supported and advanced by state sponsorship, and as a doctrine propagated in an academy or passed on by a sequence of teachers. The school of thought deriving from Zhu Xi achieved a dominant status in Yuan times in both of these respects.

State adoption of Neo-Confucianism developed gradually following the Mongol conquest first of north China, long under Jin rule, and then of south China where the Song forces held out until 1279. Initially the Mongols allowed themselves to be persuaded that China should not be converted into pastureland but should be preserved as an agricultural area to be administered by a civil bureaucracy that could generate rich tax revenues. This course of action drew the conquerors into a symbiotic relationship with the Chinese and exposed them to the indigenous administrative tradition. Later the Mongol rulers established a Chinese-style dynasty and adopted numerous practices of a Chinese state including the opening of schools with a curriculum based on the *Four Books*. The final triumph of Neo-Confucianism came in the early fourteenth century when a new civil service examination system was started (1313–15) using Zhu Xi's writings as a doctrinal core.

The intellectual acceptance of Neo-Confucianism among the Chinese literati came about without significant help from the imperial state. Beginning as early as Tang times, but becoming widespread in the Song dynasty, was the conviction shared by the Chinese scholars that the "Way" (*dao*) of the ancient sages was no longer being transmitted. Thus the learning of the Way (*daoxue*) is another name for Neo-Confucianism and the transmission of the Way or "orthodox tradition" (*daotong*), one of the Neo-Confucians' central concerns.

In the Song period it was Zhu Xi who did the most to unify elements of the Neo-Confucian perspective into a coherent body of writings. Neo-Confucians were reacting to the challenge of Buddhism and at the same time appropriating from Buddhism a vocabulary of concepts that could be used to reformulate and restate some of the core ideas of the Confucian tradition. In the process Confucianism was reborn and transformed. Zhu Xi's commentaries on the *Four Books*, a group of classical texts selected and highlighted because they served Neo-Confucian needs, lay at the center of his accomplishment. Especially important was the *Great Learning* (*Daxue*), a text that focused on the crucial relationship between the ruler, self-cultivation, government and social order. Zhu Xi's interpretations were far from transcendent at his death in 1200, but his teaching gained ground dramatically in the next two centuries.

The division within Neo-Confucianism into a School of Principle (*lixue*) and School of Mind (*xinxue*) was a product of Ming times. During the Yuan, de Bary contends, the term *xinxue* could be used to characterize Neo-Confucianism as a whole and be translated as "Learning of the Mind-and-Heart" (de Bary 1981, xv). Within this school moral self-cultivation was generally more important than the "investigation of things" (*gewu*) which became the dominant preoccupation after the early Ming.

It was the success of private scholars and teachers in spreading and developing Neo-Confucian doctrine, not state sponsorship, that solidly entrenched the new learning among the Chinese literati. Yet when the Mongols conquered China the Confucian scholars with their lofty sense of moral mission found themselves cast to the bottom of the social pyramid. Confucians (*ru*) were classified as a specialized type of household, as religious practitioners similar to Buddhist and Daoist clergy. From this modest position the Confucians grappled with the problem of how to reform Chinese society under Mongol rule. Two of the strategies they developed are worth mentioning here: direct influence on the rulers and local reform. Prolonged efforts were made to gain access to the Mongol rulers and instruct them in Neo-Confucian doctrine. The results of these initiatives were mixed at best, but they did culminate in the establishment, mentioned above, of a civil service examination system in the early fourteenth century. While this accomplishment fell short of transforming the Yuan state into an engine of Neo-Confucian purification, it did set a strong precedent for the following Ming dynasty by designating the *Four Books* and Zhu Xi's commentaries as the core of the new curriculum. This was not questioned later in the century when the Ming founder resurrected the examinations (de Bary 1981, 53–63).

Ironically, it was the other strategy, the low road of local reform, that put the Neo-Confucian scholars into the closest contact with the imperial throne. This came about when Zhu Yuanzhang recruited scholars in the Jiangnan region during his rise to power.

Studies by John D. Langlois, Jr. and John W. Dardess have given us many insights into the intellectual world of the Neo-Confucian scholars in the area around the Jinhua district in Zhejiang during the late Yuan (Langlois 1974; 1981b; Dardess 1983). It was from this area, and out of its intellectual traditions, that advisers such as Liu Ji, Song Lian, and Wang Wei were drawn. Mongol rule presented Confucian scholars with considerable obstacles to achieving the social ends their beliefs prescribed. The upper levels of the Yuan administration were in the hands of Mongols and Central Asians and the lower levels were dominated by Chinese clerks and functionaries who carried out routine bureaucratic duties but who were sorely lacking in the moral education the Neo-Confucianists believed to be the very heart of government.

One response of the Jinhua scholars to this situation was to prepare themselves for the roles available. If Confucians could not enforce their norms at the highest levels of government they could at least have a positive input at the lower levels. Confucians could be trained in practical administrative skills to serve as clerks and functionaries. They developed the idea of an "authentic scholar" (*zhenru*) who would combine Confucian learning with expertise in the law. Langlois credits these developments in the Jinhua area to the influence of a "merit and profit" or "utilitarian" (*gongli*) school of thought and a statecraft tradition that sought a rational understanding of emperorship. Toward the end of the Southern Song these elements fused with the dominant tradition of Zhu Xi's idealism to produce a unique philosophical perspective. It differed from Zhu Xi's teaching in the belief that "authentic scholars" could make the dynastic institutions function well even if the rulers did not undergo moral transformation (Langlois 1981b, 140-84).

The Jinhua thinkers put their loyalty to the Way ahead of their loyalty to a particular dynasty. They were willing to serve the Mongols if such service could contribute to institutional reform that would benefit the community (or people) as a whole. The mechanism they proposed to use to clean up the corruption and disorder surrounding them was law. Their writings reflected a preoccupation with legal institutions which Langlois characterizes as follows:

> One approach seems to have informed Chin-hua [i.e., Jinhua] literati's attitudes toward the political problems fostered by Mongol rule, despite the continually changing nature of that rule. This was the stress on the employment of law as a means of transforming Mongol domination into orderly government. Law in pre-modern China meant first of all the will of the sovereign—commands of the emperor issued in the form of edicts. Law also meant the regulations that were set down to guide the behavior of persons in their various social and political roles in the hierarchical order. It also meant penal law, the specified criminal acts for which society demanded punishment in accordance with the hierarchical principles of Confucian ethics (Langlois 1981b, 165).

In the late Yuan years the Jinhua elite undertook reform on the local level at their own initiative. The rebel upsurge of the early 1350s created ample opportunities for the Confucian literati, acting under the banner of loyalty to the Yuan ruler, to organize anti-rebel forces. The fall of the Yuan leader Toghto in 1355, however, doomed the enterprise (Dardess 1970, 548–9; 1983, 86). Without at least token support from the Yuan court the Jinhua scholars faced a difficult choice. They could remain loyal to the legitimate Yuan ruler whose cause appeared lost or throw in their lot with one of the regional rebels seeking to establish a new order. This was the situation when Zhu Yuanzhang's forces took control of Jinhua. Zhu appeared to be just what they wanted: he was able, had a sense of mission, and eagerly sought out scholarly advice. By 1360 the leading Jinhua thinkers were in his camp. They were in a position to become, as Dardess puts it, "theoretical founders of the Ming autocracy" (1983, 5).

Early Ming legislation grew out of the changing circumstances of Zhu Yuanzhang's rise as a regional commander when he began to address questions of statecraft in a serious way. Ambitious and intelligent, Zhu looked beyond the problems of the moment to the prospect of founding a dynasty. Crucial to his success was his decision to surrounded himself with learned advisors who tutored him in the essentials of statecraft. During these years, as the core of a central administration took shape, he listened to presentations, studied classical texts and talked endlessly with his advisors about the ends and means of good government.

Learning to Rule

Already in 1353 Zhu had asked Li Shanchang (1314-1390) to assume responsibility for administrative affairs (Massey 1983, 26). Li's background is somewhat obscure, but his official biography suggests that he was familiar with the writings of the Legalist school. Li appears to have been more of an executive than a scholar, regularly occupying the highest administrative offices. He did, however, play a leading role in overseeing the compilation of the new Ming law codes and in designing ceremonial guidelines in the first years of the new dynasty (DMB, 850–54). Liu Ji, Song Lian, Zhang Yi, Ye Chen, Wang Wei, Tao An and Zhan Tong were important early advisers (Massey 1983, 28). Liu Ji and Song Lian were the most influential. Liu Ji (1311–1375) and Song Lian (1310–1381) joined Zhu's service in 1360 (Langlois 1983, 101). Liu Ji, a degree holder and former official under the Yuan, was an able astrologer who gave Zhu important advice on military and political matters during the latter's rise to power. Liu is credited with persuading Zhu to disassociate himself from the regime of Han Liner (DMB, 932–738; Chan 1968; Chan 1974; Dardess 1983, 133–47).

Song Lian came from a more modest background than Liu Ji but he may have had more intellectual impact on Zhu Yuanzhang than Liu. More concerned with scholarly and ideological matters than with political decisions and statecraft, Song played a role in educating both the Ming founder and his son, the heir apparent, Zhu Biao. Song was one of the strongest links between the new regime and the school of Confucian thought associated with the Jinhua area in Zhejiang (DMB, 1225–31; Dardess 1983, 156–73). A native of Jinhua, Song Lian had studied in Pujiang and taught at the famous school of the Righteous Zheng Clan (Danjo 1982a; 1982b). Thus Song has been seen as a conduit between the thought of the Jinhua Neo-Confucian elite and the Ming founder. He wrote extensively on questions concerning the nature and influence of spirits, for example, a topic vitally interesting to Zhu Yuanzhang (Langlois and Sun 1983, 103–6).

Despite his apparent influence with Zhu Yuanzhang Song Lian did not enjoy the renown in later years that Liu Ji did. Liu Ji, whose accomplishments were not more outstanding than Song Lian's, became something of a Confucian cult figure. Araki Kengo, who studied this matter, concluded that the reason Song Lian was not highly regarded was due to the fact that Song's thought was eclectic in nature (Dardess 1983, 10; de Bary 1981, 155). This fact may also help to explain why Song Lian was as influential as he was in the early Ming period because Zhu Yuanzhang was himself more of a syncretist than he was a partisan of the Confucian position.

Liu Ji and Song Lian are two of the scholars at Zhu Yuanzhang's court whose service was crucial to the success of Zhu's drive to save China. They helped him to organize and run his government, providing both tactical and strategic advice on a wide range of policy issues. They were instrumental in writing the documents that gave the Ming government an image of legitimacy in terms of traditional Confucian cultural values. They also tutored the new emperor in the content and meaning of classical texts and philosophical doctrines.

After consolidating control over his base in the lower Yangzi Zhu followed the same pattern as numerous other regional commanders by upgrading the status of his regime. In 1361 the title Duke of Wu was conferred upon Zhu, signifying that he had serious political ambitions. In 1364 he installed himself as Prince of Wu, a logical preliminary to declaring himself emperor (MSLHW, 175).

In the tutorial sessions he held with his advisors Zhu began to explore the historical record for models upon which to base his actions. To judge from the accounts of his actions left in the *Veritable Record* the Han example was much on Zhu Yuanzhang's mind before he assumed the throne. In 1364 he consulted with Song Lian and Kong Keren about how historical conditions had constrained the Han founder's opportunity to return to the ideal government of the past (MSLHW, 95–6). A year, later in conversation with Kong Keren, he explicitly compared his own situation to that of the Han founder (MSLHW, 224–5). In 1366 he asked his Confucian advisors who was better, Han Gaozu or Tang Taizong (MSLHW, 302–3). Zhu gave the judgement to the Tang ruler.

The role of law in government was a central concern in the discussions Zhu Yuanzhang held with his advisers prior to the founding of the Ming. A number of these conversations, recorded in the *Veritable Record* over the decade from 1358 to 1367, show Zhu patronizing Confucianists, seeking instruction from them, and discussing with them the problems of pacifying the empire (MSLHW, 70, 74, 75, 79–80, 80, 93). In 1363 an Office for Honoring Worthies (*Lixianguan*) was established to regularize the employment of Confucian advisers (MSLHW, 153–4). Four years later Zhu ordered his officials to gather together a reference collection of new and old books so as to benefit from the learning of the past, especially the teachings of Confucius (MSLHW, 287). In these early years the critical question was how to govern. Talking about the administration of territory newly acquired in 1358, Zhu stressed the importance of using penal law in moderation. He compared law to medicine that is supposed to cure the patient but which, if taken in too heavy a dose, can cause death (MSLHW, 63–4). In 1364, two days after taking the title Prince of Wu, Zhu Yuanzhang spoke to his officials about the founding of a state. His remarks at that time identified rites and law as the basic principles of state (*jigang*, lit. net ropes of the state), the first matters to be dealt with in forming the state (MSLHW, 176–7). The neglect of law was explicitly cited in the Ming founder's explanation of what went wrong in the Yuan dynasty. In 1365 he addressed the officials of his court on the shortcomings of law under the Mongols:

> The Yuan were originally Barbarians [*Huren*] who arose in the deserts and came into control of China quite suddenly, uniting all within the seas. At the onset of their dynasty the officials who assisted them were worthy and those recommended for appointment were all men of virtue. At that time government was harmonious and credible. But later on morally inferior persons [*xiaoren*] assumed authority and evil persons clambered for advancement. They selected their relatives and cronies and formed cliques so that officials in both the Capital and the provinces became avaricious and shameless. From that point on the legal system was relaxed and the first principles of state were not vigourously applied [net ropes were not shaken, *jigang bu zhen*]. Eventually the situation collapsed to a point where it could no longer be saved. Now, at the outset of a founding, if we do not firmly establish a legal system in order to eliminate evil practices I fear in the future officials will follow the old ways and will be unable to straighten things out. It is imperative to employ the virtuous and able in order to foster good government. When you recommend persons for office be careful about the selection (MSLHW, 211).

Central to this passage, and to Zhu's views on good government, is the relationship between official virtue and the legal system. In this early statement the emphasis was on the moral quality of the agents of government, but the legal system was accorded a central place. Social order was pictured as a mesh or network of threads which were the norms or laws. The act of governing involved shaking the tangles from the net, i.e., applying the first principles of state (Dardess 1983, 196). Later, as he encountered difficulties in dealing with subordinates, Zhu Yuanzhang would place less emphasis on the morality of officials, whom he came increasingly to view as prone to evil, and more on laws and rules that could keep them in line.

In the months before he took the throne Zhu Yuanzhang repeatedly discussed his philosophy of government with senior advisors. On one occasion in 1367 he advocated a lightening of penal measures that amounted to guilt by association. Yang Xian, an official whose differences with Zhu's judgement were eventually to lead to his execution, advocated repressive laws:

> Yang Xian: "Former kings have employed punishments sometimes heavily and sometime lightly. The Yuan government was indulgent and people thought nothing of breaking the law. Without stern rule the transgressors will multiply." Emperor: "The people doing wrong is like clothing that has become filthy, it needs to be washed to become clean again. People who have been stained with evil need correct guidance to become new again. To make the

> people afraid to transgress by intimidating them with capital punishment is a superficial policy. To plead for one's life under repressive laws is like being a tethered fish in a pot, it is hard to stay alive. Under less repressive laws it would not be necessary to plead for one's life and death would not be the outcome" (MSLHW, 362).

As he prepared to found a dynasty, Zhu Yuanzhang energetically explored questions of statecraft in discussions with his advisors. The institutions of the regime he headed were initially similar to those of the Yuan dynasty he was trying to overthrow. His program of world salvation aimed at ending the chaos of civil war and restoring Han Chinese cultural practices. The ideals that were to guide his restoration were to be found in the past, in classical texts and historical precedents. But history and the traditional canon spoke with many voices. Precedents could be found for a wide range of policies. In the choices he made, Zhu turned to the Confucian great tradition and was heavily influenced by the views of the Jinhua scholars with their penchant for reliance on law. There is little indication, beyond the selection of the dynastic name Ming, that he was influenced by the doctrines of the radical religious movements (Dardess 1970, 557–58). His populism appeared, as in the pious exchange cited above, in the form of a concern for the common people and their suffering. Later, after he had been on the throne for more than a decade, he was to develop a keen hostility to scholars and officials whose self-serving behavior he considered a threat to the people's welfare and an obstacle to good government. How that change came about is the story of the Ming dynasty's first dozen years.

CHAPTER THREE

CREATING THE NEW ORDER

Zhu Yuanzhang was forty years old in 1368, the year the Ming dynasty was founded. During the first dozen years on the throne, Zhu was preoccupied with the optimistic and constructive work of putting the new empire on a solid footing. In that span of time great progress was made on the main agendas of world salvation, restoration of the past, and enculturation of the people. Pockets of Yuan resistance were suppressed and outlying territory was pacified. The people were spared the horrors of civil war, abandoned lands were resettled, and agricultural production was encouraged. Mongol customs were replaced by traditional Chinese practices, radical religious cults were outlawed, and orthodox Confucian learning was fostered in new schools. A comprehensive program of legislation and ritual regulations sought to define the social hierarchy in minute detail.

From the start, special attention was given to rewarding his followers and members of the imperial family. Toward this end the peasant generals of the Wu state were transformed into a hereditary nobility to reside in the capital and wait on the emperor at court (Taylor 1976). The status of the imperial clan was elevated by honoring the emperor's deceased father as a corecipient in imperial sacrifices to heaven and earth (Langlois 1988, 118–719). Imperial offspring and all future descendants were to be princes and princesses of varying degrees. Continuing practices of the Yuan dyansty (Huang 1977), the populace at large were divided into commoner (*min*) and military (*jun*) families with a few smaller specialized categories such as artisans (*jiang*) and physicians (*yi*). According to their categories the people were to supply the government with taxes, corvee service, military service, construction work, and the like.

The new regime engaged in extensive social engineering, transferring criminals and landless elements to regions in the north left depopulated by warfare in the last years of the Yuan. Military colonies were established along the northern frontier to provide security against the persisting Mongol threat. Paper currency, salt certificates, and grants of land and oxen were all used to bolster the repopulation and defense of the north at minimum cost to the state. Culturally, early Ming legislation aimed at the erasure of persisting Mongol practices and a return to Han Chinese standards in such matters as marriage, dress, and names.

A few examples will serve to illustrate the complexity and range of ways that the past was used to guide and to justify legislation in the early years of the Ming Dynasty. Despite claims that he was restoring the past, Zhu in fact followed Yuan practice closely in the early years of his rule. Later, he borrowed freely from the Han, Tang, and Song while disguising his debt to the Mongol rulers of the Yuan (Langlois 1981b, 177; Dardess 1983, 194–6).

In the first years of its existence Zhu Yuanzhang's regime was a militarized insurgency fighting to control a share of territory within the deteriorating Yuan empire. At that time many titles and institutional arrangements were borrowed directly from the Yuan. Thus the dynasty formally founded in 1368 closely resembled the Yuan in its table of organization. As time passed, however, substantial changes took place, the great upheaval of 1380 marking the most dramatic and permanent departure from the practices of the preceding Mongol government (Hucker 1985, 72). From the central down to the local levels Ming institutions took on distinct forms and nomenclature. The military system is an example of a Ming institution that was obviously influenced by Yuan precedent (Dreyer 1982, 76-87). It was built around a hereditary category of military households (*junhu*) who provided the state with men for military service in lieu of other forms of taxation. Military personnel were supported by a system of colony fields and commanded by members of a hereditary nobility. Romeyn Taylor has demonstrated how the system of guards and battalions (chiliads) was adapted from Mongol practice, noting that the debt was not acknowledged in the official *Ming History* account (Taylor 1969, 24–25).

An instance of borrowing from precedents in the Han Dynasty is the decision in 1370 to grant regional titles to the founder's sons and to set them up with small armies of retainers at strategic positions along the frontier. The resulting mixture of "feudal" and "prefectural" elements was unique to the early Ming but it drew consciously on the early Han system of commanderies and domains. Despite superficial appearances, the Ming and Han enfeoffments were distinct in purpose. The Han network of princedoms and marquisates had had the initial effect of dispersing power throughout the empire. The Ming system, by contrast, was designed to extend the emperor's power via his family members to outlying areas (Yang 1969; Hucker 1985, 13–14).

Classical and historical precedents were much on the mind of the founder and his advisers in the early years of the new regime. In 1369 the emperor, concerned that his new dynasty still had no ritual institutions, ordered a group of Confucian scholars to compile a book of ritual. Officials in the provinces were to select and send to the capital knowledgeable men of good character in their fifties. Their task was to examine historical precedents and fashion a new system for the Ming (MSLHW, 875).

In the same month, the history of the preceding dynasty, the *Yuan shi*, was completed, confirming the legitimate place of Mongol rule in the orthodox succession of dynasties while at the same time consigning it to a safe location in the historical past (MSLHW, 863–65). In these years Zhu Yuanzhang was already worrying about the weight that would fall upon his successor's shoulders, and in 1370 we find him lecturing his eldest son, the heir apparent, on responsibility for the welfare of the empire (MSLHW, 1059). A year later he instructed the heir apparent to read the *Yuan shi* with attention to the account of the dynastic founder, Shizu, i.e., Khubilai, as a negative example: "Although Shizu was able to establish a dynasty his institutional arrangements were very crude. Because he knew nothing of ritual and music his policies fell short of the Han and Tang. How could he restore antiquity [*fu gu*] (MSLHW, 1197) ?"

Like the Han, the Tang Dynasty loomed large in the historical record and offered a natural source of precedents for the new Ming state. It was to the Tang that Zhu Yuanzhang turned when he ordered that Ming subjects abandon the use of the Mongol language, Mongol names, hair styles and conventions of dress (Wu Han 1948, 110; MSLHW, 525). In 1370 it was necessary to issue a clarification about the style of caps to be worn by men and women, officials and commoners. During the first three years of the Hongwu era there were numerous discussions and rulings on matters of dress and ceremony. In prescribing the sumptuary and ceremonial regulations for the nobility of merit the Tang and Song practices were used as guides (MSLHW, 903–904, 1157).

The explicit intention to return to the practices of an earlier Chinese dynasty reflected the conviction that the era of Mongol rule just ended had robbed ethnic Chinese of their true cultural identity. In 1369, a year after the dynasty was founded, Zhu called for the establishment of schools which could revive Chinese customs. The text of his edict to the Secretariat conveys his concern:

> Instruction in the schools became extremely poor during the Yuan Dynasty. This has caused the ancient rulers' teachings on dress and decorum to become confused with those of the barbarians so that distinctions between superior and inferior are utterly destroyed. Of the schools formerly founded only the names remain; the substance was gone. How much worse the situation since the hostilities commenced. Men have become accustomed to fighting: they know only weaponry and are ignorant of the sacrifices. I have always maintained that in ruling the state education comes first and that schools are the basis of the way to education. Today there is only a National University in the Capital; the schools throughout the empire have not been revived. An order should be sent to the districts to establish schools and to respctfully engage Confucian scholars to instruct students in the way of the sages. The people thereby will gradually become educated and the ways of the ancient rulers will be restored, eliminating polluting customs. This is an urgent matter which ought to be carried out quickly (MSLHW, 923–24).

Ten days later the emperor ordered local units of government to establish schools (MSLHW, 924–5). The priority given to the matter of schooling reflects both the concern the Ming founder felt about repairing the cultural damage caused by Mongol rule and the sense that Chinese should properly conform to norms associated with the ancient rulers (*xian wang*). Central to the latter element was the assumption that enculturation (*jiaohua*) taught people forms of dress and deportment that would clarify the distinctions between superiors and inferiors. The way of the sages (*shengdao*) was an instrument for social stratification.

During the early years of the Hongwu era the emperor constantly made minor adjustments and devised rules and practices that would ensure order and secure his rule. After an unsatisfactory start the examination system was suspended in 1373. Early versions of the *Ming Code* and the *Ancestral Instruction* underwent revision, and various rules, injunctions and compilations were issued to guide the conduct of palace women, princes, nobles, officials and eunuchs. Particularly important, in terms of symbolically elevating the emperor's status were measures to honor the imperial clan. In 1369 a hall in honor of his ancestors was erected just to the east of the palace gate. The emperor also made the spirit of his late father part of the sacrifices to heaven and earth and to the spirits of grain and soil, thus associating the imperial lineage with the most fundamental forces (Langlois 1988, 124–37).

In 1371, shortly after the dynasty was founded, the first Ming emperor elaborated on his views of law in discussions with officials in the court. On one occasion he corrected his minister of rites on the place of punishments in the reform of popular behavior (MSLHW, 1248–9). The moral transformation of the people, he said, was primarily a matter of ceremonial and not a matter of administering punishments. On another occasion he refuted a censorial official who had advocated the use of harsh punishments (MSLHW, 1233). Zhu Yuanzhang rejected harsh punishments as counterproductive. Such a policy, he said, would only increase the number of persons incriminated. In making his case the emperor spoke of the ancient sage king Yao who had achieved order with moderate measures whereas the cruel tortures employed by the Qin had provoked the people of the empire into rebellion.

Codification

The first dozen years were filled with energetic measures to rebuild the social and political order, conscious efforts to distance the new dynasty from the Yuan, wide-ranging searches for classical and historical precedents, and a considerable amount of trial and error. The annals of the imperial court, the *Veritable Record* of these years, portray a still optimistic ruler studying the human condition and the lessons of history with the intention of creating a dynastic order that could endure for many generations. Several tasks that were on the emperor's mind run through the entries of the first decade: restoring Chinese cultural forms, making correct applications of classical and historical precedents, searching out men of talent and virtue, lightening the burdens of the common people, educating the next generation for rule, clearly marking social and political differences through sumptuary and ceremonial regulations, and strengthening and protecting the social order with a systematic body of laws. These concerns all reflected the need to create a new institutions where none existed. A number of them are evident in the codifications of the first decade.

In 1367, just before the Ming was founded, Zhu Yuanzhang ordered the compilation of the *Code* (*lü*) and the *Commandment* (*ling*) (MSLHW, 389–90). The Left Chief Councilor Li Shanchang was given primary responsibility. He was to be assisted by over two dozen others, including Liu Ji, Yang Xian, and Tao An. The emperor noted that the Tang and Song dynasties had fully developed statutes to decide criminal cases but that the Yuan had not followed suit. The past practice of making particular decisions into a body of articles (*tiaoge*) made it easy for officials to practice corruption. A new system of fixed statutes was needed. Zhu Yuanzhang put it this way:

> In establishing laws the important thing is that the language be simple and the principles clear so that it will be easy for everyone to know. If the provisions are too numerous, or if one case can have two outcomes, one lenient and one severe, villainous and greedy officials connive to do evil. It is not good law that seeks to prohibit cruelty and violence but ends up treating robbers as fine folk. It is imperative to seek moderation in order to eliminate complexity. For when fishing nets are too fine, there are no big fish in the water; if the laws are too fine a country's people cannot keep themselves whole. The ministers and others should look earnestly into this. Day by day, every law and its articles are to be brought to me for careful discussion among me and the ministers so that we can make laws that will last forever (MSLHW, 389).

This entry is followed in the *Veritable Record* by another in which Zhu amplified his views on the role of law in government in a statement to Liu Ji and two others that the first principles (lit. net ropes) of the law (*jigang fadu*) were the fundamental basis of government (MSLHW, 389–90). A month later he again spoke to his officials about the matter of law, this time criticizing the complexity and ambiguity of law in the Yuan period (MSLHW, 419-20). A satisfactory codification of the laws was not easy to achieve, however. It would be thirty years before the *Ming Code* assumed its final form.

The *Code* and the *Commandment* were reprinted and issued to officials in 1373 (MSLHW, 1465). After promulgation the emperor feared that the contents of the *Code* and *Commandment* would be too complicated for common people to grasp so he ordered that a simplified version be prepared for popular consumption. He again ordered his legal specialists to study the *Tang Code* for elements that could be adopted. The *Great Ming Code* was then revised again in 1374. The five punishments (*wu xing*) and their degrees were specified: (1) the light stick (*chi*), 10 to 50 strokes in five grades; (2) the heavy stick (*zhang*), 60 to 100 strokes in five grades; (3) penal servitude (*tu*), five grades from one to three years with strokes of the heavy stick starting at 60 and rising to 100 in intervals of 10 strokes for every six months of servitude; (4) life exile (*liu*), three grades from 2,000 *li* to 3,000 *li* with 100 strokes of the heavy stick; (5) death (*si*), two degrees, strangulation (*jiao*) and decapitation (*zhan*). The contents were divided into twelve categories following the organization of the *Tang Code*: General Principles (*ming li*), Imperial Guard and Prohibitions (*wei jin*), Administrative Regulations (*zhi zhi*), Household and Marriage (*hu hun*), Public Stables and Granaries (*jiu ku*), Unauthorized Levies (*shan xing*), Violence and Robbery (*zei dao*), Assaults and Accusations (*dou song*), Fraud and Counterfeit (*zha wei*), Miscellaneous Articles (*za lü*), Arrest and Flight (*bu wang*), and Judgement and Prison (*duan yü*) (MSLHW, 1534–5; Johnson 1979, 42).

The resulting compilation made use of 288 articles from the old *Code*, 128 new articles, 36 items converted from the old *Commandment*, 31 articles derived from rulings, and 123 articles from the *Tang Code* for a total of 606 articles, divided into thirty sections (*juan*). The emperor ordered that the draft be put up on the walls so that he could personally make changes. The Hanlin academician Song Lian presented the completed version which was proclaimed throughout the realm (MSLHW, 1534–35). Three years later, in 1376, the emperor called upon his Left Chief Councillor Hu Weiyong and Censor-in-chief Wang Guangyang to simplify the articles in the *Code*. His order was preceded by a typical reference to the past:

> In ancient times the customs were strong and the prohibitions were few. In later ages people's minds were corrupted and the laws became numerous. That was because the sage kings gave priority to leniency and did not give priority to severity. They stressed simplicity and did not stress complexity. When a state establishes its laws it should give priority to conforming to the Way [*dao*]; then people will submit and it will be transmitted to later ages. Long ago Xiao He made the nine chapters of the *Han Code*; it was very terse and convenient. Later, Zhang Tang schemed for his own selfish interest and distorted it. Not having been perfected, how could it long endure without faults? (MSLHW, 1821–22)

The order to compile the *Ancestral Instruction* (*Zuxunlu*), specifying how the establishments of the imperial princes were to be set up, was issued in 1369 (MSLHW, 818). The completed work was presented to the throne in 1373 (MSLHW, 1470–71). It was divided into thirteen sections: Warnings (*zhenjie*), Observance (*chishou*), Proper Sacrifice (*yan jisi*), Precaution on Coming and Going (*jin churu*), Prudence in Affairs of State (*shen guozheng*), Ceremony (*liyi*), Law (*falü*), Palace Regulation (*neiling*), Eunuchs (*neiguan*), Rules of Office (*zhizhi*), Military Guards (*bingwei*), Construction (*yingshan*), Provisions (*gongyong*). The emperor wrote his own preface, which is translated in appendix 1, making clear the effort he had put into revision. In addition to issuing the text to the princes the emperor ordered that it be put up on walls in the palace and that the princes should put it on the walls of their palaces as well. Minor changes to the text were ordered in 1376 (MSLHW, 1738–39).

In addition to legislation that dealt directly with the social order, the first decade of Zhu Yuanzhang's rule produced an enormous body of decrees and rulings governing such matters as dress, style of residence, deportment, titles, funeral practices, and religious ritual. The entries on these matters in the *Veritable Record* are so numerous as to preclude a comprehensive treatment. One example will suffice.

Sumptuary law, the regulation of dress, equipage, and residence styles, was a major area of concern in the early years. In the first two years, 1368–69, dress regulations were devised for the palace, for funerals, and for officials and their dependents (MSLHW, 467, 709–10, 744). More complete regulations governing dress for the various ranks were developed in 1370 using Song precedents as a guide (MSLHW, 1059, 1079, 1116, 1117). In 1371 it was ordered that functionaries should wear black (MSLHW, 1229–30). Multiple decrees, some in great detail, in 1372 stipulated the colors of clothing that could not be worn by commoners, the styles appropriate to persons of different ranks, what should be worn for weddings and funerals, and what by ladies and even musicians (MSLHW, 1330, 1337, 1343–47, 1363–64, 1364–68, 1399, 1403). Briefer decrees on dress regulations for the relatives of officials and for members of the imperial family appeared in 1373 and 1376 (MSLHW, 1532–33, 1765). The emperor stated his views on sumptuary regulations to court officials in 1370:

> When the rulers of ancient times governed the realm they fixed the ceremonial system in order to distinguish between the noble and the lowly and to manifest the styles appropriate to the various ranks. That is why Han Gaozu, when he first arose, used fine silk clothing to distinguish the ranks of soldiers and horses. In subsequent ages the same practice was followed. In recent time inherited customs have drifted into the usurpation of luxury so that the commoners in villages are dressing, eating, and dwelling no differently from nobles and high officials. Moreover, lowly slaves often are as dissolutely extravagant as high officials, distorting the difference between high and low so that there are no gradations. Defying propriety and transgressing limits caused the Yuan to lose control. The Secretariat should establish restrictions (*jintiao*) clarifying

gradations of housing and clothing and proclaim them in the capital and the provinces (MSLHW, 1076).

Instructions to Aid the World

During the first years of the new dynasty, when laws, rules, and regulations were being drafted for every aspect of Chinese life, the Ming founder must have devoted considerable thought to the kind of social order he wished to create. As time went by he moved beyond the simple and pious formulas he had discussed with his advisors and tutors prior to taking the throne and gained confidence in his own views. As he did so, serious tensions began to emerge between him and his officials. At the heart of the conflict was the Confucians' claim to expert knowledge about statecraft that entitled them to guide the ruler. The content of their knowledge was Neo-Confucian teachings relevant to governing society and bringing about social order. The Confucians shared a service ideal in the form of their special mission to bring about the moral reform of society. Dardess has characterized the Confucians as a professional group who enforced their own standards and were largely responsible for educating new professionals (Dardess 1983, 4). They were demonstrably not a regional interest, a hereditary category, or a class, but an educationally qualified service group. The most problematical aspect of the Confucians as a profession was their relationship to the ruler and his government. The Confucians did not, and according the dictates of their professional standards could not, form a government.
Their role was to provide service in the form of guidance and moral instruction to a ruler who stood above them. Ideally this ruler should be amenable to self-cultivation and the pursuit of sagehood.

The Confucian scholars looked to the ruler and the government as the proper mechanisms to put their philosophy into action. In their view world salvation would be achieved only through enlightened rule—a rule they would foster by instructing and serving a powerful emperor. Dardess, after investigating the writings of Liu Ji, Wang Wei, Song Lian, and Hu Han, concluded that there was much in their views to support the creation of a strong centralized state with a powerful ruler who could manage it. Because the Yuan bureaucracy, staffed by Mongols, Central Asians, and unscrupulous Chinese functionaries, was so corrupt, it would be necessary, in the eyes of the Jinhua scholars, for the ruler to deal harshly with his bureaucrats. Crucial to this system of government would be the strong influence of Confucian advisers:

> The Confucian advisory role is in fact the primary role in all of this, since the writers do assume that the bureaucracy will serve its own ends unless restrained by the ruler, and the ruler will satisfy his personal desires unless he is

effectively advised to do otherwise by the national professional elite (Dardess 1983, 176–80).

But in Zhu Yuanzhang the scholars may have gotten more than they bargained for. While he accepted in broad outline the Confucians' vision of a properly ordered society, particularly the need for a strong ruler who could control the bureaucracy, he was anything but the instrument of the scholars. He did listen to them and take instruction from them, but he was not a pliant pupil. The Ming founder exceeded the Confucian requirements of the ideal ruler. He indeed saw himself as the instrument for world salvation and accepted the proposition that he needed to restrain the bureaucracy on behalf of the general welfare, but he did not feel bound by Confucian guidance. Far from becoming the tool of the scholars and their ideology, he saw the scholars as *his* tools. They were simply one of a number of functional groups, like eunuchs or soldiers, who played a role in the work of the state. Confucianism, too, was but one of a number of ideologies that played a role in the social order.

Judging from his writings and his action the Ming founder was more of a syncretist than a Confucian. He outlawed the White Lotus and Manichaean movements that had flourished in the waning years of the Yuan but he continued to respect conventional forms of Buddhism and Daoism. He set up agencies to regulate ordination of clergy and oversee their activities. He formally recognized the leading Daoist adept but in so doing changed his title from Celestial Master (*tianshi*) to Great Perfected One (*da zhenren*) thereby preserving his own exclusive right to speak on behalf of heaven (Langlois 1988, 114). In an audacious series of actions starting in 1369, the Ming founder reorganized the pantheon of local gods of the walls and moats, subordinating them to his authority by giving them titles of nobility. A year later these military titles were abolished and the temples of the city gods were ordered made over in the style of civil offices, presumably so they could keep track of local officials (Taylor 1977, 40–41). In 1375 Zhu undertook to personally write a commentary on the *Daodejing*, taking note of its rejection of harsh punishments as a sound method of rule (Langlois 1988, 134–35). Romeyn Taylor has translated and analyzed a brief and rather cryptic essay, written sometime between 1368 and 1384, in which Zhu spells out his ideas on syncretism of the three teachings, i.e., Confucianism, Buddhism, and Daoism (Taylor 1983). All three are seen as legitimate; each has its role to play. Buddhism and Daoism are seen as essential complements to the netropes of the law. But Confucianism is in effect assigned a lower status by virtue of being restricted to the temporal realm whereas the other two teachings partook of the supernatural.

Zhu Yuanzhang sought to situate himself in a dominant position above all three doctrines. He took his role as teacher so seriously that he turned the tables on his learned Confucian advisers and would-be instructors. On numerous issues critical to the integrity of the Confucian vision Zhu Yuanzhang boldly asserted his own opinions. Instead of deferring to the expert knowledge of his Confucian scholar-advisers Zhu Yuanzhang claimed his superiority over them, even in the realm of the social theory that was their specialization. A good illustration of Zhu's perspective on these matters is provided by his essay *Yuzhi zishi tongxun* (Comprehensive imperial instruction to guide the age), completed in 1375 (MSLHW, 1664). In it the Ming founder's views on the social order were made explicit.

Zhu claimed to be transmitting the learning of the ancient sages directly to the world (ZSTX, 1447). The *Zishi tongxun* takes the form of a colloquy between the emperor and a learned visitor. In the course of the dialogue Zhu Yuanzhang gives us his approved view of how each element in the community should behave. Zhu made his intention clear in a statement to his courtiers:

> Rulers are the masters of the officials and the people, responsible for governing and instructing them, and enforcing the way of ancient rulers in accord with heaven. In unifying the world I have rested neither night nor day in restoring the customs of the people and reviving the ancient ways of government. Now I have written this document as a warning (MSLHW, 1664).

The essay is divided into fourteen sections starting with the ruler at the top of the social hierarchy and descending through the officials and scholars to the people. The section on the ruler is followed by that on the official, which is in turn followed by two sections on the people (*minyong*). As we will see below, these three turn out to be the principals in the political equation. Nobles, who presumably come just below the ruler in the social hierarchy, are not even mentioned. After the sections on the people there occur four sections on the traditional quartet of scholars, farmers, craftsmen, and merchants (*shi, nong, gong, shang*). That this is not just a repetition of a classical formula is confirmed by the fact that the section on merchants, traditionally the bottom of the social order, is followed by one on Buddhist and Daoist clergy. As the text notes, these two elements in the social order did not exist in ancient times (ZSTX, 1468–71).

In authoring this essay Zhu Yuanzhang was setting himself up as an expert on the very knowledge that gave the Confucians their professional status. He went on to offer his own definitions of the two roles that Confucians might play, those of minister and of scholar. According to Zhu, the minister (*chen*) was essentially an instrument created by the ruler. He stated this view in a discussion of the three obligations (or recompenses, *bao*) of the minister. The first was the obligation to the ruler, the second that owed to parents, and the third that owed to the people (*min*):

> Heaven and Earth have produced common people in a great multitude. Without a ruler there would be chaos. So Heaven produced the sovereign to rule over them. The ruler establishes the various officials in order to help manage them. The people, fearing the tyranny of the many over the few and the oppression of the weak by the strong, rejoice in paying taxes to the court hoping that parents, wives, and children can be free of worry. The ruler receives the taxes and apportions them to the various officials so that they may eat without tilling the soil and be clothed without practicing sericulture. They are given high positions and their families are richly rewarded so that they will be just and upright in the court. Thus the people rejoice in their happiness. If officials accept this employment, practice the Way, settle disputes among the people, and look into the people's sufferings, they can enjoy good fortune and longevity without limit (ZSTX, 1454–55).

The effect of this passage is to reduce the official to the status of an instrument facilitating the purposes of the people and the sovereign, two Heaven-created entities. The dependence on the ruler and ultimately on the people is clearly stated. This is Zhu's selective interpretation of a passage in the *Zuo zhuan* that gave heaven credit for creating the people and the ruler to superintend them. In the original, heaven was given rather more credit for establishing the officials (Watson 1988). De Bary points out that the passage in the *Zuo zhuan* adds that the ruler was to be assisted and criticized as a check on arrogance and willfulness (de Bary 1991, 19). This was hardly Zhu's view of the matter.

If the minister's status in Zhu Yuanzhang's estimate is modest, the scholar (*shi*) fairs poorly indeed. In the same essay the question is posed as to why it is that those who are called able scholars (*neng shi*) are not employed. The sad answer is that since ancient times most scholars have lacked relevance; they have been able in name only. In the founder's eyes the truly able scholar was rare indeed (ZSTX, 1461–63). In an essay on the social order he ventured the opinion that most scholars were useless braggarts, lacking in practical knowledge and prone to offering up confused double talk:

> I said to the visitor: "Well known able scholars throughout the ages did not have appropriate positions. Why is that?"
> The visitor responded: "They were all well known, able scholars throughout the ages in name only, not those who understood the times. How could either man or spirits offer them a position? And those 'well known scholars' who sit looking on in the market and the village, bragging of their own ability, enjoying flattery from the ordinary people, when did they ever experience or witness anything? They wrote books and established their views, busily crafted their language, thus confusing later scholars. When asked about managing affairs they were utterly ignorant. They merely spouted empty rhetoric, thinking it ability, but making no contribution to affairs." (ZSTX, 1461–62)

Following his discussion of the social order, the essayist goes on to consider the causes of social disorder. For Zhu, it was a matter of knowledge and ignorance. He understood knowledge to be moral knowledge, or knowledge of the *li* (natural moral principles) (ZSTX, 1471–72). Ignorance (*yu*), consequently, is ignorance of the *li* and is a result of environmental factors, particularly the absence of moral instruction in youth. Seven antisocial kinds of ignorance are enumerated: not knowing the *li*; as a consequence of not knowing the *li*, unfilial behavior; not knowing shame; harm to others without reason; being a robber; subversive activities; being an idiot. That the relationship between ignorance and idiocy (*chi*) is a causal one is spelled out in the following passage:

> Question: "Are ignorance and idiocy different?"
> Answer: "Initially, ignorance is nothing more than not knowing the principles of the sages and the ancients, and as a consequence acting always without restraint. Idiocy is not necessarily formed at birth, but it may arise from prolonged ignorance."
> Question: "What is the cause of idiocy?"
> Answer: "Doing what is not allowed, that is idiocy. This is the idiocy that arises from ignorance. It is not caused by cold and hot weather; it is a disease arising from the five viscera." (ZSTX, 1471–72)

The implication of this view, the attribution of moral turpitude to social causes and not to inherited attributes or systemic dysfunction, is that environmental factors are of primary importance in forming the individual's social character. An unstated premise is the assumption that each individual is teachable, but will only become properly socialized if made aware of the moral principles of the ancients. Thus, correct teaching was crucial to the individual's proper development and to the welfare of the society as a whole. In support of this conclusion, the Ming founder enumerated the disastrous consequences of rebels who advocated false doctrines from Han times to the Song.

One respect in which Zhu Yuanzhang's views on education contrast with the thrust of Confucian doctrine is that he did not assume a natural correlation between social status and moral virtue. There is a striking populist strain running through his statements. It is manifested in a suspicion of experts, i.e., scholars and teachers, on the one hand, and a faith in the goodness and collective wisdom of the common people on the other. A representative statement of this latter perspective is to be found in this passage dealing with the instruction of children (*jiao zi*):

> I said to the visitor: "There are parents who are neither especially worthy nor especially ignorant and yet their children, without a teacher, still attain perfect virtue (*ren*). They are harmonious with their relatives, filial toward their par-

ents, younger brothers defer to elder brothers, among friends there is fidelity, and they are friendly toward neighbors. Farmers are industrious in farming and scholars diligent in their studies. They are broadly accomplished in human affairs. What is the reason for this?"
Answer: "Although parents may not be especially worthy or especially ignorant they are persons of pure heart. Although it is not manifested outwardly, principle [*li*] resides within them. While their children do not attend a teacher, it must be that the parents serve as one in the home and themselves instruct on broad accomplishments in human affairs. Once they have got some basic instruction at home the children may inquire of numerous others. Although they do not have a particular teacher, learning the strong points of numerous others and accumulating them in their minds, is vastly superior to studying with a single teacher, and it surpasses ordinary people. Moreover, the learning of a single teacher is nothing more than the views of one individual. When they are attentive to the knowledge of numerous others will they not have broad accomplishment in human affairs?" (ZSTX, 1472–73)

The fact that the longest section of the *Zishi tongxun* is devoted to the topic of false doctrines indicates the importance that the Ming founder attached to the ideological underpinnings of the state (ZSTX, 1473–77). In this discussion he considered the fact that many persons in history had lead uprisings but failed to establish states. The reason for their defeat was ignorance and falling under evil influences instead of studying correct doctrine (*daoli*). The decisive factor in the failure of some regimes and the success of others, the Ming regime in particular, was the favor of heaven. Through heaven's action a chosen one (*zhenren*) acted as a divine instrument (*shenqi*) to unite the empire. Those in the past who proclaimed false doctrines, such as that of the Maitreya Buddha, were destroyed. Calamity was visited upon the people (*minhuo*) when men or women promoted false doctrines or resorted to criminal acts. One transgression led to another until calamity unfolded. Heaven's retribution in such matters was inescapable. It was the emperor's institution of proper laws and punishments which could bring good fortune. In addition to governmental action the people were expected to learn from each other, to keep an eye on each other and to keep order in their ranks. The conformist ideal the first Ming emperor held up for his subjects is outlined in his description of the people's good fortune (*minfu*):

I said: "What is meant by the people's good fortune?"
He said: "Take for example a village or a town of a thousand or ten thousand families who are neighbors; if there is one man or one woman whose parents are well instructed and who are virtuous in their persons, the family fortunes are prosperous, affairs are in order, and if an ignorant or wayward person in the neighborhood wants to cause trouble or do evil the virtuous persons will know of it before it happens and so will instruct and correct them. This will be

> a common occurrence. The people of a village or a town having received instruction, their markets and villages will be free of unexpected calamities and guilt by association. They will enjoy a time of great peace. This is what is meant by the people's good fortune."
> I said: "Can this bring wealth for one's whole life and for sons and grandsons?"
> He said: "Under the scrutiny of August Heaven they will be blessed again and again, and be certain to attain great prosperity. How could it amount merely to wealth?" (ZSTX, 1479–80)

This essay reveals Zhu Yuanzhang's growing confidence in his own understanding of the philosophy of government. It amounts to a statement of independence from his scholarly tutors: he was now revealing the truth to them through the words of his imaginary interlocutor. He set forth his understanding of the sources of good and evil and how people should behave. He assumed that people fell naturally into functional categories or roles and for each role he prescribed idealized standards of deportment. Social disorder came about because of ignorance, moral failure, belief in false doctrines, and environmental influences. Consequently, the solutions he proposed stressed teaching, self-discipline, moral suasion, penal sanctions and collective security measures.

The Issue of Trust

A decade after the founding, the first Ming emperor was not happy with the government he headed. Despite his heroic efforts as a legislator, the social order he desired remained elusive. Zhu had energetically formulated ritual regulations and penal laws but he could not get people to observe them. What went wrong? No doubt some of the problem was caused by the chaotic social conditions of the dynastic transition. The cultural level of the people was generally low and hard times encouraged the baser instincts. Human nature might be cited as another cause. Zhu Yuanzhang was impatient for change and intolerant of failure. Perhaps he demanded more of his subjects than it was reasonable to expect. In his "Instructions to Guide the World" (*Zishi tongxun*) the emperor revealed that he held most scholars in low regard and believed the common people to be often in the grip of moral ignorance.

Others placed the blame at the emperor's door. Ye Boju, Zheng Shili, Xiao Qi, Lian Zining, and Xie Jin were among the officials who ventured to criticize their ruler for his frequent and arbitrary use of harsh punishments (Langlois 1988, 136, 150, 156–57). Zhu ignored his own homilies about using punishments sparingly; he made wholesale use of torture, cruel punishments and execution to terrorize officials and commoners alike. But the most serious shortcoming of early Ming rule was probably the weakness of the relationship between the ruler and his ministers. Zhu Yuanzhang failed to develop a relationship of mutual trust with those who served him. How much of this was due to the subordinates is hard to say, but it is clear from the historical record that Zhu was extremely distrustful of those around him.

Much of the early Ming legislative program was aimed at safeguarding the emperor against the dangers that lurked on every side. Zhu was the sole survivor of a prolonged period of dog-eat-dog competition that destroyed all of his rivals. He survived in part because he was ever vigilant. His armies were always in the field putting down opposition and expanding his territory. His bodyguards were never far from his side. The *Ancestral Instruction* is full of warnings to his successors to be careful about their movements and to be on the lookout for signs of trouble. Once on the throne he had to worry about challenges to his authority from within his own regime. The *Ancestral Instruction* promulgated in 1373 was designed to keep the imperial princes in line and safeguard the line of succession (Langlois 1988, 132–33). The nobility were governed by regulations issued in the same year and posted on iron placards (Langlois 1988, 133–34). Zhu's strongest statements of distrust were made against officials.

An early indication of Zhu's suspicion of his officials was the famous Blank Seal Case or Prestamped Documents Case (*kongyin an*) of 1376. The emperor was outraged when he discovered that official seals were being applied to blank reports of tax receipts so that the figures could be filled in later after delivery to reflect losses in transit. This was apparently a routine bureaucratic practice that made it possible to report tax receipts promptly instead of waiting weeks for documents to make their way back to the provinces to be stamped and then sent to the capital. The emperor chose to see in this a conspiracy to deceive the throne and ordered that all the officials whose names appeared on such documents be put to death (DMB, 1575; Lin 1979, 18).

The Prestamped Documents Case was not a major purge but it had a strong impact on the emperor by heightening his suspicion of officialdom. It paved the way for the bigger cases that were to follow. It helped to shift the emphasis from legislation to prosecution and punishment that would characterize the period after 1380.

CHAPTER FOUR

DISILLUSION, CRISES AND ADJUSTMENTS

The founding period of Ming rule was followed by a series of crises that tested the initial institutional arrangements of the young dynasty. The greatest of these occurred in 1380, when the Senior Grand Councilor, Hu Weiyong, was executed for plotting to usurp the throne (Langlois 1988, 138–49). The Hu Weiyong affair precipitated a political and institutional crisis that shook the Ming court to its foundations and marked a watershed change in Chinese imperial history. The picture of government that emerges from the records of this period shows the darker side of Ming politics. We see the founder, shaken by the failure of his early institutions and ever more distrustful of his subordinates, searching for levers of power to check the evils threatening his empire. Investigations into the alleged conspiracy spread throughout the government as thousands of officials and their families came under suspicion and were executed.

Hu Weiyong was an early follower of Zhu Yuanzhang who had risen through a series of offices to head of the Secretariat. From surviving records it is impossible to determine exactly what crimes he committed or why he was put to death. A brash and somewhat reckless man, he apparently overstepped the powers of his office by diverting the flow of memorials to the throne through his own office and by acting independently in matters involving rewards and punishments. He fell under suspicion and was imprisoned in the fall of 1379 (DMB, 638–41). Hu Weiyong's case took on a different light on February 8, 1380, when a high censorate official reported to the emperor that Hu Weiyong was plotting rebellion and the investigation of his misconduct widened (MSLHW, 2043-48). Whatever Hu Weiyong's real crimes may have been, it seems likely that the charges against him were exaggerated. He was accused of having poisoned an ailing Liu Ji but most shockingly of having contacted the Japanese, and perhaps Mongols, Koreans and even Southeast Asians for help in overthrowing the dynasty (DMB, 640). The charges against Hu Weiyong provided a ready pretense for incriminating anyone the emperor wanted to dispose of. The purge went on for years and was revived spectacularly a dozen years later when surviving military leaders, most notably Lan Yu, were implicated and executed or driven to suicide (DMB, 641, 790-91).

Reorganization

The execution of the grand councilor was followed by a fundamental reorganization of the institutions of the central government (Farmer 1976, 79-84). The office of grand councilor, in essence a prime minister, was eliminated, as were the highest offices in the parallel censorial and military branches of the government. The elimination of the office of prime minister was the single most important step in the strengthening of Ming autocracy. It left the emperor as the sole central agency with authority to coordinate the activities of the six ministries, the five regional military commissions, and the various censorial bodies. The new constellation of central government offices had the effect of decapitating the bureaucracy, at one stroke removing from the outer court the one office that could serve as a voice of the officials as distinct from the throne and that could provide unified direction to the government through the mechanism of a trained civil servant. Ultimate administrative power was now lodged in the person of the hereditary emperor.

On February 17, 1380, the emperor ordered a comprehensive restructuring of the central organs of the government, eliminating the office of grand councilor, replacing the Secretariat with the six ministries and the Central Military Commission with the five regional military commissions (MSLHW, 2051–53; Hucker 1985, 72–74). For help with the heavy administrative burden that fell upon his shoulders the emperor established the short-lived system of the Four Advisors (*si fuguan*; Hucker renders this Four Supports), choosing low ranking but intellectually able scholars who were to serve him directly (MSLHW, 2114–16, 2121). Later, increasing use was made of the grand secretaries who were designated according to the various halls in the palace and who only partially were able to fill the vacuum created by the elimination of the grand councilors. As early as 1382 the founder warned against the danger of eunuchs interfering in governmental affairs outside of the palace, a problem that was to reach colossal proportions in later reigns (MSLHW, 2523).

During this phase the emperor, now in his fifties, reorganized the government along lines that suited his own view and enhanced his personal control. If high officials could not be trusted he would manage the bureaucracy directly from the palace. One form the exercise of personal power took during this period was the employment of the imperial princes as the emperor's surrogates along the northern frontiers (Farmer 1976, 73–79, 86–92). As his sons began to come of age they were sent to fiefs on the frontiers, where they constituted an extension of the imperial family into the heart of the strategic defense commands and a check on the generals who led the largest armies outside the capital district.

While some of the activities of earlier years, such as the development of sumptuary regulations, continued to be carried on, the emphasis of imperial action was decidedly different. The dominant concern was the quality and reliability of the official class. Particular attention was given to the effort to locate men of virtue and talent. Calls went out to search the empire for able scholars and students who might serve as officials, and the nobles and military officers were urged to send their sons to the national university (MSLHW, 2142–43, 2387–88, 2141). Once in the national university students were to study the *Shuo yuan*, a text the emperor said he found to be a source of guidance, and the *Code* and *Commandment* that embodied the law of the land (MSLHW, 2159). In 1381 more than 860 recommended persons arrived in the capital, where they were ranked into five grades (MSLHW, 2133–34, 2137). The pressure of the talent search was sufficient that the emperor found it necessary in 1384 to caution his officials not to impress able teachers into administrative duties (MSLHW, 2453).

Education was another area that received attention. In 1382 a set of twelve regulations governing students was proclaimed, and a month later the examination system, abolished in 1373, was revived when a seven part recommendation was approved calling for students to be examined in six fields (MSLHW, 2299, 2301–02, 2321–24; Langlois 1988, 131, 147). In 1384 the Ministry of Rites was ordered to issue detailed regulations for the examination system that specified a three-year cycle of testing based on the core Neo-Confucian texts such as the *Four Books* and Zhu Xi's commentaries (MSLHW, 2467–69).

Concern for the quality of his government led Zhu Yuanzhang to lecture repeatedly on the importance of virtue in his officials (MSLHW, 2299, 2395, 2414, 2249–50, 2653–54). Despite his efforts Zhu found that those who were sent to him were too often lacking in moral fiber (MSLHW, 2574–75). The emperor alternately lectured his officials on the importance of virtuous service (MSLHW, 2099, 2113, 2115) and cautioned them against doing wrong. To this end in 1380 he ordered the compilation of the *Chen jie lu*, a text that recited 220 famous cases of official wrongdoing from throughout history (MSLHW, 2100). Six years later the *Xinggong lu*, an extract from the longer ritual work the *Cunxin lu*, was issued to instruct officials on matters concerning portents (MSLHW, 2684; DMB, 956, 1265).

Given his dissatisfaction with the performance of his officials it is not surprising that the Ming founder devoted a great deal of attention to enforcement of the law. Many small adjustments were required in a system that seemed never to be satisfactory (MSLHW, 2144, 2162, 2165–66, 2189–90). In 1381 the Court of Judicial Review (*dali si*) and the Punishment Reviewing Office (*shenxing si*) were revived (MSLHW, 2202–3). This institutional change reflects in part the importance of reviewing, altering and reducing sentences, prominent activities in the administration of justice. The emperor repeatedly gave his views on particular cases and on judicial practice in general. Upon occasion he talked about the nature of law enforcement, usually stressing the limits of penal measures as tools of government (MSLHW, 2204, 2417). In 1383 he advised the heir apparent and the princes that rewards and punishments were the two great powers for ruling the realm (MSLHW, 2384).

Early in 1384 the minister of justice was executed for complicity in the Hu Weiyong affair (MSLHW, 2447–49). Four months later the emperor issued an eight-point directive on the administration of justice to be published throughout the realm (MSLHW, 2496–98). At the end of 1384 he consolidated the administration of the penal system under the Ministry of Justice strengthening the provisions for review of sentences at various levels (MSLHW, 2559).

The enforcement of military law also received attention. Statutes on military law (*junfa dinglü*), promulgated in 1382, were to be read regularly at the various levels of command (MSLHW, 2253). In 1387 the emperor tried to restrict the illegal torture of offenders by the Embroidered Uniform Guard (MSLHW, 2722–23).

In his search for alternatives to unreliable civil officials the emperor apparently made increasing use of Buddhist and Daoist advisers. Langlois notes that a leading Confucian official criticized the emperor's use of Buddhist monks (Langlois 1988, 146). But the picture is not entirely clear. Regulation of Buddhist and Daoist clergy was tightened when the "academies" (*yuan*) established in 1368 were replaced by "registries" (*si*) to oversee the activities of those two religious communities (Langlois 1988, 114, 146; MSLHW, 2262-63). Sumptuary regulations governing the dress of Buddhist and Daoist clerics were issued the next year (MSLHW, 2368). Within three years the Ministry of Rites reported that the number of Buddhists and Daoists stood at 20,954 and that the number seeking to register was growing. Their motive was said to be to escape corvee service. A strict system of triennial registration was proposed and adopted (MSLHW, 2563). In 1387 persons over twenty were prohibited from becoming Buddhist priests and a triennial examination system was instituted at the capital for those who wished to be registered (MSLHW, 2771).

To enhance ideological control the emperor energetically promoted Confucian schooling. On several occasions in 1382 Zhu Yuanzhang expounded on his ideas about China's first teacher and the importance of his doctrine (MSLHW, 2276–77, 2278, 2281–82). A guide for sacrifice to Confucius (*Shidian xianshi Kongzi yizhu*) was issued to standardize ritual practice in schools throughout the empire (MSLHW, 2282). Zhu advised his officials that the works of the sages gave instruction in three important categories: respect for heaven, loyalty to the ruler, and filial piety toward relatives. In 1383 a text, the *Jing cheng lu*, was completed in three *juan*. It consisted of excerpts from these classical texts: the *Book of Changes*, the *Book of Documents*, the *Odes*, the *Record of Rituals*, the *Classic of Filial Piety*, the *Analects*, the *Great Learning*, the *Doctrine of the Mean*, the *Zuo Zhuan*, the

Guoyü, and the *Mencius* (MSLHW, 2386-87). The Ming founder's faith in the doctrines of the sages was reiterated in 1384 when he ordered that a school be erected in Liaodong. He rejected the notion that schooling was inappropriate to a frontier region, reasoning instead that it could potentially reach anywhere. Arguing that human nature was not different but that environmental influences were crucial in determining customs the emperor advocated classical education for the military officers and their sons on the frontier lest they lose their cultural identity (MSLHW, 2567).

The local community was also a target of imperial action in the 1380s. We can see in these enactments many of the elements of the local order referred to in the *Placard of People's Instructions* in appendix 3. The compilation of yellow registers of labor service (*fuyi huangce*) in 1381 entailed the reorganization of villagers into groups of 10 and 110 households, *jia* and *li* respectively, with headmen called *jiashou* and *lizhang* (MSLHW, 2143-44). Two months later the village wine-drinking ceremony (*xiang yinjiu li*), originally revived in 1372 (MSLHW, 1342–43), was reinstituted in a systematic fashion (MSLHW, 2146–47). Specific guidelines for the ceremony were issued two years later (MSLHW, 2436–38). In 1383 the common people were ordered to set up community schools (*shexue*) under their own control to avoid the abuses that had occurred earlier when local officials had tried to establish schools (MSLHW, 2436). Official abuse and unfair administration of the tax and labor systems were natural concerns of the central government. Another problem on the emperor's mind was the fear that people would change their occupations or their place of residence. Both were forbidden in 1386 (MSLHW, 2687–88, 2691).

The Grand Pronouncements

A second crisis was touched off in 1385 by the arrest of the vice minister of revenue, Guo Huan, for theft of a massive amount of government grain (DMB, 387). It was not in fact a single crime or a single case but a series of charges that spread out in widening circles, far beyond Guo Huan, until tens of thousands were involved. We have no biography of Guo Huan, but Lin Tai-yung has pieced together the outlines of the affair from subsequent imperial statements (Lin 1979, 27–69). Corruption was massive and widespread. Officials from top to bottom of the government, including the provinces, had embezzled tax receipts in grain, cash, silver, and paper currency in sums equivalent to millions of piculs of rice. The emperor's most generous estimate of the losses was 24 million piculs of grain, an amount that exceeded the empire's annual grain tax revenue (Lin 1979, 40). In the persecution that followed Guo Huan's execution, the central government was devastated for the second time in less than a decade. Hundreds of co-conspirators were executed and 7 million piculs of grain were recovered (Li Guangbi 1957, 29).

The scale of the Guo Huan affair stunned the already suspicious emperor and prompted him to issue the first of his famous *Grand Pronouncements*. Between 1385 and 1388 Zhu issued the *Grand Pronouncements* (*Da gao*) in four groups (Langlois 1988, 152–56, 159–60). Organized into a sequence of discrete items the *Grand Pronouncements* were statements of Zhu's own views about what was wrong with the world. In them we can still detect the impassioned quality of his voice as he decried the evils pervading the empire. The *Grand Pronouncements* represented a new tactic in Zhu's ongoing battle against evil, and their issuance marked a new stage in his rule. He was no longer content just to cite the ancient sages and worthies. Increasingly, he presented his own views on his own authority. The title *Da gao* was taken from the *Book of Documents*. In using it, Zhu Yuanzhang was in effect claiming a status equal to the ancient sage rulers (Langlois 1988, 154).

The first text, the *Yuzhi da gao* or *Imperial Grand Pronouncement*, was completed November 3, 1385. Zhu's lament makes clear the depth of his frustration. His whole program of world salvation was foundering:

> Chinese culture has been lost and the norms of behavior overthrown. Since taking the throne I have fixed the rites and music and established the laws and regulations, changed gowns and caps and ceremonial dress to rectify the moral order and clarify superior and inferior, to completely restore the way of former kings, causing the people to be enlightened with ceremonial and not dare to violate their stations or evade the law (MSLHW, 2665-66).

He wrote the *Grand Pronouncement* in his spare time and ordered it be proclaimed throughout the realm. He also said:

> Loyalty to the ruler and filial piety toward relatives, in ruling the people to cultivate the self, this is the essence of it. If it can be carried out it will foster good fortune; if it cannot be carried out disaster will result. Proclaim it to the officials and commoners as an instruction forever. (MSLHW, 2666)

The *Grand Pronouncements* were issued in four groups over a span of four years. The first text, the *Yuzhi da gao*, consisted of seventy-four items in no particular order. A *Supplementary Grand Pronouncement, Yuzhi da gao xubian*, was issued in 1386 (MSLHW, 2682). It was made up of eighty-seven items and was the largest of the four groups. A third text, the *Yu zhi da gao sanbian*, consisting of forty-seven items, appeared in 1387 (MSLHW, 2715). Later that year the emperor repeated his intention that the *Grand Pronouncement* be used to instruct the common people (MSLHW, 2753). In 1388 a version of the *Grand Pronouncement* aimed at military officers, the *Da gao wuchen*, was issued (MSLHW, 2808–9). It had only thirty-two items and was written in simple language that unlettered soldiers could understand (Langlois 1988, 159).

It would be an overstatement to call the *Grand Pronouncements* a code or codes in the same sense as the documents translated in the appendices. The four collections comprise a total of 236 items which tend to be more discursive and less focused than the articles in a code. The entries range in length from less than 100 characters to more than 600, most falling in the 300–400 character range. The jumbled and varied contents of the *Grand Pronouncements* are a rich source of information on early Ming society and government and provide many insights into Zhu Yuanzhang's state of mind and style of rule. Lin Tai-yung translated the table of contents for the first three groups of pronouncements and analyzed their contents (Lin 1979, 6–10, 290–98). A majority of the entries in the *Grand Pronouncements* refer to crimes and misbehavior by officials and commoners that came to the emperor's attention. The longest entry in the third collection catalogues the names and crimes of hundreds of degree holders the emperor felt moved to condemn at a time when his slaughter of officials was at its peak (DGSB, 114–26, item 2). Lin notes that the crimes mentioned in the pronouncements are most heavily concentrated in the capital district and nearby provinces (Lin 1979, 255). Some items take the form of directives and regulations and had been proclaimed earlier or were subsequently issued elsewhere. The items most relevant to this study are those concerned with moral exhortation.

In addition to the litany of crimes and official transgressions the first group of pronouncements restates a number of familiar themes. An indictment of Mongol rule appears in the third entry as the emperor again rails against the damage that ninety-three years of barbarian overlordship had done to Chinese customary practices (DG, 34–35). A specific instance of undesirable Mongol influence is cited in Section twenty-two on marriage. Mongol marriage practices struck at the very heart of the Chinese social order, but outlawing them provided an opening for official corruption:

> First cousins of the same surname married, younger brothers inherited their elder bother's wives, and sons got their father's concubines. These were the Mongol customs of the former Yuan. After I brought peace, an exception was made for marriages already concluded under the Yuan. From my unification the old regulations of our Chinese Former Kings were set forth. The essence of it was that there must be familial feelings between father and son, rectitude between ruler and minister, distinction between husband and wife, hierarchy between old and young, and sincerity between friends. It has been eighteen years already. There are those who are perverse and wayward who distort the meaning of my *Commandment* and *Code*, who conspire with greedy officials and corrupt underlings to take advantage and lay false charges against those boys and girls married in the Yuan but who despite the fixed regulation have

> not registered. It has reached the point were those who have been married for decades but lack money have all fled and those who have money are safe. This kind of malefactor commits a new crime every day, losing their lives and destroying their families. They should repent and reform. How have Mongol customs come down to this. The elder brother takes the younger brother's wife, the younger brother gets the elder brother's spouse, the son inherits the father's concubine. There was a woman who married the father and gave birth to a son. After the father died she became the concubine of the son who was without a wife and she also bore him a son. This completely destroyed the basic relationship of distinction between husband and wife. How could this accord with the instructions of the Chinese sages? In establishing the *li*, past matters are often a source of difficulty. This is the reason we do not deal with affairs of the Yuan dynasty. From now on if there are transgressions of the institutions of the Former Kings the crime will be punished without mercy.(DG, 39–40)

More central to Zhu Yuanzhang's concern than even the fundamental family bonds was the relationship between the ruler and his ministers. In the very first entry in the *Grand Pronouncement* he made this statement:

> In ancient times a minister realized his station in concert with the ruler. His exertion of loyalty completed and perfected his ruler. Whether eating or sleeping he never forgot his government. And what is government? It is nothing more than bringing about good fortune for the people, making up the ruler's shortcomings, restraining the ruler's excesses, and repairing the ruler's faults so as to glorify his ancestors down below, delight his parents in the present, and bring glory to his wife and children in the future. Life and reputation are precious; do not destroy them. Just exert your loyalty and fulfill your station. The wise man knows this. What is difficult about it? Today's officials are not so. They obscure the ruler's brilliance, extend the ruler's mistakes, and treacherously conspire in factions almost without cease. Everything they do are fatal schemes, prescriptions for rushing into the fire or plunging over the cliff. (DG, 34)

The *Grand Pronouncements* were directed at a broad spectrum of the population from high officials down to village leaders and heads of families. Zhu Yuanzhang's strategy was to enclose the people in networks of social and religious obligations. Thus, he could lecture officials on their obligations to their parents (DG, 40–41, 24), Buddhist and Daoist clergy on the need to obey the strictures of their faiths (DG, 43, 30), and commoners on their need to reciprocate the benefits they enjoyed from the bounty of nature (DG, 43–44, 31). In this latter case we see the emperor enlisting a cosmic principle, recompense (*bao*), to regulate the behavior of the people. The people needed to give thanks to the gods of soil and grain in much the same way that the emperor did. As the emperor ritually propitiated the altars of soil and grain, *she* and *ji*, so the common people needed to make local sacrifices to the same spirits. Sacrifice acknowledged what mankind had received:

> In ancient times the wise kings set up altars to worship the *she* and the *ji*. Solemnly, reverentially, and respectfully they made offerings. They dared not be remiss. Why was this? Because *she* is the Gods of the Five Soils and *ji* is the Gods of the Five Grains. The Five Soils produce the Five Grains so that the people may sustain their lives. The Son of Heaven cannot sacrifice everywhere in the realm. Thus the various offices erect altars in their respective locations and perform sacrifices on them. Moreover, a Great Soil Altar and a Great Grain Altar are erected to the right of the Pheasant Gate, close by on either side of the Ancestral Temple, so that in the spring the emperor can sacrifice at the Soil Altar and pray for a good grain crop, and in the autumn sacrifice his recompense can be complete. The good people who keep order, wherever they reside, all consume the benefits of the Soil. Irrespective of whether it is a lot or a little, in their hearts they daily wish to give back something. How is this sincere intent made actual? By using the Soul and Grain Altars to stand for the beneficence of Heaven's command. (DG, 43, 31)

But the welfare of the people is not just a matter between themselves and the gods; the ruler is also involved. The disasters that can visit them are both natural and human in origin. A critical element in the people's welfare is the extension of recompense in their reciprocal relationship with the ruler:

> When the ruler sends injustice the little people consider it their misfortune and do not understand that it is their recompense. If they want to extend sincerity to recompense the *she* and *ji* and be the ruler's subjects, when the ruler gives a command they will hasten to serve and obey. And when he sends someone to collect taxes they all respond. Sincerity like this is recompense for eating the bounty of the soil and the [imperial] favor that sustains their lives. (DG, 43–44, 31)

At this point Zhu Yuanzhang offers a formulation of a sort of social contract that tied the ruler and people together by mutual obligation:

> *Xian* [31st chapter of the *Book of Changes*?] says: "The ruler nourishes the people." How does he foster them? The ruler's food and clothing are all provided by the people. Food and clothing are what the people provide. But how does that nourish the people? The ruler nourishes the people with the five teachings and the five punishments. The five teachings foster the people's peace. They are familial feelings between father and son, rectitude between ruler and minister, distinction between husband and wife, hierarchy between old and young, and sincerity between friends. When the five teachings are instilled there will be peace. (DG, 44, 31)

Those who fail to follow the five teachings will have social ills of every kind visited upon them. The solution to waywardness in such cases was the addition of the five punishments which, once proclaimed, could persuade evil persons to give up their corrupt ways. The stupid people who put their lives and families in jeopardy would be subject to oversight by both human and divine agencies.

One of the most remarkable features of the *Grand Pronouncements* was the emperor's attempt to check official abuse at the local level by establishing a direct link between the local community leaders and the throne. It was at once an expression of his concern for the common people and his distrust of officaldom. The *Grand Pronouncements* explicitly permitted village leaders to travel to the capital for audiences with the emperor:

> Elders and commoners of every province, prefecture, subprefecture, and district [may] proceed to the capital to present reports to the emperor in person. Although they have not travel documents (*wenyin*), if the number of travelers is great, be it thirty or fifty persons, more than one hundred persons, or up to three or five hundred persons, when they come to a pass, ford or guarded defile and report that they are going for a personal audience they shall be let through. Do not stop them. Those who stop them shall be punished for violation of the article in the *Code* on Interception of Sealed Government Documents [*Code* 262]. (DG, 49, 46)

Not only did the *Grand Pronouncements* entitle villagers to report grievances directly to the emperor, it also authorized them to arrest underlings who oppressed the people (DGXB, 49–50, 10). To encourage wide distribution and popular knowledge of the *Grand Pronouncements* it was stipulated that households possessing a copy would be entitled to a one degree reduction in punishments of beating or penal servitude should they come before a court for sentencing. Those lacking a copy would be subject to one degree increase in the normal punishment (DG, 61, 74). In issuing the second group of *Grand Pronouncements* it was stressed that

> Every household must possess it. If there are those who have it but do not respect it, they are not people transformed by my rule. They shall be banished beyond the pale of civilization and never allowed to return. This is to be taken seriously. (DGXB, 105, 87)

The issuance of the *Grand Pronouncements* in the latter half of the 1380s marked the high tide of Zhu Yuanzhang's effort to personalize government through direct appeal to the populace. These same years also saw him inflict some of the most indiscriminate and inhumane atrocities on thousands of officials and subjects, guilty and innocent.

Despite the tenor of the times and the demonic cruelty that accompanied his purges the Ming founder never abandoned his program of legislation. A major revision of court protocol was enacted in 1387 with the issuance of the *Liyi dingshi*, or *Fixed Regulations on Ceremonial* in twenty-six articles (MSLHW, 2789; Franke 1968, 179). The next year a massive revision of the sacrifices was ordered (MSLHW, 2836–55). In 1389 the *Great Ming Code* was revised in a way that cleared up confusing additions and brought its contents into closer alignment with the *Commandment* (MSLHW, 2955–56). The *Code* now had seven major divisions: one devoted to terms and general principles and six corresponding to the sequence of the ministries. Its 460 articles were divided into thirty *juan*.

Succession

A new phase of the Ming founder's rule might be dated from around 1390. In that year there was an uprising in the capital. Zhu Yuanzhang responded harshly to the threat by executing many officials and conducting a massive purge of the capital population. Two years later, when the emperor was sixty-five years old, his eldest son and heir apparent died with the result that the next ranking male in that line, the senior imperial grandson, was elevated to become heir to the throne. This event, with its potential to destabilize the imperial family, introduced an additional element of uncertainty into the future of the young dynasty. In the following year, 1393, a second major purge was unleashed in a revival of the Hu Weiyong case. This time the able general Lan Yu was charged with complicity in the earlier plot and fifteen thousand suspected conspirators were put to death in a seven month period. So pervasive did the distrust become among the government officials that the emperor was obliged to end the purge and declare a general amnesty for all those not yet charged. In 1390 Li Shanchang, one of the senior generation of officials, was implicated in the decade-old Hu Weiyong affair and ended his life by suicide (MSLHW, 3023–24, 3026–27).

In the last decade of his life the Ming founder continued to refine the organization of the government and add to his body of legislation by revising and issuing a number of codes intended to introduce a degree of stability into the badly shaken political system. Both the Ministry of Revenue and the Ministry of Justice were reconfigured so that four sections were subdivided into twelve sections corresponding to the provinces.

In 1391 a detailed restatement of sumptuary rules governing dress was issued (MSLHW, 3110–19). Two years later the *Zhusi zhizhang* appeared. It was a formal prescription for the organization of the central government following the Tang model (MSLHW, 3308; Franke 1968, 178). Shortly thereafter the *Jizhi lu* was issued (MSLHW, 3310). Based on Han, Tang, and Song precedents, it codified the rules governing the nobility of merit. Ceremonial regulations applicable to the nobility of merit were proclaimed in 1396 (MSLHW, 3598–99). A comprehensive set of regulations governing deportment at court came out a few days later (MSLHW, 3329–44). In

1394 two books of guidance for princes and officials were issued. These were the *Yongjian lu* and the *Shichen zonglu* respectively, works that detailed historical examples of good and bad conduct by those classes of persons (MSLHW, 3370). In 1397 protocols were developed for greetings between members of the imperial nobility and others and between officials of various ranks and others (MSLHW, 3602–3, 3637–38). The purpose of all these protocols was to clarify and reinforce differences in rank and status.

The local level also received attention in the 1390's. On several occasions the emperor ordered that elders be recruited as officials or sent on missions, particularly for relief work (MSLHW, 3032, 3040, 3046–47, 3065). Local granaries were ordered established in 1394 consolidating the earlier relief work by the elders (MSLHW, 3375). Revisions of the yellow registers was undertaken in 1390, adjusting for changes in wealth since the original classification of households (MSLHW, 3043–44). In 1394 the responsibility of elders for managing disputes was increased (MSLHW, 3396). A census of wealthy commoner households was conducted in 1397 in a search for talent (MSLHW, 3643). In the same year villages were ordered to establish wooden bells and to designate aged or disabled persons to walk through the lanes six times per month calling on villagers to behave properly (MSLHW, 3677–78). This practice became a regular provision in item 19 of the *Placard of People's Instructions*.

The ideological concerns of the 1380s continued to be on the emperor's mind in the 1390s. In 1391 new constraints were placed on Buddhism and Daoism and the number of temples was restricted (MSLHW, 3109–10, 3125). The emperor noted that Buddhism was originally a foreign faith and that it undercut the dictates of filial piety. The prohibition on Buddhists and Daoists recruiting children was repeated in 1394 (MSLHW, 3372–73). Persons over the age of twenty were to take examinations in the capital to gain admission to ordination. In the following year it was ordered that Buddhists and Daoists be tested to make sure that their teaching was in accordance with the canonical works of their faiths (MSLHW, 3524). On one occasion when a Daoist adept offered the emperor advice on government the emperor rejected it saying that the learning which he could use was the way of the sages (MSLHW, 3482–83).

In ideological matters primacy was given to Confucianism over Buddhism and Daoism (MSLHW, 3121). In the Confucian schools the curriculum included Confucian classics such as the *Spring and Autumn Annals* and practical subjects such as archery, calligraphy and mathematics (MSLHW, 3181, 3482). It was about this time that Liu Sanwu was directed to prepare an abridged version of the *Mencius*, the *Mengzi jiewen*, to be used for the civil service examinations (DMB, 957). In addition to these traditional subjects, the Ming founder added content of his own creation. Students were ordered to study the *Grand Pronouncement* and the *Code* (MSLHW, 3158). Here we can see the influence of Zhu Yuanzhang's normative agenda on formal education. The same agenda was extended to informal education as well. In 1391 forty-three students of the Directorate of Education (*guozi jian*) were sent to the guard units around the capital to read out the *Grand Pronouncement for Military Officers* (MSLHW, 3105). In order to encourage obedience from an early age, boys throughout the empire were encouraged to memorize the *Grand Pronouncement*. The Ministry of Rites was to rank them according the amount they had mastered and reward them accordingly (MSLHW, 3159). The result of this order must have been very gratifying to the aging ruler. In 1397 more than 193,400 teachers and students who had studied the *Grand Pronouncement* came to the capital to get their rewards (MSLHW, 3652).

The tone of legislative actions in the 1390s suggest that the Ming founder was increasingly concerned with the survival of the system he had put in place. When asked in 1391 and again in 1395 to reconcile inconsistencies in the laws, the emperor declined to do so. He noted that the statutes (*lü*) of the *Code* were good for all time and that rulings (*tiaoli*) were exigencies of the moment growing out of particular situations (MSLHW, 3144–45, 3456–57). Four months later he insisted on the primacy of the *Code* and *Grand Pronouncement*. At that time he repeated prohibitions against cruel punishments and the establishment of a prime minister and restated the authority of the *Ancestral Instruction* over judicial matters relating to the conduct of the princes and members of the nobility (MSLHW, 3477–79). Three months later, on October 2, 1395, the revised *Ancestral Instruction* was issued. The emperor made reference to the experience of the Han dynasty in stressing its importance to the survival of his house. In December, 1395, the *Lizhi jiyao* was completed (MSLHW, 3529–30; DMB, 957). It was a text that clarified the status hierarchy among officials.

On May 29, 1397, the *Da Ming lügao* was issued. This was a combination of selected elements of the *Grand Pronouncement* attached to the *Code* to make it more comprehensible to the common people (MSLHW, 3647–48; Lin 1979, 14–15; Huang 1977, 155–207). The emperor was emulating the ancient ideal of using punishments so as to do away with punishments and, at the same time, personalizing the content of the codes. It was an action that aptly embodied Zhu Yuanzhang's innovative legislative style.

The Jianwen Era (1398–1402)

In his thoughtful essay on Chinese despotism, F. W. Mote makes the point that the use of terror in Ming government was confirmed largely by historical accident (Mote 1961, 39). The rule of the Ming founder was followed by that of the Jianwen emperor, a gentle and scholarly man sympathetic to notions of Confucian reform. It was the usurpation of the throne by the Yongle emperor that led to the revival and continuation of the harsher elements of the founder's rule.

The Ming founder was succeeded on the throne by his grandson, Zhu Yunwen (1377–1402) whose reign title was Jianwen (DMB, 397–404). The brief Jianwen period was a tantalizing might-have-been in the history of late imperial China. The names alone are emblematic of the kind of change the new reign was to usher in. Jianwen, which means "Establishment of Civil Virtue," contrasted starkly with the founder's era name, Hongwu, "Vast Military Power." Zhu Yunwen himself is described in the surviving record as a gentle and bookish young man devoted to the Confucian ideals of good government. The possibility existed, had he been able to hold the throne for a long time, that he could have promoted a more humane and temperate style of government than that which had prevailed under his grandfather. As his reign title suggested, he could establish a civil (and civilized) standard of administration. Toward this end he summoned to his service the eminent Confucian scholar Fang Xiaoru who was only too eager to propose reforms in the Hongwu system of government.

In the later years of the Hongwu era, Fang Xiaoru emerged as the leader of the Confucian scholars. As a student of Song Lian, and as Song Lian's anointed successor, Fang carried on the traditions of Jinhua thought (Langlois 1981b, 141–2; Dardess 1983, 264–65). According to Dardess's account, Fang's philosophy shared the concern of the older generation with world salvation to be achieved by Confucian influence exerted through a centralized state (1983, 279–82). Where he differed from his teacher and the Ming founder was in his understanding of how Confucian ends were to be attained. Fang would have placed less emphasis on punishment and active administration by the ruler and more on fixed institutions to manage the affairs at the district level. It might be argued that the Ming founder was already moving in this direction at the time of his death. The issuance of the *Ming Code*, the revival of local control institutions, the revision of the *Ancestral Instruction* and a treatise on the ritual system could all be taken as evidence that the founder was interested in leaving behind a strong set of institutional arrangements.

Prior to Zhu Yuanzhang's death, Fang Xiaoru discretely avoided public confrontation with the aging despot. Instead, Fang built up a network of like-minded scholars who looked to him for intellectual guidance. He found safety in the enlightened court of the learned Prince of Shu, Zhu Chun, in Chengdu. Shortly after the Ming founder died, Fang was called to the court of the new Jianwen emperor, where he assumed a position of intellectual leadership. The court in the years immediately after 1398 embarked on a course of institutional reform which, had it succeeded, might have given China a considerably moderated despotism. Fang Xiaoru led the way toward reform, arguing that the founder's *Ancestral Instruction*, which forbade any institutional changes, could be violated to achieve a still higher purpose, that of dynastic survival, which was the founder's paramount concern (Dardess 1983, 285). Unfortunately for Fang, and perhaps for Ming

China as well, the Jianwen emperor's reign was cut short in 1402 by Zhu Di's coup d'etat.

The failure of the Jianwen emperor to survive was largely due to factors originating in the Hongwu period. First of all, Zhu Yunwen was too young and inexperienced, just over twenty years of age, to effectively take charge of a dangerous situation. Even though he had been coached in the arts of government by his aged grandfather, Yunwen was not able to handle the problems that confronted him when he took the throne. Secondly, he lacked loyal and experienced generals who could have rallied the armies to his cause and put down the opposition. This weakness of the imperial establishment was due in no small part to the purges carried out by his grandfather. When Zhu Yuanzhang turned on Lan Yu in 1393 his motive may have been in part to secure the throne for his grandson. What was not foreseen was that the imperial princes, the new ruler's uncles, would pose a serious problem once the founder died. The third factor, then, was precisely the power and military experience of the princes, especially the senior surviving prince, Zhu Di, who as Prince of Yan was well established at Beiping (Beijing), the old Yuan capital in the north.

Usurpation

Zhu Di's usurpation of the throne in 1402 cut short whatever modifications of the Ming system were underway in the Jianwen era. The fact that Zhu Di was a usurper has helped to obscure our understanding of many matters. Once in power as the Yongle emperor, Zhu Di tried to erase the record of his predecessor: documents were altered to eliminate reference to the Jianwen reign name by extending the Hongwu era to 1402. Particular attention was given to rationalizing Zhu Di's seizure of the throne as an effort to save the dynasty from the hands of evil advisers. This involved citing language in the *Ancestral Instruction* that sanctioned a prince coming to the aid of a new emperor (*Instruction*, art. 56). Succession to the throne by a prince not in the line of the founder's eldest son also involved the *Ancestral Instruction's* stipulation that sons of the wife were to be given primacy (*Instruction*, 57). In Zhu Di's case there is reason to doubt that he was in fact born of the Empress (DMB, 355–65).

In addition to obscuring the historical record the Yongle usurpation also provoked substantial ideological problems. Because Zhu Di was a usurper, many upright officials and scholars were unwilling to serve him. Fang Xiaoru's was the most famous case of this type. After declining to aid Zhu Di he was tortured and executed as were hundreds of relatives, friends and followers. His writings were proscribed during the Yongle period. Denied the service of many high minded Confucians, Zhu Di was forced to rely on those who were willing to serve him. Persons who had betrayed their emperor to aid the Prince of Yan in his seizure of Nanjing now found themselves in favor. The increased use of eunuchs for imperial business, of whom the great navigator Zheng He is the most celebrated, was stimulated in part by Zhu Di's need for agents willing to do his bidding. Some of those who had reservations were put to work on the *Great Yongle Encyclopedia* (*Yongle dadian*) allowing the emperor simultaneously to patronize scholars and search out dangerous literature (DMB, 554–58, 1561–65).

In order to legitimize his rule Zhu Di portrayed himself as defender of his father's sacred system. This meant that changes in laws such as the *Ancestral Instruction* or the *Ming Code* were out of the question. Furthermore, Zhu Di took a number of ideological initiatives that strengthened the Neo-Confucian rationale for the despotism. In 1409 the *Shengxue xinfa*, which de Bary renders "The System of the Mind-and-Heart in the Learning of the Sages," was compiled. Following the style of earlier Neo-Confucian works, the *Shengxue xinfa* was addressed to Zhu Di's relatives and to posterity. It stressed the link between the ruler and heaven with the implication that the ruler need be bound only by his own conscience. By tying the ruler to heaven Zhu Di placed himself above institutional restraint while at the same time insisting upon loyalty from his ministers (de Bary 1981, 158–63).

In 1414 Zhu Di ordered the compilation of the "Great Compendia of the Five Classics, Four Books, and Human Nature and Principle" (*Wujing sishu xingli daquan*) that provided an official version of important texts for the examination system. With this work, that included the writings of leading Song thinkers together with the classics, the link between the Ming state and Neo-Confucianism was complete. The imperial endorsement was not without cost for Neo-Confucianism since it may have deprived the "Learning of the Mind-and-Heart" of a great deal of its vitality. In his preface to the "Great Compendia" Zhu Di underscored the ruler's obligation to make the Way known to his people and thereby bolstered his own credentials as a sage (de Bary 1981, 164–68). It was another victory for the Chinese throne and another loss for the independence of Chinese scholarship.

CHAPTER FIVE

FOUR MING CODES

Years ago Charles O. Hucker directed attention to Zhu Yuanzhang's many codifications, noting that in compiling and issuing rules and regulations, the first Ming emperor probably surpassed all other dynastic founders in Chinese history (Hucker 1978, 44; Yang 1992). Four codes have been selected from the body of Zhu's legislation to exemplify his program of social regulation. They are the *Great Ming Commandment* (*Da Ming ling*), the *August Ming Ancestral Instruction* (*Huang Ming zuxun*), the *Placard of People's Instructions* (*Jiaomin bangwen*), and the *Great Ming Code* (*Da Ming lü*). The full text of the first three of these documents and the table of contents of the fourth are translated in the appendices.

These four codes were all designed to shape Chinese society to the emperor's specifications by stipulating behavioral norms for rulers, officials, and commoners. As codes they shared certain common features. Each was issued in the form of an imperial edict after drafting by the emperor's advisors. Each begins with a brief statement of the emperor's views on the importance and purpose of the regulations being enacted. Each is divided into articles that have been given sequential numbering in the translations attached as appendices. In their internal organization, however, the four codes show some variation. The 145 articles of the *Commandment* are divided under six subheadings corresponding to the six ministries. This pattern is followed by the *Ming Code*, the longest and most complicated of the documents. Its 460 articles in seven sections (an introductory section and six sections corresponding to the six ministries), each with subheadings, provide specific penal sanctions for the general guidelines spelled out in the *Commandment*. Like the *Commandment* and the *Code*, the *Ancestral Instruction* is also divided into sections within which its ninety-six articles are grouped. But the *Instruction* is more loosely organized than the *Commandment* and the *Code*. Although it is shorter, its contents fall under thirteen headings that lack the formal order of the functionally designated six ministries. The *Placard of People's Instructions* is the shortest and simplest in its arrangement. Its forty-one articles are not subdivided and they display no obvious sequence.

Taken together the four codes sought to govern a wide cross section of the Ming population. Perhaps the clearest contrast among them is to be found by identifying the populations whose behavior they were designed to regulate. The *Instruction* aimed at the imperial establishment: future emperors; the imperial family; eunuchs, servants and imperial bodyguards; some officials of the outer court; and the extensions of the imperial family in the provinces, the princely establishments. The *Commandment* directs its regulatory force at the officials and the population at large. Some items are simply regulatory guidance to be applied within the government, while others apply to aspects of civilian life. The *Code*, too, is aimed at officials and commoners, about the same range of the population as the *Commandment*. The *Placard*, by contrast, is aimed only obliquely at the district level of administration and more directly at the subdistrict leadership of the local community and its population. We have, then, in these four codes a mix of regulations spanning the full range of Chinese society from top to bottom. The spread of their coverage can be represented in tabular form. (see table 1).

TABLE 1

The Coverage of Three Codes Compared

Codification	Parts of Population Governed
Ancestral Instruction:	Emperors
	Imperial Relatives
	Empresses, Consorts
	Princes, Princesses
	Eunuchs
	Imperial Bodyguards
	Nobility of Merit
	High Court Officials
	Princely Establishments
Great Ming Commandment (and *Great Ming Code*):	
	Civil Officials
	Central
	Provincial and local
	Subofficials
	Military Personnel
	Population at large
	Tax Payers
	Various Occupational Groups
	Families and their members
Placard of People's Instructions:	County Officials
	Subofficials
	Rural Population
	Community Heads
	Tithing Chiefs
	Villagers

The kinds of behavior covered by the codes are also quite varied. The *Instruction* stresses such matters as imperial policy, organization of the court, court ceremonial, religious ritual, security, and management of the affairs of the imperial family. The *Commandment* is focused on the organization of the civil bureaucracy, the tax system, marriage and family organization, official religion, criminal law, and, very marginally, regulation of the economy. The *Code* regards these same matters from the perspective of deviance, prescribing punishments for actions that violate the social order spelled out in the *Commandment*. The *Placard* is concerned with the administration of justice, community governance, maintenance of social hierarchy, ideological indoctrination, and promotion of agriculture at the local level.

The structure and contents of the codes will be taken up one at a time.

The Imperial Ancestral Instruction

In the preface to the *Ancestral Instruction*, Zhu Yuanzhang states what was on his mind and what he intended in having the document compiled. Since the states of ancient times founding rulers had established the laws, thereby bringing peace and security to the people and extending benevolence and authority throughout the land. The Ming founder recalled the distress and disorder he had experienced in his early career before noting the role law codes had played in bringing order to the world. Order was to be achieved by enacting codes and teaching people to obey them. The *Instruction* appears to have been closely associated in Zhu's mind with the law codes. He refers to it as a family law. Its purpose, he asserted, was to bind the actions of his descendants forever. In its final version the *Ancestral Instruction* had been through numerous drafts and was offered in a definitive form as a protection against the facile and crafty interpretations of those who like to twist the law. Not a single word was to be changed.

As a family law the *Ancestral Instruction* was intended to regulate the imperial clan in all subsequent generations, e.g., future emperors, their households, and their relatives. A glance at the contents of the *Huang Ming zuxun* reveals the thinking of the authors: the headings used indicate their understanding of areas of concern, and the numbers of items may be taken as an index of relative importance. The order of the headings also provides a modest clue to the authors' assumptions. As with many other Ming documents, items dealing with morality, sacrifice, and ritual generally come before materials dealing with penal law and routine administrative matters, while construction and supplies are relegated to the end of the list. Thirteen categorical headings are used to classify the ninety-six items in the code. These are, in order of appearance: First Section, Observances, Proper Sacrifice, Precautions on Coming and Going, Prudence in Affairs of State, Ceremony, Law, Palace Regulations, Eunuchs, Rules of Office, Military

Guards, Construction, and Provisions. The First Section, the longest part of the *Ancestral Instruction*, as measured by its seventeen items, was added to the document in its final version. It is the most personal part of the *Instruction* and the most varied in its contents, reflecting the founder's effort to set down the lessons he had learned after years on the throne. Other sections of the code deal with discrete categories. If we rank these headings by the number of items assigned to them it is easy to see what the main concerns of the *Instruction* were (see table 2).

The emphasis on Ceremony, Law, and Rules of Office is on defining the status and obligations of imperial princes. The second cluster of headings on Military Guards, Palace Regulations, Proper Sacrifice, and Provisions are concerned with routine administration of the imperial and princely establishments. What is immediately apparent is the mixed nature of the contents of this code. It spans the range from imperial policy and court procedure to mundane matters of household management. This range of concerns in a single document is illustrative of the degree to which the imperial clan was imbedded in the structure of the Ming state. Because the Ming empire was a hereditary monarchy there was no line between the government and the emperor's family. Imperial family or household law could, without any inconsistency, combine matters relating to the external relations of the empire, the abolition of the prime minister, the court ceremonial and the regulation of the emperor's harem.

TABLE 2
Headings in Instruction Ranked by Number of Items

Heading	Items
Ceremony	16
Law	15
Rules of Office	11
Military Guards	10
Palace Regulations	7
Proper Sacrifice	6
Provisions	6
Eunuchs	2
Prudence in Affairs of State	2
Construction	2
Observances	1
Precautions on Coming and Going	1

Another way to approach the contents of the *Huang Ming zuxun* is from the perspective of the objects of its regulative intent. If we inquire as to the locus of the regulative impact, the items of the code may be divided into three spheres of interest; the palace, the court or capital, and the fiefs of the imperial princes. The breakdown of contents in this regard is summarized in table 3.

TABLE 3
Locus of Actions Covered by Instruction

Locus of Regulation	Items
Palace	13
Court/Capital	30
Fiefs	53

At once we see that the greatest weight of this document is directed toward the princes in their establishments outside the capital. The point is reinforced if we ask whose behavior was affected by the regulations (Farmer 1987, 16, 23-26). The following listing indicates the number of items in the *Ancestral Instruction* that are directed toward eight categories of persons. Since some items affect more than one class of person the totals exceed the number of items. The figures, in declining frequency, are depicted in table 4.

Here we can see the heaviest concentration on the emperor (23) and his offspring (47). If we add the number of regulations dealing with palace ladies (6) and eunuchs (5) there is a total of eighty-one items oriented toward the imperial household versus only forty-nine items affecting other agents of the central government and commoners.

TABLE 4
Contents of Instruction by Category of Person Governed

Category	Items
Imperial Offspring	47
Civil Officials	24
Emperor	23
Military	17
Imperial Ladies	6
Eunuchs	5
Guards/Messengers	5
Commoners	3

A similar sort of analysis can be made of the types of behavior governed by the *Ancestral Instruction*. Obviously the categories of behavior cannot be determined with the same degree of objectivity as the locus of regulation or the classes of individuals listed above. Recognizing the somewhat arbitrary nature of the distinctions being made, seven types of behavior are listed in order of frequency of occurrence in the *Ancestral Instruction* (see table 5).

The number of items devoted to organization and titles reflects the interest in institutionalizing practice within the imperial family and household. Institutionalization was one way of keeping people in their place. The regulations dealing with movement and security protected the emperor by limiting access to him and by restricting the movement of the princes who were his potential rivals for the throne. Ceremonial and ritual practices were used to reinforce desired social relationships. Judicial and penal measures provided sanctions where the desired order was threatened.

TABLE 5
Types of Behavior Covered by the Ancestral Instruction

Type of Behavior	Items
Movement/Security	20
Ceremony/Ritual	18
Organization/Title	16
Judicial/Penal	12
Policy/Administration	12
Resources	9

The First Section of the *Ancestral Instruction* stands out from the rest of the text both in the varied nature of its contents and the scope of the questions addressed. Here we find the emperor speaking to future generations on lofty matters of state. In the first article, for example, he specifically charges his descendants not to use cruel punishments. His intention to give this injunction the force of constitutional law is made manifest in the stipulation that those officials who in the future suggest using such punishments should themselves be executed. In the fifth article he claims the mandate of heaven for himself and urges those who follow him to continue to be worthy of heaven's favor. Effective rule is the theme that runs through articles on concern for the people's welfare (6), disaster relief (7), choosing able ministers (12), hearing lawsuits (13), and awarding achievement (14). Other items are of a more personal and cautionary nature, advising future emperors how to survive. From these very general remarks about the *Instruction* let us turn to a consideration of the *Commandment*.

The Commandment

The opening statement of the *Great Ming Commandment* is quite brief. It consists of an edict issued by the emperor proclaiming the *Commandment* early in 1368. In it the Ming founder discourses briefly upon his philosophy of law. The ideal law from his point of view is a simple codification the people can readily understand and obey. He sees the proper role of law as an instrument to encourage good behavior, presumably by putting people on notice, so that enforcement of penal sanctions can be minimized. The distinction is made between commands (*ling*) and statutes (*lü*), the former operating before behavior takes place and the latter after. Thus, the *Commandment* is seen as a didactic instrument to prevent criminal actions and the *Code* as more of a punitive instrument for dealing with criminal actions if they occur (Farmer 1993, 185-87). The tone, and to some degree the contents, of the *Commandment* seem to support this distinction. The *Commandment* often states matters in a positive way, requiring a certain mode of action, while the *Code* specifies punishments for transgressions.

Presumably the edict introducing the *Commandment* is the only part of the text that can be attributed to Zhu Yuanzhang. It is the only part which quotes him directly and is stated from his point of view. The rest of the document is a dry and often technical recitation of the details that give no hint of authorship.

The text of the *Great Ming Commandment*, which was first presented to the Prince of Wu in December, 1367, shortly before he took the throne, consists of 145 articles divided under six major headings (MSLHW, 422–23; Yang 1992, 176-78). It is here for the first time that we see the functional categories of the six ministries—Personnel, Revenue, Rites, War, Justice, and Works—used to organize a legal code. Later, these categories were to be applied to the *Great Ming Code* in what amounted to a major departure from the arrangement of the old *Tang Code*. The sequence of the categories, as with the ministries, is always the same, reflecting a view of the stature and priorities in government affairs. Personnel ranked first since the selection and use of people is at the heart of the political process. The second place ranking for revenue and the third place given to rites also accord with a view that placed substance ahead of form. Military affairs, preeminent before the founding of the dynasty, fell to fourth place in the hierarchy of ministries. The functions of justice and works were clearly of lower stature than the other four.

Some sense of the content of the *Commandment* can be gained by looking at the number of articles under each heading in table 6. The fact that nearly half of the articles in the entire code are classified under the justice rubric, the next to the last in the sequence, is a clear indication of the degree to which the *Commandment* was meant to embody the outlines of a law code for the population at large. The substantial sections on personnel, revenue and rites are mostly of a regulatory nature, aimed at both officials and civilians. The modest number of articles dealing with military and public works matters shows those areas to be of marginal concern in this document.

TABLE 6
Number of Articles Under Each Heading in the Commandment

Heading	Articles
Personnel	20
Revenue	24
Rites	17
Military	11
Justice	71
Works	2

A different perspective on the *Commandment* can be gained by looking at the categories of people mentioned in the code. While it is difficult to avoid some overlap and imprecision, a count of the number of articles in which various kinds of people are mentioned helps to bring the document into focus in at least two ways. First, the categories of persons affected are markedly different from those dealt with in the *Instruction*. The *Commandment* is directed toward a much wider segment of the population than is the *Instruction*. Second, the frequency with which different categories of persons are mentioned is a good indication of the principal aims of the document (Farmer 1993, 188). A count of the number of articles that make substantial reference to the actions of various categories of people has been summarized in table 7.

TABLE 7
Categories of Persons Governed by Commandment

Categories	Items
Civil Officials (all levels)	67
Central Level only	5
Provincial/Local Level only	19
Military Officers	11
Subofficials	14
Populace at large	59

These figures, which count some articles in the *Commandment* more than once and others not at all, are at best a rough approximation because of the varied ways groups are mentioned in the text. What does become apparent, however, is the degree to which the *Commandment* is focused on the mass of the people rather than the imperial family and court, the primary concerns of the *Instruction*. Indeed, the emperor and his circle all but disappear from view. There is only one mention of a eunuch (51) and one mention of the servants and retainers of imperial relatives, nobles, or high officials (131). Where officials are mentioned they are more likely to be local officials than part of the central administration in the capital. The small number of articles referring to military officers and the nature of their involvement confirms that the *Commandment* is not concerned with military affairs in a substantial way. Although the number of items dealing with subofficials is only slightly larger, the contents of those articles verify that low level administration was a central concern of the *Great Ming Commandment*. Indicative of this concern is the large number of local officials and lesser functionaries mentioned in the text. For example, we learn of the staff supervisor (*shouling guan*), the staff foreman (*sili*), writers (*tieshu*), sealkeepers (*zhiyin*), couriers (*xuanshi*), agents (*zouchai*), functionaries (*li*), and five different kinds of clerk (*dianli*, *lingshi*, *shuli*, *yuan*, and *yuanli*). These titles represent the underside of the government bureaucracy that reached to the county level. There is only one passing reference to the community head (*lizhang*) at the village level (143).

The concern of the *Commandment* with the administration of justice is evidenced in the number of offices of functionaries in the legal system, both civil and military, mentioned in the text. In addition to a judge (*tuiguan*) and a warder (*siyu guan*) there are two kinds of jailers (*jinzi*, *tilao guan*), guards (*yuzu*), ushers (*zhihou*), constables (*gongbing*), accusation writing clerks (*shuzhuan renli*), coroners (*wuzuo*), and messengers (*xingren*).

Articles in the *Commandment* that deal with revenue and justice matters are the ones most likely to be phrased in all-inclusive language that applies to officials and civilians alike. Nevertheless, there are numerous points at which specific groups within the population are singled out. Of the registration categories into which the populace of the Ming empire were divided, commoners (*min*) are mentioned more frequently than military families (*jun*), artisans (*jiang*), physicians (*yi*), and geomancers (*yinyang*). Groups mentioned by occupation include merchants, shopkeepers, brewers, brokers, hostel keepers, Buddhist monks, Daoist priests, and matchmakers. Robbers and thieves constitute another category that might not quite fit the definition of an occupation. Masters, servants, and male and female slaves are other descriptions that fall short of telling us what work people were engaged in. Some entries refer to people simply by their condition, e.g., the young, the aged, the sick, widows, widowers, orphans, and women.

The *Commandment* often sees people in terms of family relationships. In many articles individuals are defined by their standing in kinship units. The most frequent references are made to sons and grandsons followed by parents, wives, fathers, and daughters. Excluding article 50, which consists largely of a long catalogue of relationships, mention is made at least once of clan heads, grandparents, grandfathers, mothers, guardians, husbands, concubines, younger brothers, bastard sons, children, sons-in-law, nephews, grandchildren, and relatives.

As with the *Instruction*, so too it is possible to ask what kinds of behavior were regulated by each of the articles of the *Commandment* (Farmer 1993, 189-90). The outcome of such a survey is markedly different than the figures related above for the *Ancestral Instruction* (see table 8).

TABLE 8
Types of Behavior Governed by the Commandment

Type of Behavior	Items
Judicial/Penal	67
Policy/Administration	28
Ceremony/Ritual	16
Resources/Taxation	15
Family/Marriage	9
Movement/Security	7
Organization/Title	3

The greatest contrast with the contents of the *Instruction* is the relative importance of the judicial-penal category. The next most obvious differences are the de-emphasis under the heading organization-title and the increase under policy-administration. This contrast reveals the regulatory nature of the *Commandment*. Whereas the *Instruction* is concerned with defining the status of members of the imperial establishment, the *Commandment* merely sets out rules for the operation of a bureaucracy whose structure is already known. The resources-taxation heading in the *Commandment* is a bit more prominent thanks to mention of the tax collecting function of officials as well as the tax paying and service obligations of commoners. The activities of commoners also account for a family-marriage heading that was not needed in cataloging the contents of the *Instruction*.

The articles that fall under the judicial-penal heading in the *Commandment* constitute a brief but comprehensive criminal code. Articles on the five punishments (73), the ten abominations (74), the eight considerations (75), commutation (76), and penal instruments (77) provide the basic definitions of crimes and punishments upon which the penal system was based. The technical details of court procedure and pleading are covered in articles on accusations (83, 107, 138, 139); interrogation (85); confession (95, 99, 117); investigative reports (86); rules governing testimony by dependents (130); substitutes pleading for the old, the infirm, or the disabled (90); and provisions for autopsy reports (97, 116). The participation of the public in the criminal justice system was encouraged by rewards to those who captured robbers or thieves (94). Some restraint was shown, however, in a requirement for investigation of cases in which victims of a robbery pursued and killed the robber.

The Placard

The *Placard of People's Instructions* was issued in 1398, the last year of the Ming founder's rule. As with the two codes discussed above, the *Placard* begins with an edict giving the emperor's rationale for its enactment. In the edict Zhu Yuanzhang recounts how he brought order to the world and reconstituted the government at the central and provincial levels. Despite these efforts, the moral quality of the officials and functionaries remained an obstacle to the reform of the empire. People continued to bring their complaints to the capital. The main purpose for issuing the *Placard*, therefore, was to distinguish clearly which matters were to be handled at the community level among the people themselves and which matters were to be referred to the officials. In general the village elders and *lijia* elders were to judge minor disputes involving marriage, land and brawls while the more serious offenses such as adultery, robbery, fraud, or loss of life were to be reported to the authorities in the government office.

Jurisdiction for enforcement of the *Placard* was given to the Ministry of Revenue. The reason for this assignment is undoubtedly because the revenue ministry was the one charged with the population census, land survey, household registration, and the tax and labor service assignments which brought it most directly into contact with the civilian population in the villages. As we shall see, however, the *Placard* was concerned with a great deal more than just the generation of revenue; it touched upon the social structure of the community, ideological indoctrination of the population, community solidarity, judicial administration, and the promotion of agriculture, to name the main issues.

When the *Placard* is compared with the *Ancestral Instruction* and the *Great Ming Commandment*, numerous contrasts are at once apparent. The locus of its authority is limited to the lowest level of the rural community. There is none of the interest in the imperial, court, provincial, or military affairs that fill the other two codes. The *Placard* concerns itself almost exclusively with villagers, mentioning county level officials primarily to exclude them from involvement in village affairs. Finally, the *Placard* is undifferentiated in its contents, consisting of a single list of forty-one articles with neither subheadings nor an explicitly stated order.

The most fruitful angle from which to analyze the *Placard* is the classification of the types of behavior which it was designed to control (see table 9). The large cluster of items under the judicial-penal heading clearly depicts the extent to which the *Placard* is concerned with keeping order in the local community. One theme stressed in this group of articles is the jurisdictional authority of the community leaders, i.e., the *lijia* elders. Minor matters, such as those involving marriage, land, brawls, and disputes, were to be decided by the *lijia* elders in the village (1).

TABLE 9
Types of Behavior Governed by the Placard

Type of Behavior	Items
Judicial/Penal	18
Ceremony/Ritual	6
Resources/Taxation	6
Policy/Administration	4
Organization/Title	3
Family/Marriage	3
Movement/Security	1

A punishment of sixty blows is prescribed for those who took such minor matters to the county officials. The intent of this legislation was twofold: to free the local officialdom from involvement in a sea of petty matters and to build up a judicial capability within the village community itself. The problem is to clarify the distinction between the two levels of authority. The second article spells out a list of nineteen specific offenses which are to be judged by the elders. These include domestic conflicts, petty crime, and disturbances of the public order and the agricultural economy—a variety of activities that we might call misdemeanors. Those who are not satisfied with the ruling of the elders and the *lijia* and willfully take matters on to the officials are to be executed and their families exiled to the frontiers (12). Serious matters—adultery, robbery, fraud or homicide—are to be sent to the officials for judgement (10). Yet the line is hard to draw. Some cases of adultery, robbery and homicide not involving one of the ten abominations can still be handled in the village by the elders (11). The emperor's exasperation shows through at one point when he notes that the people of the areas closest to Nanjing were overly fond of litigation and too often carried their quarrels directly to the capital (23). In such cases the elders are simply to arrest the offenders and enforce the jurisdiction of their local authority.

The Ming Code

A discussion of early Ming social legislation would not be complete without some consideration of the *Ming Code*, the largest and best-known example of the Ming codification. However, the *Code* is too formidable a topic to be treated in detail here. In the long history of Chinese penal law it ranks second only to the great *Tang Code* from which the bulk of its contents derived (MacCormack 14). The *Ming Code* is essentially a reaffirmation of the Tang vision after a period of Mongol rule; many of its articles are carried over from the *Tang Code*, sometimes in identical language, sometimes restated or rearranged. In its earliest version, presented with the *Commandment* to the Prince of Wu in 1367, the *Code* consisted of 285 articles based on the *Tang Code*, but with additions and deletions. Its contents were listed under the six categories as follows: Personnel 18, Revenue 63, Rites 14, Military 32, Justice 150, and Works 8 (MSLHW, 422–23). In the early versions of 1373 and 1374 the *Ming Code* had reverted to the same organization as its Tang model. It now consisted of 606 articles arranged as follows: General Principles, Imperial Guard and Prohibitions, Administrative Regulations, Household and Marriage, Public Stables and Granaries, Unauthorized Levies, Violence and Robbery, Assaults and Accusations, Fraud and Counterfeit, Miscellaneous Articles, Arrest and Flight, and Judgement and Prison (MSLHW, 1534–35). But by 1389 the contents of the *Code* were reorganized in its 460 articles under new headings: a statement of terms and general principles and six categories corresponding to the functional hierarchy of the six ministries (MSLHW, 2955–56). This structure comes directly from the *Great Ming Commandment*, which spells out in general terms the legal norms for which the *Code* provides detailed and specific punishments. The *Ming Code*, which took its final form in 1397, has fewer articles and is more tightly worded than its predecessors or its earliest versions.

The concerns as well as the contents of the *Code* parallel those of the *Commandment*. The distribution of articles under various subheadings provides a profile of the matters covered (see table 10).

The distribution of articles in the *Code* closely resembles the allocation of contents in the *Commandment* (Farmer 1993, 187). In both cases the justice category is the largest. If the articles under Terms and General Principles in the *Code* are added to those under Penal Law, the percentage (47%) is very close to the percentage of Justice Regulations in the *Commandment* (49%). The ratios for the Revenue category, 16% in the *Commandment* and 20% I n the *Code*, are very close and both codes assign scant attention to the Works category, 1% in the *Commandment* and 2% in the *Code*. Significant variations appear in the Personnel, Rites, and Military categories. That the *Commandment* assigns 13% of its contents (20 items) to Personnel while the *Code* assigns only 7% (33 items) underscores the fact that the *Commandment* is concerned with specifying the staffing levels and organization of government offices, whereas the *Code* is aimed at criminal conduct by officials. Likewise in the Rites category the *Commandment* devotes 11% of its contents (17 items) to prescribing ceremonial and ritual practices essential to the dynastic order, while the *Code* assigns a mere 7% of its contents (26 items) to miscellany of ideological misdeeds. The reverse can be said of the Military category which occupies only 7% of the *Commandment* (11 items) but fully 16% of the *Code* (75 items).

TABLE 10
Subdivisions of the Great Ming Code

Headings and Subheadings	No. of Articles	
I. Terms and General Principles (*ming li lü*)		(47)
II. Administrative Law (*li lü*)		(33)
a. Administrative Regulations (*zhizhi*)	15	
b. Standards of Official Behavior (*gongshi*)	18	
III. Civil Law (*hu lü*)		(95)
a. Family and Corvee Service (*hu yi*)	15	
b. Landed Property (*tianzhai*)	11	
c. Marriage (*hunyin*)	18	
d. Granaries and treasuries (*cangku*)	24	
e. Taxes and tariffs (*kecheng*)	19	
f. Money lending (*qianzhai*)	3	
g. Public markets (*shichan*)	5	
IV. Ritual Law (*li lü*)		(26)
a. State sacrifices (*jisi*)	6	
b. Ceremonial regulations (*yi zhi*)	20	
V. Military Law (*bing lü*)		(75)
a. Imperial palaces and guards (*gong wei*)	19	
b. Administration of armed forces (*junzheng*)	20	
c. Frontier guard posts (*guanjin*)	7	
d. Horses and cattle ([*jiumu*)	11	
e. Postal services and transport (*youyi*)	18	
VI. Penal Law (*xing lü*)		(171)
a. Violence and robbery (*zei dao*)	28	
b. Homicide (*renming*)	20	
c. Assault and battery (*dou ou*)	22	
d. Abusive language (*mali*)	8	
e. Accusations and suits (*su song*)	12	
f. Bribery and squeeze (*shoucang*)	11	
g. Deception and conterfeit (*zha wei*)	12	
h. Sexual violations (*fan jian*)	10	
i. Miscellaneous offenses (*zafan*)	11	
j. Arrests and flight (*bu wang*)	8	
k. Trial and imprisonment (*duan yu*)	29	
VII. Laws on Public Works (*gong lü*)		(13)
a. Public construction (*ying zao*)	9	
b. River conservancy (*hefang*)	4	

The *Commandment* describes the organization of military agencies, while the *Code* presents an extensive catalog of crimes.

The *Code* was aimed at officials and commoners. Little mention is made of the nobility or the emperor. When the imperial establishment is mentioned, it is most often indirectly, as in laws against shooting arrows at palaces (211), stealing wood from imperial estates and tombs (286), or quarreling in the palace (327). Typically it is an official whose actions are governed by the *Code's* language. Beyond the office holders are underlings, family members, and then the mass of common people. As a guide to social life the *Code* is much less concerned with what ought to be done than with what ought not to be done. Where the *Commandment* lays out principles and guidelines for organizing the government, religious activities, social intercourse, and family life, the *Code* says what may not be done and what penalty is appropriate for doing it. Article 439 requires that officials passing sentence in criminal cases specify under which article in the *Code* or *Commandment* they are acting. Where the *Code* lacks a specific punishment, Article 409 provides one for violation of anything prescribed in the *Commandment*. Where neither the *Commandment* nor the *Code* provides specific guidance, Article 410 of the *Code* fixes a punishment for violations of common sense, "that which ought not to be done" (*bu yingwei*).

The *Commandment* as it is translated in appendix 2 dates from the year before the Ming dynasty was founded. Its form and contents can be taken as a reflection of the thinking of Zhu Yuanzhang and his advisors in 1367. The *Code*, on the other hand, presents a much more complex picture. Not only were many of its contents carried over from the *Tang Code*, it also underwent thirty years of revisions before assuming its final form. Organizational changes in the *Code* may represent nothing more than a process of rationalization through incremental improvements. Changes in the content of the *Code*, however, reflect altered historical circumstances. One can ask what happened during the three decades of the Ming founder's rule to bring about changes in the law. Unfortunately, we lack detailed documentary evidence on earlier versions of the *Code*. Nevertheless, by comparing the *Ming Code* to its Tang ancestor and by looking at the events of the Hongwu reign, we might venture a few observations. First of all, there is Taizu's effort to use law codes as instruments of moral education. Article 63 requires officials to be familiar with the provisions of the *Code* and *Commandment* and censors to test their knowledge (HMZS, 1772–73; MacCormack, 79). Students were encouraged to memorize the *Code* and the *Da gao*. A simplified version of the laws was prepared for popular consumption. The coupling of the *Code* and the *Grand Pronouncement* appears to have been an effort by the emperor to elevate and enforce his own views by linking them to the penal code. It was a particularly forceful attempt at moral reform.

A perusal of the articles in the Ming *Code* that are not in the Tang *Code* suggests some of the legislator's concerns. The largest number of new articles have to do with government revenue and property. New provisions are added to protect currency and coinage (125, 126, 382), regulate tax collection and expenditure (127, 130, 131, 132, 135, 136, 137, 138, 267, 288), and prevent misuse of government materiel and production (451, 452). A whole section is added on salt and smuggling (149-164, 166, 167). Some of the articles are suggestive of the mistrust Zhu developed in the famous Prestamped Documents Case (*kongyin an*) of 1376, when he discovered that official seals were being applied to blank reports of tax receipts so that the figures could be filled in later after transport (Langlois 1988, 135–36). A number of articles dealing with government files (72, 73), seals (76–79), and document delivery (259–64) may have grown out of that experience. The founder's mistrust of officials is witnessed by a number of new administrative regulations dealing with selection, appointment, and influence (48, 49, 50, 54, 58, 59). Also apparent is a regard for security and safety of the imperial person (60–62, 80, 207, 210, 213, 215, 220, 283), concern clearly manifested in the *Ancestral Instruction*.

Old provisions for protecting social distinctions are strengthened by a number of new articles. Article 119 prohibits officials from taking musicians as wives or concubines. Marriages concluded prior to the dynastic founding are exempted (HMZS, 1837). Officials and their sons and grandsons are to be punished for patronizing entertainers (398). The purchase of commoners' children to be entertainers or musicians is likewise outlawed (398). Buddhist and Daoist clergy are forbidden to marry (120) or to have sexual relations (396).

A number of new articles reflect the Ming founder's concern for ideological dominance. Officials and scholars are required to regularly perform ceremonies honoring local spirits (178), while common people are banned from farming or pasturing animals on the tombs of previous rulers (179). Witchcraft and heterodox teachings are outlawed (181), as is the possession of political books, the private practice of astronomy (184), and prediction of good fortune or disaster by soothsayers (197; Farmer 1990). The emperor's status is enhanced by the requirement that imperial edicts be properly announced (186). At the local level the traditional community wine drinking ceremony (*xiang yinjiuli*), designed to reinforce the social hierarchy, is given the force of law (201). Legal protection was also extended to the pavilions (*shenmingting*) where official announcements are made and the notice boards (*banbang*) where documents are displayed (400). An interesting extension of the law in the area of oral expression is the addition to prohibitions against cursing within the family of articles making illegal cursing of higher officials by lower (348, 349), or cursing by anyone at all (347).

The four codes described here were important parts of the Ming founder's ambitious effort to remake Chinese society. Taken as a whole they constituted a comprehensive set of guidelines intended to impose order on the royal family, the nobility, the officials, and the mass of commoners. They testify to the systematic character of Zhu Yuanzhang's legislative program. In the next chapter the strategy and content of the legislation will be discussed.

CHAPTER SIX

A LESSER EMPIRE: HAN CHINA RESTORED

Laws are the products of legislative processes and thus tell us more about those who write them than those they are intended to govern. They are evidence of how legislators want others to behave. In the present case, the laws of the early Ming dynasty are the products of the founding emperor's effort to reconstruct China. The codes translated in the appendices are statements of intentions rather than descriptions of actual social practice. They were chosen for what they can tell us about Zhu Yuanzhang's view of the ideal Chinese social order. In a real sense they are the design specifications of the Chinese world that Zhu, acting pursuant to heaven's mandate, set out to create from the ruins of the Yuan dynasty. In this body of legislation we can find statements of some of the principles upon which the Chinese social order was supposed to be based and many details about the specific forms it was supposed to take.

Han China

Benedict Anderson defines the nation as "an imagined political community—and imagined as both inherently limited and sovereign" (Anderson [1983] 1991, 6). He contrasts the nation with religious communities and dynastic realms, the cultural systems which preceded it. In those regimes, small literate elites connected by sacred written languages could use their claim to divine truth to dominate centralized orders. In China, Mongols and Manchus who mastered the cultural system could be regarded as legitimate rulers (Anderson [1983] 1991, 12–14). In such an order, "the fundamental conceptions about 'social groups' were centripetal and hierarchical, rather than boundary-oriented and horizontal" (Anderson [1983] 1991, 15).

While Anderson's definitions succinctly capture the main contrasts between imperial dynasties and the modern nation, they miss an important ambivalence within the Chinese traditional order: that between the Han and non-Han dynasties. Rather than viewing the Ming and Qing dynasties as a block because of their institutional continuities, a case can be made that the Ming and Qing represent two distinct configurations, two poles of the Chinese imperial tradition. At times in its history China has taken the form of a "universal empire," expanding its territory to enfold peoples of different cultures. This form of Chinese identity was most fully realized under the

Mongol and Manchu conquest regimes of the Yuan and Qing. In contrast to this imperial and imperialistic configuration there existed a narrower definition of China as a culturally homogeneous Han people. This vision of China as the central states or middle kingdom surrounded by a sea of barbarians tended toward nationalism or culturism, a China that was "boundary-oriented" and, while socially hierarchical in some respects, culturally horizontal.

Between these two views of China, the imperial or the cultural, Zhu Yuanzhang tended toward the limited, homogeneous community. In his vision China was essentially a self-sufficient, ethnically uniform Han society defending itself against the outside world while inwardly pursuing a hierarchical model of moral perfection. The Ming founding provided Zhu with the opportunity to give this Han community its clearest definition. When it was overwhelmed by Manchu conquest in the mid-seventeenth century it lived on within the multinational Qing empire. In the twentieth century it has lived on within the multinational People's Republic of China, a Chinese nation within a Chinese empire.

The Ming dynasty embodied a conscious effort to recreate an ethnic community of Han people who would be true to the core principles of the Chinese great tradition. While the Ming regime was by no means an example of modern nationalism it did manifest some proto-nationalistic elements. Complaints that China had been abused and humiliated under Mongol rule sound much like the grievances that inspire contemporary nationalists everywhere. Hostility to foreign domination was not just an issue for the educated elite who found their learning devalued: it was shared from top to bottom. The most strident charge against the Yuan had to do with marriage practices, violations of norms that cut across class lines. Mongol customs for absorbing widowed women into family units, well adapted to the conditions of nomadic life in the steppe, were anathema to Chinese of all social strata. The awareness Han Chinese shared of the wealth of their common history, territory, language, and culture provided ample fuel for patriotic appeals.

Requirements that Ming subjects give up Mongol styles and customs in favor of Chinese practices was part of an effort to strengthen an ethnic identity. Beyond the effort to return to traditional practices, such as a Tang dynasty dress code, there appears to have been an effort to assimilate remnants of the Mongols and Semu who had until recently ruled China. article 122 of the *Code* reads as follows:

> Mongols and Semu [i.e., non-Mongol collaborators] shall marry with Chinese persons. (It is essential that both parties be willing.) They are not permitted to marry within their own kind. Violators shall be punished by eighty blows of the heavy stick and both men and women shall be enslaved by the state. If Chinese persons do not wish to marry Qincha Muslims [whose physical ap-

pearance is different from Han Chinese] they may marry each other among their own kind; the prohibition above is not applicable (HMZSb, 1839–40).

The new empire claimed descent from its Chinese predecessors and sought to distance itself from the Mongol Yuan. It was consciously modelled on the historical past, especially the Han, Tang and Song dynasties. Classical references and historical analogies were used to justify the new arrangements as consistent with an ongoing cultural tradition. History was a guide and a source of legitimacy, but it was subject to interpretation. Despite the extensive use of precedents, Zhu Yuanzhang did not hesitate to innovate when it suited his purpose to do so. A case in point is the elimination of the office of prime minister. In the final version of the *Ancestral Instruction* this matter is taken up in the second article. There, Zhu boldly rejects the authority of the entire span of imperial history by asserting that there had never been a prime minister in antiquity and that the office had been created by the Qin, which had expired soon after instituting it. In an obvious breech of consistency he failed to make the same observation about the position of emperor.

In the extent of its territory the Ming empire more closely resembled the Northern Song dynasty than it did the Han or the Tang. The Han and the Tang were ages when Chinese power and influence thrust outward to Korea, Vietnam and Inner Asia. The Song controlled a smaller territory and took a more defensive posture toward its neighbors. In his relations with the outside world the Ming founder also urged caution. The fourth article in the *Ancestral Instruction* warned his successors against the dangers of adventurism on the frontiers and mandated instead a strong defense. It is true that after Zhu Yuanzhang died the Yongle emperor undertook an expansion of Chinese power and influence through military campaigns and naval expeditions, but his was an innovation that could not be sustained. Expenditures for the great sea voyages conflicted with the needs of northern border defense and were soon abandoned. Efforts by Yongle's successors to play an active military role along the frontier culminated in the Mongol capture of the foolish Yingzong at Tumu in 1449. Later in the dynasty the Ming returned to the defensive foreign policy of the founder and a cultural style that was inward and backward looking. Zhu Yuanzhang's Ming empire was a lesser China, a Han state that sought to retrieve the best from its past and shield itself from outside influences.

High and Low

Zhu Yuanzhang thought of social order as a hierarchy. What he stressed most in laying down laws to govern the social order was the importance of hierarchical distinctions within every sphere and between spheres. This was the central organizing principle that applied to all, from the imperial clan and nobility at the top down through the officialdom to villagers and their families at the bottom. Social legislation clarified relative standings, specified ways to mark positions in a pecking order, and provided sanctions to enforce conformity.

Relative centrality was a second dimension of the status hierarchy congruent with elevation on a vertical axis. If the social order was a pyramid the emperor's position at the apex was also at the center: positions farther from the center were necessarily farther down the hierarchy on the vertical axis. The highest positions in the society were in the palace, the capital, and the central provinces and at lower levels in princely establishments and the administrative seats of provinces, prefectures, subprefectures, and districts. Just as a member of the royal family could be cast down to the bottom of society by being reduced to commoner status, an official could be posted to a remote location, or a criminal could be sentenced to life exile at a great distance or even sent to the frontiers beyond the pale of civilization.

The *Ancestral Instruction* devotes a great deal of attention to symbolic elevation of the emperor. When the emperor is addressed in a memorial by members of the imperial clan they are required to use special terminology that makes clear their relationship to the emperor and empress (36). The emperor's birthday is to be celebrated by princes in their fiefs (31). On the first day of the new year princes and civil and military officials are required to don their best gowns and congratulate the emperor in a ceremony of twelve obeisances (30). The *Commandment* requires that officials be arranged in order of their rank and grade in all court audiences (45) and that congratulatory memorials presented to the son of heaven be elegantly written and contain no taboo words (46). Sumptuary regulations in the *Commandment* reserve the gold embroidered five-clawed dragons and dragon and phoenix motifs for imperial clothing, curtains, saddles and carriages (51). These are but a few examples of the myriad ways in which terminology, symbols, and symbolic acts were used to enhance the emperor's superiority.

Just below the emperor are his offspring, the princes in their scattered fiefs. Because the princes are blood relatives of the emperor it is necessary to insure that they receive the respect due them. The *Ancestral Instruction* stipulates that commoners, whether of military or civilian household registration, who reside in the territory of an imperial prince and venture to be rude to that prince are to be arrested and sent to the capital (47). Those who might dare to accuse the prince of a crime are to be executed and their families banished to the frontier (54). The *Instruction* specifically disavows any intention on the part of the throne to cause offense to the princes through statements of court representatives sent to the fiefs (55). The fear here is that officials at the court might try to cause misunderstanding between the prince and his ruler. In order to clarify the superior status of the imperial family it is explicitly set down that all high officials passing the fief of a prince shall pay their respects to the prince and make obeisance before him. The penalty for evading this responsibility is execution (34).

The fusion of the princes with the civil and military apparatus of the central government is reflected in the many items in the *Ancestral Instruction* concerning the management of the princely establishments. An example is an article which requires that civil and military officials in the vicinity of the prince's fief pay court on the prince on the first and fifteenth days of the month (35). The princes play a role in recruiting their own military commanders and in disciplining their subordinates but are not allowed to expand their staffs or foster the advancement of self-promoting schemers (51, 53, 81). Attention is also given to the status of the military forces in the prince's jurisdiction and inspections are to be made to control defections (58). The civil and military organization of the fief staffs is specified in detail, both titles and ranks being given (83, 84). As extensions of the imperial household, the princely establishments also are assigned eunuchs just as is the heir apparent in the capital (71, 72). Princesses also are allocated a minimal complement of eunuchs (73).

As extensions of the ruling family in outlying areas, the princes have to display a style of life and show evidence of power sufficient to awe the people with the grandeur of the imperial clan. The princes' stipends are paid annually from central government sources; the salaries of civil and military officers are to be paid monthly (98, 99). A schedule of stipends due imperial relatives begins with 10,000 piculs of rice for an imperial prince and descends to 200 piculs of rice for minor princesses and their consorts (100). The entourage of the fief holder includes a specified inventory of ceremonial weapons, musical instruments, and pennants for purposes of show (94). The greatest public spectacle the princes make is their annual pilgrimage to the court to pay their respects to the emperor. When the prince leaves his fief his heir is to manage the establishment (86). The size of the retinue is subject to negotiation since it all has to be paid for by the prince and can not be imposed upon the districts through which the party will pass (87, 97). While it is in the interest of the ruler to have his offspring make an impressive show when they travel to the capital it is not desirable that their lifestyle become too grand. The size of princely palaces is limited, and, while it is permitted to add courtyards for sons and grandsons, the construction of detached palaces and other facilities is not allowed (95, 96). Abuse of the princes' residences in the capital by unscrupulous officials is also to be severely punished (50).

The power of the state to shape the organization of society through the use of symbols is best seen in the elaborate sumptuary regulations spelled out in article 51 of the *Commandment*, the second longest in the document, which specifies the styles of clothing, residences, equipage, dishes, and tombs suitable for persons of each rank. Certain symbols, especially the dragon and the phoenix, are reserved for imperial use. It is noteworthy that the sumptuary regulations so carefully described for civil officials and commoners do not necessarily apply to military personnel. This is a minor indication of the relatively high status the military enjoyed at the time of the dynastic founding. Closely related to the sumptuary laws are the titles and posthumous titles conferred upon those who have served the state at the highest levels (60, 61).

Questions of status figure prominently in only three articles in the *Placard.* Villagers more than fifty years of age with good reputations are to be named elders and charged with settling disputes (4). If they have neither the experience nor the capacity to make the necessary judgements they are to be called elders in name but not required to handle cases. When civil disputes are to be settled a panel of elders and *lijia* is to be convened in the exhibition pavilion (*shenming ting*) with strict attention being given to the order of seating (3). The most explicit ranking of villagers is that required for the community wine drinking ceremony, a public event in which the participants are arranged by age and moral worth (27). It is a mandatory group acknowledgment of the social order.

In 1383 a diagram of the community wine drinking ceremony was issued with the order that the ceremony be held in Confucian schools throughout the empire in the first and tenth months. In a formal intersection of officials and local elites (*shidafu*), the senior official played the role of host while a retired official played the role of guest (*bin*) and a virtuous and accomplished elder that of honorary guest (*zunbin*). The instructions for the ceremony underscored the social hierarchy by specifying the location and direction in which the participants were seated, the guest and honorary guest on the north facing south and the host on the east facing west, as well as the sequence in which vessels were washed and wine and food presented. At the heart of the ceremony was a reading from the *Code* and the *Commandment* during which miscreants were required to stand in a central location and listen. In 1389 it was ordered that those who had committed crimes should be clustered on the outer edge of the assembly and not allowed to sit among the good people (MS, 1419-21).

Security Measures

The First Section in the *Ancestral Instruction* alludes to the emperor's need for security. Articles in this section include admonitions to be always on guard (8), to keep weapons and riders always at the ready (9), to listen for noises in the night (10), and to be moderate in eating and drinking (11). Clearly the emperor's lot was neither an easy nor a safe one. In article 25 future emperors are enjoined to use divination before setting out on a journey and to be alert to the possibility of warning signals from heaven of dangers that might lie along the way. The palace and the court are full of traps for the unwary ruler. Article 18 warns against drinking and consorting with actors, against allowing wives and concubines to influence the ruler's judgement, and against acting on the advice of a single official, especially when that advice is offered in a moment of relaxation. Articles 26 and 27 warn future rulers to be alert to the possibility that officials might cut the emperor off from information or might misrepresent their own virtue.

Physical isolation is another device that protected the emperor by shielding him from contact with others. The *Ancestral Instruction* is much concerned with the operations of the imperial household. Strict measures provide for the insulation of those within the palace from the outside world. Private documents may not be exchanged with outsiders, and even in the event of sickness physicians are not to be allowed into the palace (60, 63). Ladies in the palace are not allowed to grant audiences to officials, but they are allowed to come to court twice a month and on some special days (64). The ladies of the palace are under the jurisdiction of the empress, who is expressly barred from intervening in any affairs outside the palace (62).

The cardinal concern of the *Ancestral Instruction* is the need to control the members of the imperial clan. The class of relatives that constituted the greatest threat to the ruler are the imperial princes (*qinwang*) because they are potential rivals for the throne. The Ming solution to the problem of the princes, which is also a partial solution to the problem of frontier defense and of controlling armies at a distance from the capital, is to follow the Han precedent of enfeoffing the princes at strategic locations distant from the capital. Sixteen locations are specified in this version of the *Ancestral Instruction* (95). A major advantage of this arrangement, from the emperor's point of view, is to remove his sons, except for the heir apparent, from the capital so that they can not meddle in court politics. A weak rationalization is offered in article 15, which notes that the princes are happier in their fiefs than is the emperor in his capital, burdened down with the problems of governing the realm. More ominous statements follow in articles 16 and 17, specifically warning the princes and nobles about the dangers of not keeping their places and of subverting the court.

Spatial separation from the capital and the emperor is an important device used to control the princes. While enfeoffment at remote locations assures that the princes will not be able to meddle in court affairs, the very fact of their remoteness creates control problems on another level. How is the emperor to guarantee their loyalty and prevent their misconduct? Many articles in the *Ancestral Instruction* touch upon this problem. Part of the solution is to require that the princes make annual visits to the capital to pay their respects to the emperor in person. They do not come all at once but the oldest first, with precedence given to the offspring of the principal wife (37). Military emergencies along the border are recognized as a reason for departing from the schedule (38), and princes who happen to be uncles of the emperor are excused from paying court after the age of fifty (41).

Communication between the emperor and the princes is a sensitive matter. Messengers sent to the court by a prince are supposed to be granted immediate access to the palace, and officials are not allowed to detain them or prevent the emperor from being notified of their arrival (52). The emperor, for his part, can summon the princes at will by sending a senior official or a eunuch bearing an imperial command and a golden tally (45). Six sets of travel tallies are to be maintained by each prince for reporting to the throne (92). Particular care is to be taken when there is an allegation of wrongdoing on the part of the prince (44). In such cases reliable emissaries are especially important. The emperor has to guard simultaneously against the possibility that a prince will intercede on behalf of a transgressing subordinate and the possibility of unsubstantiated charges levelled against the prince by the censors (48, 49).

Fear of subversion, conspiracy and rebellion are undercurrents that run through the *Ancestral Instruction*. The Ming founder came to his throne by force of arms and had not been long upon it when this document was first drafted. All sorts of dangers and abuses are anticipated but none is more sensitive than the transfer of power when a new ruler takes the throne. Succession to the throne is to fall to the sons of the wife, the younger being elevated when the elder brother dies (57). If attempts are made to manipulate the succession in favor of the son of a concubine, regardless of relative age, the latter is to send notification to the son of the wife so that the conspiracy can be ended. These are provisions premised upon the assumption that the junior imperial offspring represent a threat to the throne. In another article it is contemplated that a new emperor might find himself the prisoner of evil officials in the capital and that the princes with their armed forces should be summoned by a secret edict to come and rescue the emperor (56). It was this provision which, after the death of Zhu Yuanzhang, provided the Prince of Yan with a pretext for usurping the throne.

The *Instruction* devotes considerable attention to the military role of the imperial princes. The princes represent an extension of the emperor's family out into the territory of the empire as a political and military presence. As commanders of military forces the princes are both a safeguard and a danger to the emperor in the capital. The military forces of the prince's fief are of two kinds. First there is the guard unit that patrols the walls and gates of the prince's compound. This force consists of 15 officers and 672 men divided into three equal units for duty rotation (85). There are also escort guards under the command of the prince. These are distinct from the local garrison forces which have their own commanders (89). The relationship of the prince to these regional defense forces is a strategic matter of the utmost sensitivity. An important reason for enfeoffing the princes in strategic locations in north China is to give the court a politically reliable check on military commanders in areas where strong garrisons are stationed far from the capital. Commanders of frontier garrisons can not move their troops on their own initiative or even on the authority of a court command alone. They are required to have a parallel command sent to them through the nearest imperial prince. If a command from the capital comes to the garrison commander only, an immediate notification of the prince is required, whereupon the prince is to notify the emperor directly (88). This provision reveals the concern of the Ming founder and his advisors for the reliability of their military forces and the relative trust they placed upon the imperial offspring, a concern underscored by the next article, which stipulates that in a strategic area the prince, in time of emergency, may assume direct authority over the garrison forces (89). The prince can not intervene in the affairs of the garrison by favoring certain individuals, however (90). Under normal circumstances the princes and their escort guards are kept ready for action by hunting expeditions to take place during the fall and winter months and to drill them five to eight times every month (91, 93).

Attention to the control of movement appears at a number of points in the *Commandment*, but not as a central concern. There is no mention of the security matters that figure so prominently in the *Ancestral Instruction*. Generally speaking, travel was tightly restricted in early Ming society. The chief exceptions are merchants, criminals undergoing banishment or exile, and persons on government business, and these are the ones we see in the code. Hostels are required to keep a register of merchants staying with them and to show it to the local authorities monthly (32). At the national and provincial capitals travel permits are issued by the military authorities and at the local level by civilian officials (71). Regular check points inspect travel documents. Although common people are not allowed to travel freely, allowance is made for persons sentenced to life exile to take members of their family and household with them. When the exile dies, the dependents are allowed to return to the original place of registration except in the case of the most severe crimes (113).

The emperor's reach is weakest at the local level, where the officials who are supposed to act on his behalf are the hardest to control. Zhu Yuanzhang tried to solve this problem by forging an alliance with the community leaders. In the *Placard* we can see signs of the tension that exists between the court and the lower officialdom and the role that the villagers are to play in helping the ruler bring his agents into line. The elders are to identify persons of virtue and merit and report their names to the court (17). Officials who fail to pass the information on are to be punished. The people's voice is to be listened to in matters of official deportment (22). If large numbers of people support or denounce an official it is to be taken as a good sign of his virtue or vice. Elders, having failed to reform a wayward official through remonstrance, are empowered to arrest him and take him to the capital.

The matter of public education was doubtless a painful one for Zhu Yuanzhang. Early in his reign the founder had ordered that village schools (*shexue*) be established for instruction of commoners' children (32). Later, however, the schools apparently became a burden to the people when officials compelled attendance by the sons of families who could not afford to spare them from the fields. For this reason the *shexue* were abolished and the people are allowed to organize their own schools. The appeal of complaints up the administrative ladder is to proceed one level at a time without bypassing lower levels (38).

The last article in the *Placard* grants permission for elders with judicial matters to report to proceed directly to the capital without the usual travel documents (41). This provision illustrates as clearly as any how the emperor relied on the rural leadership as a check on the lower levels of his own bureaucracy. By giving villagers permission to come directly to Nanjing, the emperor in effect bypassed his officials and forged a direct link to his subjects.

Ritual and Sacrifice

As the son of heaven, the emperor was the only one qualified to make the sacrifices to heaven and earth. The status of the imperial line was elevated by associating the imperial ancestors with the highest sacrifices (*Commandment* 20). A cluster of articles in the *Commandment* briefly specify when and under what circumstances some of the principal official sacrifices are supposed to take place. These include the Temple of the Three Emperors, the Altar of Soil and Grain, the Temple to King Wu and King Cheng, and the Confucian Temple (56, 57, 58, 59). These articles govern the relation of the Ming regime to the spirit world. Provisions dealing with the emperor's sacerdotal obligations stress the need for sincerity and self-control while sacrificing (19). Before major sacrifices the emperor is required to bathe, change clothes and reside in the fasting hall for up to five days (20, 21, 23). Even in the case of minor sacrifices that are performed by officials, the emperor has to cleanse himself and fast for a day before sending the official (23). The household sacrifices can be performed by eunuchs (24).

Since the empire was viewed as an extended system of spiritual forces unified and brought into harmony by the ritual practices of the emperor in the capital it stands to reason that the princes should play a parallel ceremonial role at their fiefs in the provinces. Ancestral temples, altars of the soil and grains, and other temples are to be erected outside the gates of the princes' palaces (28). Within the palace complex the various domestic sacrifices are to be carried out to the gods of the household, hearth, buildings, gate, and well (29). These activities are merely scaled down versions of the ritual activity of the palace in the capital.

Religious orthodoxy was protected by measures in the codes that outlawed heterodox practices (Farmer 1990). The imperial establishment was protected by a law against setting up shrines and worshipping the dipper in the palace (*Instruction* 61). Officials were not allowed to consult soothsayers (*Code* 197) and commoners were forbidden to impinge on the emperor's exclusive right to communicate with heaven (*Code* 180). Books of prophecy were outlawed (*Code* 279) as was the possession of astronomical instruments (*Code* 184). Shamanism generally, and appeals to the Maitreya Buddha, the White Lotus Society, Manichaeism, and other cults, were explicitly prohibited (*Code* 181).

Six articles in the *Placard* deal with ceremonial and ritual matters broadly defined. To make sure that the message reaches clear down to the individual villager it is specified that old, handicapped, or blind persons led by children shall parade through the village ringing a bell and proclaiming an uplifting message six times per month. The gist of the message is to get along with others, respect authority, and work in peace (19). To instill the emperor's ideas in the hearts and minds of the people, children are ordered to study the texts of the *Grand Pronouncements* as a way of avoiding future trouble (26). In addition to ideological exhortation and public ritual the Ming founder tried to get the power of the spirits behind his blueprint for local community order. Villagers are reminded that the ghosts and spirits keep track of human behavior, and are enjoined to perform sacrifices to the appropriate spirits so as to avoid tragedy (28). A warning is given against the teaching of heterodoxy and teachers are urged to follow the doctrines of the former saints and worthies in preparing their charges for careers in official service (34). The villagers are reminded that the *Placard* is a living document telling them what the imperial court wants them to do (39). It is their duty to put it into action.

The Patriarchal Family

The primary approach to the problem of keeping order among the imperial princes was to force them into an idealized status hierarchy based upon the fundamental assumptions of traditional kinship organization, employing principles of generation, age, and sex. As the founder of the dynastic line, Zhu Yuanzhang specified in the *Instruction* sets of twenty characters to be used in the names of the offspring descending from each of his sons (43). Inheritance of titles within the imperial clan follows a principle of primogeniture for the offspring of the wife. Unlike property, which was commonly equally divided among sons in commoner families, a title has to be passed to a single individual. Absolute preference is given to the sons of the wife, the oldest of them receiving the title (57, 74). Very strong sanctions are to be employed against any attempts to raise the sons of a concubine in favor of living sons of the wife. Younger sons of the wife, sons of concubines, and daughters of all kinds are given lesser titles in a descending order that gradually degrades the status of secondary lines as the generations pass (74, 76). A certain wariness toward officials is reflected in the article concerning the selection of mates for children of the imperial clan: they shall not be accepted from high officials if offered (65). The complicated business of keeping records of the imperial relatives and policing their actions is the duty of the Imperial Clan Court (77, 79).

The possibility that a prince might be senior to the emperor in age or generation, or both, is a case in which the requirements of the family system comes into conflict with the requirements of the state. How can the son of heaven retain his full authority while acknowledging the seniority of his older relatives? Two articles deal with this question. Article 39 stipulates that regardless of age differences the prince and the emperor must conform to the proper ruler-minister relationship. By an ingenious fusion of the political and the kinship institutions the emperor's position is protected. As son of heaven the emperor is to be given the same respect as the founding ancestor; he is to have an inscribed tablet that identifies him with the "law-giving ancestor designated by heaven" (39). The prince, even if he is older than the son of heaven, has to pay reverence to the holder of the tablet. Item 40 allows for a multiple ceremony system in which princes visiting the capital will first formally make obeisances while the emperor holds the tablet and later move to another part of the palace where the emperor will make obeisance to the prince as a senior family member (40). Thus are the demands of kinship and court protocol reconciled.

A significant group of articles in the *Commandment* concern the way the state regulates the family system. The longest single article, running eighteen pages in the Chinese text, is the one that provides the official Ming definition of the grades of mourning (50). By classifying family relationships—both through descent and through marriage—under the headings of the ancient forms of mourning observance, the *Commandment* in effect provides a legal definition of the Chinese kinship system. Referring to this article, it is possible to determine how closely two people are related by finding the degree of mourning that is required of each upon the death of the other. Built into the classifications is an elaborate set of assumptions about the ideal social hierarchy.

An assertive aspect of the *Commandment's* legislation of family affairs is the support for desirable behavior and the curtailment of its opposite. An element crucial to the integrity of the male-dominated lineage system is the willingness of women who marry into a family to remain loyal to it. For this reason women who are widowed before the age of thirty but hold to their vows until after they are fifty are to be recognized with publicly posted citations and their households excused from labor service (31). Filial sons, obedient grandsons, righteous men, and chaste women are likewise to be recognized with public placards (49). In official families special emphasis is placed on the requirement to care for aged parents and grandparents even if this means leaving office (48). A grandson who gains official position thanks to his grandfather's government service is required by the regulations to observe a three-year term of mourning when the latter passes away (37). This protection privilege (*yin*) is one of the many junction points where the state system intersects with family structures (55).

A number of articles in the *Commandment* aim at regulating the family system of the population at large. Here we can see the state's power exerted in support of the preferred norms of family organization. Marriages are to be arranged by parents and grandparents and the condition under which engagements can be broken off are spelled out in some detail (23). Parents are not supposed to pledge their children in marriage before birth, but the ages at which men and women are permitted to marry are not specified (43). The seven traditional grounds for divorce and the three reasons for denying divorce define the legal limitations of the marriage bond (28).

The strongest concern running through the articles on family and marriage is for the continuity of the family unit. The problem is to provide for family survival in the face of the mortality of its members. Sons and grandsons whose parents and grandparents are still alive are not to divide their wealth and residences unless the members of the elder generation give their permission (35). A widow who has no son by the time her husband dies is, if she remains faithful to her vows, to defer to the head of her husband's clan to designate an appropriate heir to carry on the family line (25). Those who have no sons are to bring in a nephew to act as heir (24). Failing that, any relative of the same surname is acceptable so long as the generation is correct. A family without a son can also contract with an outsider to join the family so as to continue its line and care for the parents, but such a son-in-law, even if he changes his surname, may not carry on the ancestral rites (26). Only sons are forbidden to hire themselves out in this manner. Daughters inherit property only when there are no suitable heirs in the lineage and the family line is cut off (27). Normally, land and other property is to be equally divided among the sons of the wife, concubines, and slaves (22). An exception is made in the case of families with official protection in which case the eldest son or grandson of the wife is given special consideration. This is a trace of the practice of primogeniture that characterizes the inheritance pattern of the nobility and the imperial family.

Family matters also take up three articles in the *Placard*. The first of these illustrates with great clarity the official view of the centrality of family relationships in socializing the individual (33). Explicit reference is made to the *Grand Pronouncement* and its stress on the importance of mutual respect and support within the family system and the obligation of family members to play their assigned roles. The idea of family membership as a social contract between parents and children is brought out in a standard prayer text attached to the article. In that text the household members are required to ritually report their sense of obligation to the spirits of their ancestors. Respect for one's seniors, whether relatives or not, is to extend from the household to the whole neighborhood so as to build harmony and community solidarity (35). When a family is in economic need such that they have to sell their land, relatives and neighbors in the same *li* are required to participate in the process by signing their names to the bill of sale (36).

Agriculture and Resources

The imperial household, a small city unto itself, was run by eunuchs bureaucratically organized into directorates for specialized purposes, including sanitation, seals, tombs, provisions, apparel, equipage, supplies, ceremonial, horses, credentials, and cleaning (67). Others were charged with gatekeeping, or providing music or fuel (68, 69). Finally, there were a number of eunuch bureaus and storehouses to provide armor, weaving and dyeing, clothing, uniforms, gardening, wine and flour, storehouses, treasurehouses, and eunuch supplies (70). The emperor exercised control over disbursements of large amounts of valuable items, eunuchs and censors being employed to keep him informed of misappropriations (59).

Nobles and officials were expected to live on their salaries and to refrain from indulging in commercial activities. However, it is clear from the emperor's preface to the *Jigu dingzhi* (Regulations for the nobility) that many were so engaged (HMZSb, 2291-94). Violations of sumptuary law and profiteering were linked initially to the Hu Weiyong plot but it was clear that the problem still existed in 1396 when the preface was written:

> Among the civil and military officials of Our Dynasty there are those who do not follow ceremonial regulations or law and yet enjoy generous stipends. Furthermore their greed is endless. They everywhere order their sons, younger brothers, slaves, and servants to engage in commerce and snatch profits away from the common people even to the point of producing salt. They rely on their governmental power to coerce the officials. They interfere with proper order and break laws in many ways. Now I order the Hanlin to consider the Tang and Song systems and fix grave and tablet size, house dimensions, and prohibitions on commerce by families on stipends. Compile them in book form to be respected forever. Alas. Respect and obey my words and forever enjoy the prosperity of great peace. (HMZSb, 2293–94)

The concern for the economy in the *Commandment* has two primary foci. One is the regulation of the economy so as to produce revenue and the other is the control of the officials who levied the taxes. The standardization of weights and measures is an essential element for an orderly tax collection system (40). The requirement that all households register with the officials and stay in their categories is another fundamental condition for a sound tax system (21, 34). Mention is made of a sales tax on land, houses and livestock and of a tax on brewer's grains (29, 33). The most important tax is the land tax. The local magistrate is to keep a register of all land transactions and report them annually to the prefecture (41). The regulation appears to prohibit the sale of surface rights while retaining the tax obligation with the original owner. Taxpayers are explicitly prohibited from presenting the title to their land to imperial relatives or other powerful persons so as to escape the tax collector's net (36). Compassion is shown in the regulations for the aged who might hire someone to perform their labor service or be excused altogether (30) and widowers, widows, orphans, and the childless who were to be given a monthly grain allowance and an annual cotton allowance (42).

The commoners and their livelihoods are viewed by the government as resources to be managed and extracted as needed. Some commoners are required to provide specialized services. Along the main routes of travel the government maintained a network of water stations and express stations with boats and soldiers supplied by local households (63, 64). Those travelling on official business are entitled to a specified retinue and a standard issue of grain at the points where they stop (68, 70, 72). Most commoners engaged in farming, which provided the most important source of taxes. The desire to control the revenue-raising activity of officialdom is evident in a number of articles. Officials are not allowed to squeeze what they need from the people but are required to pay the going rate to merchants (38). When requisitions and deliveries are permitted they are to be managed in a uniform manner (44). Taxes are not to be levied without authorization from the Secretariat (39). Military officials are not allowed to impress into the ranks commoners who do not come from military households (66). The procurement of weapons and fabrics is to be carried out with special attention to quality control (144, 145).

Six articles in the *Placard* are devoted to economic resources and taxation. The court was anxious to promote agricultural production. Toward this end, each village is instructed to establish a drum that can be beaten in the early morning during the farming season to call the people to work (24). The elders are required to supervise the population and punish any who do not work. Every household has an obligation to plant mulberries, dates, persimmons and cotton, and to produce silk and cotton (29). These measures are required in order to provide families with economic security. Failure to produce is punishable by exile to the frontiers. Villagers are expected to work together and help each other out by pooling contributions to help meet the unusual expenses of marriages and funerals (25). The elders are to play a managerial role in planning and coordinating community efforts in water conservancy (30). The people are urged to pay their taxes and perform their corvee duties promptly (31). When officials or community leaders take bribes and subvert the tax system, the people are authorized to collectively arrest the offenders and send them to the capital for punishment. The duty to identify draftees for military service and the apprehension of draft evaders falls on the elders and the *lijia*. (37).

Graded Justice

Ming justice was very much concerned with the social status and condition of those whom it governed. The *Ancestral Instruction* provides for crimes by imperial relatives and high nobles to be judged by the heir apparent and members of the imperial clan, with recommendation forwarded to the emperor (3). Special articles provide for the investigation of crimes by the heir apparent and the imperial princes (44, 48). Both the *Commandment* (75) and the *Code* (3,4) contain the Eight Deliberations (*bayi*), categories of high ranking or outstandingly virtuous persons entitled to special consideration in the judicial process. A number of articles in the *Code* segregate crimes by civil and military officers and the parents and grandparents of persons entitled to the Eight Deliberations (4, 5, 6, 7, 8, 9).

The judicial process described in the *Commandment* gives consideration to the aged and the sick even if they had been in good health at the time a crime was committed. By the same token, a crime committed in youth is still to be judged as a crime by a youth if it is discovered and comes to trial after the criminal has come of age (136). Women are given consideration at several points. A woman guilty of a crime less serious than murder is spared jail if she can be held in the custody of close relatives. On the other hand, a woman is barred from lodging complaints in the court so long as there is a husband or son to act on her behalf (137). Buddhist and Daoist clergy who are convicted of crimes lose their special status: they are returned to the lay world to perform labor service.

Questions of jurisdiction figure prominently among the concerns in the justice articles in the *Commandment*. The status and regulations have the force of law from the moment of their proclamation, even applying retroactively to crimes committed before their enactment (134). Imperial edicts, however, might outlaw a certain action on a temporary basis, but unless they are codified as statues and regulations officials are not allowed to add them to the body of formal law (132). Care is to be taken that cases are not decided by the wrong authority. Where two jurisdictions are involved, the officials where the complaint was first lodged are to request allocation of jurisdiction from the home district of the accused person (82). Officials are expected to practice avoidance in deciding cases involving their relatives, teachers, or old antagonists (10, 140). Transient officials passing through an area on government business were not allowed to hear local cases (92). The independence of local judges (*tuiguan*) is specifically protected in the regulations (80). Likewise, the local magistrate is precluded from interfering with the censors' investigation of the staff supervisor (*shouling guan*).

The status consciousness of the Ming legal system can be seen in several provisions of the *Commandment*. Serious crimes, as classified by severity of punishment, are to be decided at higher levels of the administrative hierarchy, with the court making a determination in cases involving banishment and life exile (78). In a similar manner, crimes involving officials of the sixth rank and below can be handled by the censors at their discretion but cases involving officials of the fifth rank and above have to be referred to the throne (87). The censorate was also authorized to handle routinely the prosecution of low ranking military officers but has to memorialize about higher ranking officers.

Without becoming overly judgemental about the quality of Ming justice, it is fair to say that the regulations reveal a greater concern with sentencing—the assignment of punishment for a crime—than they do with the determination of guilt. Where more than one crime was committed, the *Commandment* specifies that the more serious offense be used as the basis for punishment (89). The Ming magistrate, in his capacity as judge, has to calculate the value of bribes and stolen goods in deciding upon the proper sentence (100, 101, 114, 127). Ill-gotten goods are either to be returned to the original owner or confiscated by the government (106, 115, 121). Out of consideration for the family system, however, ancestral tombs are not to be included among the items seized when a criminal's property is taken (120). Compassion or lenience is manifested in the many provisions which mitigated the severity of punishment. For example, if stolen property is returned to the owner before the crime was discovered the thief was to be treated like one who had made a voluntary confession. Sentences are to be reduced by lowering the degree of the punishment specified for the crime committed (108). Amnesties are important in mitigating the severity of punishments (123, 124). Good behavior, and in some cases participation in the capture of armed criminals, can hasten the restoration to the community of convicts whose sentences are up and facilitate the removal of tattoos marking them as outcasts (93). There are limits to the amnesties, however. Those who make false accusations which cause others to die can not be pardoned (133). Life exiles sent to live in distant places are not allowed to return (109). In the Ming, as today, China had a well developed system of banishment that consigned southerners to the north and northerners to the south to toil in iron smelters or salt farms, or to open new land as farmers (141, 142, 143). Humane administration of jails and prisons was the chief concern of two articles in the *Commandment* (81, 135).

Crimes by officials are treated somewhat differently than crimes by ordinary persons. An immunity is granted for those who report mistakes in government business (16). Officials enjoy a limited immunity from prosecution while in mourning (13). When they are charged with a crime, depending upon its seriousness, they can remain in office, take a demotion, or be reassigned to the frontiers (12, 96). A magistrate can redeem the punishment of a minor crime by paying copper cash (105). Former officials are not to be exempted from prosecution, nor are the servants and retainers of imperial relatives, nobles, or high officials (112, 131). Military officials are to be treated more leniently than civil officials (125, 126).

Consideration for the family system is shown in a number of items in the penal law. Leniency is shown to those who out of loyalty try to shield their masters or close relatives when the latter were guilty of crimes (10). The shielding of more distant relatives still within the mourning grades yields a reduction of sentence. This consideration is not applicable for the most antisocial acts: rebellion or assaulting a superior. When a family loses a member to murder the perpetrators of the crime are expected to pay for funeral expenses incurred by the survivors (111). When crimes are committed by family members acting as a group, the senior members of the group can be held responsible (119). In more serious crimes, however, all are to be punished without regard to family status (98). Crimes that threatened the family are singled out for strict treatment. The killing of sons and grandsons, for example, is given an article (122). Infidelity by a wife is another example (91). Women, who are normally allowed to keep on their undergarments during beatings and who are to be spared tattooing when exiled, are to be stripped and beaten for infidelity. I presume that the special attention to infidelity is related to the potential threat it posed to the continuity of the male line.

The *Placard of People's Instructions* addresses the problem of law enforcement at the local level. Already in the second article, punishment of *lijia* elders is mentioned, introducing the question of control over the elders. Elders who commit crimes and cause trouble can be arrested by other elders and sent to the capital (8). Elders who use the power of their positions to intimidate others and escape their corvee obligations are to be exiled to the frontiers with their families (9). The initial jurisdiction over elders charged with a crime lies with the other elders who are to meet and make a judgement, forwarding reports of serious transgressions to the capital (7). Officials are not allowed to arrest and interrogate elders on their own initiative (6, 7). These measures are intended to protect the elders and their villages from the undue intrusion by county level officials. At the same time there is a provision to protect individuals who can settle disputes on their own from the meddling intrusion by grasping elders (14). On the other hand, those who harbor grudges against elders and so make false indictments against them are to be severely punished (20).

The provisions for keeping the peace in the local community are rather simple. The *lijia* elders are responsible for arresting wrongdoers among the common people (15). When elders encounter conflicts of interest in judging matters involving their close relatives, they are to convene a group of elders and *lijia* from adjacent *li* for collective counsel (5). When great force is needed to arrest a criminal the elders are to mobilize the people to help out. The elders are also charged with exhorting the people to do good; the people, for their part, are to keep an eye on one another (16). The elders are to warn the people against harboring deserters from military or corvee service; such persons, when captured, are to be caged and turned over to the authorities (21). Although charged with arresting criminals, the community elders are not allowed to operate a jail (13). When troublemakers fail to reform after punishment the elders have the option of sending them to the capital (18). This link to the capital brings them into potential conflict with local officials who might try to obstruct the process. In the case of such obstruction, elders are allowed either to go in person to the capital to report to the emperor directly or to memorialize the throne about the officials involved (7, 18). To put some imperial authority behind these provisions the provincial surveillance offices are charged with seeing that provincial and local officials encourage popular knowledge of and adherence to the *Placard.*

In Zhu Yuanzhang's vision the Ming was a smaller empire than the Yuan had been. It was conceived as a homogeneous realm populated by Han Chinese who were to reclaim their historical identity by returning to the cultural practices of former ages. It was a hierarchical order intended to be immune from change. It was a state of grace made possible by heaven's mandate and the correct guidance of a sage legislator.

CHAPTER SEVEN

MING AUTOCRACY

The founding of the Ming dynasty was important in two ways that are interconnected. As a revival following a period of Mongol rule, the Ming construction of a Han identity made up of elements from the long historical memory reinforced central features of the Chinese cultural tradition. So successful was the Ming codification of official and orthodox standards for government, social life, and learning that many of its regulations and practices were carried over into the Qing dynasty by Manchu conquerors who became custodians of cultural arrangements they could neither ignore nor substantially modify. In this sense the Ming gave modern China an indelible identity that persisted into the twentieth century and elements of which to this day continue to assert themselves as contributions to contemporary Chinese nationalism. The second and related significance of the Ming founding was the enhanced concentration of power in the imperial institution: Ming autocracy. That political development was also an extension or further evolution of trends with a long historical past. The increased power of the throne was exercised in the creation of the Ming legislative program even as it was further enhanced by that legislation. The despotic, or authoritarian or absolutistic, aspects in early Ming government were tendencies continued and built upon in the Qing dynasty and even, much later, in the dictatorship of the People's Republic.

The Construction of Order

When I began this study more than a decade ago I thought that the creation of the Ming order could be understood from the perspective of social control as a rational process in which Zhu Yuanzhang devised institutional arrangements to maximize his power and ensure the survival of his dynasty. Certainly, his actions and the cohesive body of legislation he promulgated make sense from such a perspective. I have endeavored to show that Zhu's program for organizing Chinese society evolved over many years, often in response to specific events. Yet there is more to the story than just an account of a power hungry pragmatist. Beyond the superficial rationality and consistency of Zhu's program there persist questions of intent, of interest, of symbolic meaning, and of historical significance.

The question of intent is one of the central problems of intellectual history. How do we know what Zhu Yuanzhang thought and what his intentions were? In the earlier chapters I have generally treated statements attributed to the Ming founder as accurate representations of what he believed. In fact I have no sure basis for knowing what he believed. In the case of a Chinese emperor, as in the case of an American president today, public statements were often drafted by others and subsequently modified or edited. In some cases the authorship of particular imperial statements is known, while in other cases we are left to assume that what are presented in the record as the emperor's words are in fact the work of others. Rather than try to determine in each case whether a text was drafted by Song Lian or Liu Ji I have treated the whole corpus of pronouncements and legislation as the products of Zhu Yuanzhang's reign in the same way that White House statements today might be taken as representations of a president's administration if not of his person. All that was written or decreed in Zhu Yuanzhang's name is taken as a representation of his interest if not an expression of his psyche. It is a clear and fairly consistent official or public account of what the emperor wanted people to think he believed. Details of authorship are matters for another inquiry.

A second question that may be directed at Zhu Yuanzhang's tenure on the throne is the question of what interests he represented. Some would take it as axiomatic that any ruling authority must represent the interests of a particular social class. Perry Anderson sees the absolutist state of modern Europe as a carapace fronting for the waning feudal elements in a monarchical order threatened by the rising bourgeoisie (Anderson 1974, 18). Whose interests did Zhu Yuanzhang represent? Since he rose from the peasantry, that class is one possibility. Certainly there are many references to the suffering of the common people in Zhu's rhetoric, but he was no revolutionary in the sense that he gave them power. What he did do was reimpose controls over them and endeavor to create conditions which would allow them to live peacefully and productively so that they could pay taxes. That he used them as a check against abuse by minor officials in no way implies that he empowered them.

The nobility were the stratum closest to the emperor in social standing, but they cannot be considered a true class. They were artificially created from among the commoners who supported the Ming house in its rise. The titles and forms to which the Ming nobility were required to conform were rich with artifacts from earlier eras such as the Tang , ?? when great families had been influential forces in court politics. In the early Ming, noble families were assigned military roles but were carefully segregated from the garrison forces as a check against Caesarism. Their ranks were thinned by purges already during the first reign period. They never represented a danger to the Ming house.

Officials were more of a force in Ming politics, since they were the ones who carried on the work of government. But the officials were not a class. They were recruited individually into imperial service and so were the servitors of the emperor, not a hereditary interest group. Zhu Yuanzhang was ever alert to the influence they could exert and the damage they could do in the course of their duties. He viewed them as instruments, tools for his own purposes. He constantly reminded them of their dependent status and their duty to recompense the generosity of the people who supported them and the ruler who appointed them. Ceremonial and punishments were used to regulate their standing in relation to the emperor, each other, and the common people.

Scholars were even less privileged in Zhu Yuanzhang's scheme than were officials. He appears to have been hostile to scholars generally. Education was promoted at the local level and carefully supervised at higher levels. Imperial editing of the classics exerted a political control over the scholars' area of special expertise. Sending students out in investigating teams and requiring them to memorize the emperor's pronouncements were other forms of politicization of the educational realm. Buddhist and Daoist clergy fared little better. Their numbers were carefully restricted and they were required to conform to at least some of the demands of the kinship system.

Merchants and craftsmen scarcely appear in the codes, nor is there any mention of a landlord "gentry" that was to become so influential in later times. The existence of a wealthy land-owning class might be inferred from the transfers to Nanjing of old supporters of Zhang Shicheng from the Suzhou-Hangzhou region.

The two consumer groups that developed within the Ming structure and enjoyed the greatest share of imperial revenues are the imperial relatives and the eunuchs. The titles and stipends of the former and their offspring are explicitly provided for in the *Ancestral Instruction*, while the growth of the latter group was explicitly forbidden by the founder. The imperial relatives grew through reproduction, the eunuchs found their chance for imperial patronage in the Yongle period when the usurper-emperor needed supporters who would not question his legitimacy. The point to be made about these two "interest groups" is that they were both extensions of the imperial household, not social classes.

The question of symbolic meaning is the question of how the social order Zhu Yuanzhang outlined in his legislative program sought to reproduce age-old cultural forms. Even though as a dynastic founder Zhu wielded enormous power and enjoyed considerable latitude in decision making, he was not free to act in a completely arbitrary way. He was both constrained and guided by the logic and structure of the culture and society in which he lived. He was enmeshed in what Sangren calls the dialectical connection between "collective representations" and "social and cultural reproduction"

(Sangren 1987b, 2). Zhu Yuanzhang can be viewed as an actor in such a process, influenced by received cultural values even as he tried to shape social practice and define cultural identity. Sangren's point is that culture is not just a reflection of society; it is also an agent in shaping society:

> the very institutions that reproduce culture are themselves, at least in part, culturally constituted. Culture and society are aspects of a program that continuously rewrites itself in transmission from one generation to the next and in transformation from one institutional context to another (Sangren 1987b, 6).

We should be alert to the reciprocity and circularity of cultural values, legislated ideals, and social practice. Influence could run in either direction. Seen from this angle Zhu Yuanzhang the legislator was not immune to influence from his social and cultural environment. One remarkable aspect of the Ming order is the extent to which its authoritarian features echoed the hierarchical structure of order as conceived of in the traditional religious system.

Imperial sovereignty was the engine of domination over a population disposed to submission. Domination and submission were celebrated in the received "political culture" both at the elite level of Confucian classical studies and at the popular level of worship for folk heroes and gods and spirits. The poles of the relationship between the ruler and ruled were clearly symbolized by its fictional representation as a bond between parent and child. Acceptance of this authoritarian model as a true picture of the ideal relationship between the emperor and his subjects precluded any but the most submissive role for the subject. A parent is not just more powerful than a child; a parent is older, wiser, and above all due respect because parents alone give life and provide sustenance. At the top this model was a prescription for incontestable authority and at the bottom it was an invitation to popular adulation and cringing deference.

Granted that the Ming founder and his advisors set out consciously to impose order on Chinese society, to what extent were they constrained by tradition? The massive continuity of institutions and of language, most starkly illustrated by the continuity of provisions from the *Tang Code* to the *Ming Code*, provide evidence for those who would minimize change. Indeed, Ch'ü T'ung-tsu takes the view in his monumental survey of Chinese legal history that there was no fundamental change in the structure or character of Chinese society from the Han to the Qing and consequently no significant change in the legal institutions (1961, 10). Without contesting the very substantial continuity of both intention and detail that Ch'ü exhaustively demonstrates existed in the codes of various dynasties, it is still possible to argue against minimizing the changes that took place during the two millennia of imperial rule. Rather, it can be argued that continuity of terminology often tends to mask important changes that took place in the course of China's imperial history.

The Chinese penchant for portraying the world in historical terms and for analyzing contemporary events in terms of a vocabulary of precedents from the past simply confuses the situation. Historical consciousness was one of the stronger continuities in Chinese culture. Because the standards of truth and value were located in remote antiquity consistency with ancient practice was a test of veracity and worth. In his brief introduction to Ch'ü T'ung-tsu's study *Law and Society in Traditional China*, A.F.P. Hulsewé notes the mentality of Chinese thinkers who took continuity for granted:

> It should not, however, be forgotten that during all these centuries Chinese authors, notwithstanding their great historical sense, consciously or unconsciously assumed that Chinese society was static. This explains the enormous force of historical precedent. What had been applicable once, they felt, might be applied again (Ch'ü 1961, 2).

Bearing in mind the complication created by the fact of a Chinese penchant for archaic terminology and classical precedents, it is worthwhile to consider the kinds and degrees of change that took place in the imperial period. It is not necessary, nor would it be prudent, to argue that Chinese society underwent drastic transformation. Yet, the more moderate concept of "change within tradition" is also problematic because of the way it privileges tradition. One of the premises of this study is precisely that tradition itself was one of the things that was being contested, and that it was being changed, produced and reproduced, consciously. Continuity with the Han or the Tang or the Song was not something that came about spontaneously. What may appear in the long run as continuity often at the time involved choice, change, and no small degree of coercion.

By the late fourteenth century, Chinese society and culture had been substantially impacted by the centuries of northern domination in the Liao, Jin, and Yuan eras. Traces of this change are to be found in the Ming founder's legislation against Mongol practices and his effort to restore Tang forms of marriage, dress, and the like. Tradition in this case was not continuity but radical discontinuity, the Ming government used its power to stamp out foreign influence and to resurrect practices long abandoned.

Ming sponsorship of Zhu Xi's brand of Neo-Confucianism marked something of a cultural watershed. The Confucianization of Chinese law began in the ancient period, as Ch'ü T'ung-tsu (1961, 267–79) amply documents, but from the Song dynasty on the content and emphasis of Confucian teaching was substantially changed. Zhu Xi's clustering of the *Four Books* as the core of a newly interpreted canon was in itself a radical departure from the received tradition. Zhu Xi reached back more than a millennium to ground his new views in the ancient authority of Mencius. Zhu

Yuanzhang recognized Mencius but ordered an expurgated version prepared that left out passages sanctioning popular overthrow of tyrannical rulers. The Ming founder's claims of ideological authority had a decided impact on the Confucian school and darkened an already indelible autocratic imprint on political thought.

Institutional changes, such as the elimination of the prime minister in the early Ming, significantly altered the character of the imperial state. Here too the enhanced powers of the ruler affected both the legislative and administrative sides of government. The subordination of the civil service to direct imperial oversight not only led to occasional abuses such as the rise of eunuch dictators, it also removed the stabilizing influence of a semi-autonomous prime minister to counter the vagaries of hereditary rule. Political power was personalized to a greater degree than had been the case in the past. In the Ming only Zhu Yuanzhang and his son Zhu Di took full advantage of their personal power. Their reigns came closest to embodying a fully developed despotism. Later emperors were generally less forceful. Authority was wielded on their behalf by others, not by the emperors personally.

With Zhu Yuanzhang we encounter a kind of imperial populism that fostered a direct connection between the ruler and the mass of common people. This is most obvious in the many efforts of the Ming founder to communicate directly with the people. His *Placard of People's Instructions*, the creation of community schools, the promotion of his ideas through the *Grand Pronouncement*, and the sanction for village leaders to bring offending officials to the capital are all parts of an alliance between the ruler and the people. The intention of the alliance, made clear in various statements about officials, was to keep the bureaucracy in check by having the people keep an eye on them. The gods were also enlisted in the same cause (Taylor 1977, 40–41). No doubt this aspect of early Ming rule was in large part a product of the personality and social background of a man who rose from the peasantry. His was not a pattern of rule other emperors could easily repeat. The precedent, however, was taken up by Mao Zedong nearly six centuries later.

Coerced Community

In a passage quoted in chapter 1, Kamenka and Tay characterize the punitive law imposed on traditional China as a form of "external intervention" by which the imperial state tried to restore the *Gemeinschaft* in a process of "domination and submission" (Kamenka and Tay 1980, 23). The notion of external intervention aptly captures the essence of what Zhu Yuanzhang and his advisors thought they were doing when they composed and issued the codes translated in the appendices. They were wielding governmental power to control their social environment by shaping formal institutions and customary practices. I take it that this is what Bruce Lincoln means when he says that "certain specific modes of discourse" have been used "for the construction, deconstruction, and reconstruction of society itself." He hastens to make the connection between discourse and force: "Together, discourse and force are the chief means whereby social borders, hierarchies, institutional formations, and habituated patterns of behavior are both maintained and modified" (Lincoln 1989, 3).

In the course of his lifelong effort to conquer the chaos and immorality that plagued Chinese society, Zhu Yuanzhang employed a diverse arsenal of weapons. These reflected both his own understanding of life and the resources available to the government he headed. It goes without saying that none of the strategies and devices Zhu used to shape Chinese social practice was unique to Chinese government or even new with the Ming. What is striking about Zhu Yuanzhang's application of social control measures is the systematic and energetic manner in which they were applied.

The primary instrument of Zhu Yuanzhang's program of social control was the classification of the population. In any social system the power to circumscribe the individual's choices through classification is a fundamental sanction. Once a person's category is defined, he or she can be held to standards deemed appropriate for that category. In China this fundamental principle takes the form of the doctrine of rectification of names developed in the early Confucian classics. In its classical formulation the concept is applied to both political and kinship roles, neatly uniting state and family under a single patriarchal model of authority: a minister naturally owes loyalty to his ruler just as a son naturally owes filial respect to his father.

The power of the classification scheme for social control purposes rests on the assumption of the "natural" character of the behaviors which attach to certain roles. At the family level parental dominance is grounded in biology, at least until the child matures. After the child grows up sanctions of convention and law are required to maintain generational dominance. The same is true of age differences among siblings or unrelated persons. Considerable attention is given to these matters in the codes. The domination of males over females likewise requires conventional reinforcement where biological difference is insufficient to assure role differentiation. In general, male supremacy is so thoroughly entrenched in late-fourteenth-century Chinese society that the authors of the codes scarcely ever find it necessary to stipulate sexual differences. For the most part the codes describe positions, offices, and professions that are assumed to be occupied by males alone. Special rules are introduced for females in three kinds of situations: where males are unavailable for lineage functions, where judicial and penal rules designed for men have to be modified for women, and where women enjoy high social status as relatives of elite males. In no case does the subordination of females appear to be a problematic or contested question.

The same thing cannot be said of the political order and the social order. In the political sphere there is no "natural" or biological order to rely upon, hence the fabrication of a structure of fictive kinship. The emperor is father and mother to the people; the people are likened to children. The dominance of the ruler, the nobility, and the officials over other segments of the society requires considerable rationalization and the reinforcement of many sanctions, both normative and coercive. The commoners are especially circumscribed by occupational classifications that dictate both the kinds of service and tax obligations they owe the state, i.e., define their social functions, and restrict their participation in the political process to the lowest forms of local governance. The division of the commoners into four occupational specializations is an ancient formula. It is one area where the Ming founder indulges in modest innovation by adding Buddhist and Daoist clergy to the traditional four classes of scholar, farmer, craftsman, and merchant. It is ironic that Zhu Yuanzhang, who himself rose from the peasantry to the throne, should so strongly forbid others to change their classifications.

One cannot read the Ming codes without being impressed by the overwhelming importance of hierarchy in all matters of social life. Again, in both the familial and political spheres the authors of the codes are obsessed with status markers in every aspect of life. In the kinship system the mourning grades, a schematic device of hoary antiquity, fixes each individual in relationship to each other individual in an ingenious structure that anticipates every conceivable social relationship. The funereal function of the system links it to the most solemn and public of social events in a society where death and afterlife receive considerable attention. The insertion of the system into the penal law places the coercive power of the state behind what otherwise would be an obscure artifact of an ancient feudal system.

In the political sphere the concentration on forms of address, of dress, and life-style pervades the codes. From the special forms reserved for the emperor down through the gradations of imperial relatives, nobles, officials, and local leaders, the rules and regulations detailed in the codes constitute a vast system of status markers. The system is designed to fix every individual it governs into an unambiguous position relative to all possible classes of persons. Those governed are the emperor, who is set above every one else, the princes and nobles, who are distinguished from the officials, and the officials who are marked off from the commoners. Among the commoners devices such as the village wine drinking ceremony clarify the subordination of younger to older and higher to lower.

The early Ming legislative program includes elements other than penal law. Next to the classification of the population, ceremonial devices are probably the most important instruments of social control. As we have seen, the Ming founder himself linked law and ceremony as the complementary components of government, the first principles state. A broad range of activities can be lumped together under the heading of ceremony and ritual. It is probably best to leave the boundaries open and consider the variety of activities. In the main these are activities that fall under the purview of the Ministry of Rites, but there are doubtless other agencies involved as well.

Like codified law and sumptuary regulations, ceremony reinforces social hierarchy but also goes beyond rewards and punishments to shape social life in space and time. Ceremonies and rituals, formalized activities assigned extraordinary symbolic meaning, have important spacial and temporal dimensions. Religious rituals often took place in special venues—altars, halls, and walled compounds carefully sited on the points of the compass. Religious rituals and formal ceremonies in Ming China always emphasize these spacial aspects. Mention of music is frequently found in statements about ceremony but I do not know enough about it to say how it was employed. My speculation is that music may have added a temporal dimension to ceremonial activities by punctuating them into segments. The temporal character of ceremonial activities is more obviously seen in the use of the calendar to specify appropriate dates for both religious and secular events. The official Ming calendar issued by the government advised users when it was and was not auspicious to undertake various activities.

The spacial and temporal aspects of ceremonial activities are often linked to the status hierarchy. The most important ceremonies and ritual acts are reserved for the emperor, while less important tasks are assigned to subordinates. Within the imperial family the rotation of visits to the imperial capital by the princes is sequenced according to seniority.

Coercion, the use of violence against individuals or groups, is one of the most fundamental modes of achieving compliance. The legitimate exercise of violence to compel obedience to law is often seen to be a defining attribute of the state as an institution (Frank 1986, 283). In the early Ming case the application of punishments (*xing*) is one of the most widespread and routine of government activities. The fullest and most systematic statements of when and how punishments are to be applied to the Ming population are those found in the *Commandment* and the *Code*. The *Commandment* expresses desired outcomes in both positive and negative terms, stating in some cases what ought to be done and in others what ought not to be done. The *Code* is primarily concerned with specifying how and under what circumstances punishments are to be applied.

The term "punishment" (*xing*), customarily used to designate the general area of law enforcement in imperial China, differs in emphasis and implication from the contemporary American concept of "justice." While the Ming codes are not unconcerned with such matters as security of the state, the protection of property, or the physical safety of persons, the emphasis lies elsewhere. Rights are less important than obligations and the maintenance of social order. Zhu Xi's *Family Ritual* and the ancient prescriptions of mourning rites are used to specify how the social order ought to be reproduced. Carefully graded punishments are specified to discourage departures from the specified norms.

It should also be noted that "rewards" play a minor role within the structure of punishments. Persons of exemplary virtue, such as widows who remain faithful to their marriage vows, are to be honored with notices of imperial recognition, publicly displayed in their neighborhoods or villages. Honorary arches (*pailou*) commemorating virtuous individuals, among the dominating features of the architectural landscape, are tangible manifestations of social control. At times officials were to distribute bolts of cloth or other valuable items to commoners whose behavior had been exemplary or to give monetary rewards for the reporting of a crime. But for the most part, rewards were of greater symbolic than financial value.

Suasion is another important component of the Ming founder's social control program. While the emphasis on a didactic style of rule may simply reflect long established practices, it appears that Zhu Yuanzhang placed special emphasis on moral exhortation. This may derive from his sense of mission as heaven's agent of world salvation or it may be attributed to his assertive personality. Whatever the cause, Zhu was energetic and resourceful in communicating his views on social order to the Chinese populace.

The many oral statements made to court officials, recorded in the *Veritable Record*, give us a picture of a forceful and articulate advocate for correct thinking and proper conduct. Innumerable edicts, orders, commands and pronouncements relayed his ideas to a wider audience. The many normative texts he ordered compiled evidence his faith in the power of the word to influence behavior. The use made of the *Grand Pronouncement* both as a legal code and as a curricular element in formal education is the outstanding example of how far the Ming founder went to communicate his word.

Stress on the role of education is a distinctive feature of Chinese elite culture. Although he came from a modest background, the Ming founder did not question the importance of education nor its primarily normative character. He fully subscribed to the Neo-Confucian view, enshrined in the *Great Learning*, that good government derives ultimately from the self-cultivation of the ruler (MSLHW, 3035). For the ruler, education starts at home. Exemplary of his commitment to his own education is his penchant for having important texts posted on the walls of the palace where he could study them at any time.

Social control through education was to be accomplished by institutional arrangements and the preparation of teaching materials. Schools were established at the higher levels of government and, briefly at least, at the local village level. The examination system was revived, abandoned, and then revived again. At each level of education great attention was given to the preparation of texts with appropriate didactic content. In some cases this entailed the collection and publication of the classics and their commentaries. In other cases, such as the edification of princes or officials, compilations of relevant historical precedents were specially tailored to the group the ruler wished to enlighten. For the civil service examinations and the lower level schools, great use was made of the *Grand Pronouncement* and the *Code*, normative texts to be committed to memory.

The Ming founder believed in a natural and proper order and that heaven had chosen him to impose (or restore) that order on the traumatized and chaotic world in which he came to power. The opportunity history presented to him to rewrite the rules, in essence to construct a new (or reconstruct an old) China, was a rare event. It must, however, be qualified in two respects. The power to impose or legislate a new order was transitory. Succeeding emperors were not free to rewrite the constitution, reorganize the government, or make more than modest changes in the laws. And the order that Zhu Yuanzhang created existed first and foremost on paper. It was a plan, a set of demands, a statement of the ideal; we should not suppose that Zhu's laws governed everything that happened. They did not and could not. But to say this is not to dismiss them as unimportant. Laws, rules, regulations and ideals are all important components of social reality. Exactly how they affect beliefs, perceptions, motives and actions are matters worthy of investigation even if they are beyond the scope of this study.

Implications

Zhu Yuanzhang attempted, through his program of social legislation, to extend imperial influence throughout Chinese society. He wanted to create a hierarchy of state and patriarchal authority integrated at every level. Stable as the Ming system was, it was not perfect, nor did it bring an end to history by creating a changeless China. The implications of Zhu's construction of the Ming autocracy can be viewed from three perspectives: institutional stability, social change, and cultural values.

Some of the institutional deficiencies of Zhu's constitution were apparent already during his reign. The integration of imperial power with the patrilinear family system is a case in point. The clear stipulation in the *Ancestral Instruction* of the rules governing succession were intended to free Ming China from the debilitating power struggles that had plagued the Yuan court. In this regard, the *Instruction* failed its first test. The death of the founder's eldest son and designated heir resulted in the elevation of the senior grandson in the imperial line as successor to the throne. After the founder's demise in 1398, the young Jianwen emperor was overthrown in less than four years by his uncle, the senior surviving prince of his father's generation. While the Yongle Emperor's usurpation led to a jog in the line of dynastic descent it did not lead to an abandonment of the *Ancestral Instruction* or a weakening of the Zhu clan's hold on the throne. History was rewritten to paper over this initial transgression of the rules: the usurper claimed to be the son of the founder's empress and the legitimacy of Jianwen's rule was denied. Lies told about the usurpation had the effect of enhancing the authority of the *Instruction*, the script upon which the lies were premised.

Throughout the Ming there were no serious efforts by outsiders to claim the throne and none of the few revolts by princes constituted a threat to the ruling line. Following his capture by the Mongols in 1449, Yingzong was set aside in favor of his brother Daizong until a palace coup in 1456 restored him to the throne for the remainder of his natural life. This, the second transfer of rule by force, only served to confirm the importance of clan law: it restored a former emperor with a stronger claim to the throne than the incumbent who was deposed. A coup on behalf of a more junior claimant remained unthinkable throughout the dynasty.

The second disjunction in the agnatic line of descent was that caused when Wuzong died without heir in 1521. Shizong, the chosen successor, was not a brother of his predecessor but a cousin, offspring of a prince who was the younger brother of Wuzong's father. This deviation in the descent line was turned into an enormous political crisis when Shizong resisted the advice that he become the adopted son of the dead Wuzong to maintain the fiction of continuing Wuzong's line. Instead, the willful Shizong insisted on retroactively elevating his natural parents to the level of emperor and empress and so to formalize an altered line of descent from them (Fisher 1990). The court was thrown into a turmoil by the dispute, which came to be known as the Great Ritual Controversy (*da liyi*). Once again history had to be rewritten. One beneficiary, besides Shizong's parents, was the usurper Yongle, whose temple name was changed from Taizong (Great Ancestor) to Chengzu (Accomplishing Progenitor). At stake in this affair was the interest of the Zhu clan as dynasty (the fiction of an unbroken line of descent) and the Zhu clan as family (the emperor's obligation to his parents). The *Ancestral Instruction* provided ammunition for both sides in the debate and could not, by itself, resolve the issue. In the end the emperor got his way. Despotic power allowed him to reject one set of ritual obligations in favor of another. He exercised it not on behalf of the *li* of dynastic principle but the imperative of filial piety, the subjective force of human feelings (*qing*).

Elimination of the position of prime minister presented a second set of challenges to institutional stability. The massive task of providing direction to the central government required that emperors seek help in doing the work that prime ministers previously had done. For the most part this help was provided by grand secretaries, agents of the emperor who worked within the palace in the "inner court." In time their rank and status rose and they took on concurrent offices as heads of ministries in the "outer court." By building alliances, a number of grand secretaries were able to exercise prime ministerial power without achieving constitutional legitimacy. It is interesting to note that one of the most effective of all Ming grand secretaries, Zhang Juzheng, was constrained by the fact that his power was not institutionalized. When the death of his father required that Zhang leave office for a twenty-seven month mourning period, he had sufficient influence over the youthful Wanli emperor to secure an imperial order exempting him from the requirement (Atwell 1988, 526–28). In this case imperial authority was used to overrule the dictates of the patriarchal family system. This violation of filial obligations fueled criticisms which had to be suppressed by force (DMB, 58–59).

The other group who filled the vacuum of power created by elimination of the prime minister were eunuchs, some of whom were able to dominate the government. Eunuch power was necessarily informal and for the most part illegitimate in an institutional sense. Zhu Yuanzhang had anticipated the danger of eunuchs meddling in official business and caused an iron plaque to be erected directing that eunuchs stay out of government affairs on pain of death. Eight years later the founder himself set a precedent by sending a eunuch on a mission (MHY, 699). In subsequent reigns eunuchs were entrusted with many substantial assignments. As castrated servants of the imperial house, eunuchs could pose no threat to the dynasty. Their power was derived entirely from the emperor whom they in name served but whom in fact they sometimes controlled or manipulated. The greatest perversion of Ming despotic power occurred in the 1620s when the eunuch Wei Zhongxian was granted a noble title (exalted duke, *shanggong*), had temples erected in his honor, and became the object of sycophantic praise by officials (ECCP, 846–47; Atwell 1988, 608–10). Wei's abuses went well beyond corruption and the misuse of police powers. Taking noble titles for himself and his relatives and becoming the object of religious veneration seriously threatened the principles of social hierarchy enshrined in the dynastic constitution. As long as he controlled the emperor Wei could break the rules, but once the emperor died he was obliged to commit suicide.

Zhu Yuanzhang's edifice of social legislation did not prevent economic change from occurring but it may have played a role in inhibiting the degree of social transformation that accompanied developments in the sixteenth and seventeenth centuries. Late Ming China was most unlike early Ming China. Its center of gravity was in the commercialized urban centers of the lower Yangtze, not in the remote imperial capital at Beijing. As the Eurasian and African trading networks fused into a truly global trading system, maritime transport eclipsed the animal caravans of inner Asia. Coastal cities thrived, silver flowed into China from the Americas, and European merchants and missionaries arrived in growing numbers. Despite the appearance of "sprouts of capitalism," late Ming China underwent no fundamental social transformation or transition to a new stage of historical development. The wealthy merchants whose life style is portrayed in the popular novels of the late Ming were not members of an Asian bourgeoisie. The Chinese social system allowed them limited options. They could educate their children to compete in the examination system but that road led only to a prestigious life of servitude in the imperial bureaucracy. Money could be used to bribe officials, or even to purchase decrees, but it could not purchase rights. No matter how influential a merchant might become he could not legally gain autonomy or exercise governmental authority. The constitution made no provision for it.

If social change did not lead to political transformation, neither did cultural change. So jealous was the imperial government of its authority in ideological and cultural matters that a transformation as profound as the European Renaissance and Reformation is hard to imagine. Again, there was great dynamism in late Ming religion in the form of syncretic interaction between traditions and the emergence or ascension of new deities in the pantheon of popular religion. In the realm of Confucian philosophy Wang Yangming's contributions led to what de Bary has termed a "near revolution in thought" (1970a, 23). And yet those institutions which might have provided the public space for new ideas to mature inevitably attracted official interference. Religious sects were persecuted, academies were shut down, and independent thinkers were stifled.

Zhu Yuanzhang understood politics as a tug-of-war between the ruler and groups of all kinds. He consciously undertook to put each and every element in society into a state of subordination from which they could not escape. When he designed the rules of Ming autocracy he did so with the express purpose of outlawing what we today might herald as civil liberties or civil society. This was his achievement and it is his legacy.

APPENDIX 1

THE AUGUST MING ANCESTRAL INSTRUCTION[1]
(*HUANG MING ZU XUN*)[2]

CONTENTS[3]

---

[1] This is a direct translation of the Chinese title based on the assumption that *huang* means great as opposed to imperial. Teng Ssu-yu (Yen 1968, x) renders it *Family Instruction of the Imperial Ming*. For convenience I shall refer to it as *Instruction*.

[2] The text of the Instruction may be found in MCKGWX (1966, 3:1585-1671). It is followed (3:1673-1768) by the *Zu xun lu*, an earlier version of the same document. A convenient copy with slightly smaller print is that which occurs in HMZS (Tokyo edition, 1969, 2:1-21). A less legible version appears in *Huang Ming jingshi shiyongbian* ([1604] 1967, 1:69-146).

[3] I have numbered the contents for convenience in referring to the text.

22. Stars, wind, etc.
23. Lesser sacrifices
24. Household sacrifices

IV. PRECAUTION ON COMING AND GOING

25. Divination before action

V. PRUDENCE IN AFFAIRS OF STATE

26. Getting all the facts
27. False recommendations

VI. CEREMONY

28. Altars for princes
29. Sacrifices by princes
30. New Year's audience
31. Emperor's birthday
32. Emperor's birthday
33. Edict arriving at prince's fief
34. Officials owe obeisance to prince
35. Procedure for prince's court
36. Imperial clan kinship terms
37. Princes visiting the court
38. Frontier princes
39. Subordination of princes to emperor
40. Obeisance of princes to emperor, etc.
41. Age limits on relatives paying court
42. Princes banned from state banquets
43. Names to be used by princely lines

VII. LAW

44. Transgressions by princes
45. Summoning of princes to court
46. Officials serving princes
47. Popular respect for princes
48. Punishment for princes
49. Accusations against princes
50. Princely residences in capital
51. Princes punishing subordinates
52. Princes communicating with emperor
53. Officials lobbying for princes
54. Commoners accusing princes
55. Princes disciplining court agents
56. When a new emperor takes the throne
57. Succession to the throne
58. Control of military in fiefs

VIII. PALACE REGULATION

59. Control of supplies
60. Ban on communication outside

61. Ban on shrines in the palace
62. Limits on authority of empress
63. Ban on outside physicians
64. Palace ladies' contact with the court
65. Mates for imperial offspring

IX. EUNUCHS

66. Eunuch offices
67. Titles and ranks

X. RULES OF OFFICE

68. Enfeoffments
69. Inheritance of fiefs
70. Marriage of prince
71. Employment of princes' offspring
72. Titles of descendants
73. Imperial clan court
74. Court control of fief officials
75. Prince selects military subordinates
76. Court may claim princes' retainers
77. Offices in princely establishment
78. Guard organization

XI. MILITARY GUARDS

79. Organization, numbers
80. Heir commands when prince gone
81. Retinue when prince goes to court
82. Movement of troops
83. Control of garrison, escort guard
84. Contact between princes and garrison
85. Hunting maneuvers
86. Travel, messenger tallies
87. Training of troops
88. Military equipment

XII. CONSTRUCTION

89. Sites for princes' palaces
90. Restrictions on size

XIII. PROVISIONS

91. Supplies when paying court
92. Stipend payment
93. Do not request additional payments
94. Stipend rates
95. Grants for daughters, etc.
96. Declining succession in secondary offspring

THE AUGUST MING ANCESTRAL INSTRUCTION

PREFACE[4]

I have observed that since ancient times, when states established their laws it was always done by the ruler who first received the Mandate. At that time the laws were fixed and the people observed them. Thus was the imperial benevolence and authority extended throughout the realm; the people could enjoy peace and security. This was because at the outset of the founding the ruler endured hardships, saw many men and became experienced in handling affairs. In comparison with a ruler born and bred deep within the palace, unfamiliar with the world, or a hermit scholar living alone in the mountains or forests considering himself enlightened, how different it was. When I was young I was orphaned and poor, and grew up amidst warfare. At the age of twenty-four I joined the ranks and was ordered about for three years. Then I gathered together able followers and studied the ways of training soldiers, planning to compete with the warlords. It was trying and worrisome. I was apprehensive and on guard for nearly twenty years until I was able to eliminate the powerful enemies and unite the empire. Of human deceit I have known plenty. Therefore, drawing on what I have seen and done, together with the officials I have fixed the law of the land. This has eliminated the indulgent rule of the Yuan Dynasty and those who defiled the old customs. The warlords were powerful and deceitful. They were hard to govern, but I have governed them. The people, encountering disorder, tried by all manner of evil means to pass through the unrest. They were hard to manage but I have managed them. Now since the pacification of Wuchang[5] there was discussion about enacting the Code and the Commandment. The additions, deletions, and changes have been innumerable. Ten years have passed and we accomplished the task.[6] They were promulgated and gradually the people came to know the prohibitions. In order to teach later generations the Ancestral Instruction was also created. It was set up as a family law. It was written in big characters in the Western Corridor and was read day and night to make the text perfect. From start to finish it has been six years.[7] It went through seven drafts and is now done. How difficult! Many shallow scholars affirm the past and decry the present. Evil officials constantly twist words and bend the law. If I had not selected the able from the masses and made decisions

---

[4] The author is Zhu Yuanzhang, founding emperor of the Ming.

[5] Wuchang, in Huguang, was taken on March 20, 1364. See Taylor (1975), 48.

[6] This statement would place the writing of the preface around 1374. The earliest version of the *Instruction* was completed in 1373, but careful scholarship by Huang Zhangjian (1961, 119-137) has shown that the surviving text was a revision of 1381. The Instruction was issued in its final form in 1397.

[7] Obviously the span from 1373 to 1381 is more than six years. The discrepancy may be due in part to the fact that Western calendar years overlap with Chinese calendar years.

resolutely I would have been confused by them and unable to accomplish anything. Now I have ordered the Hanlin to compile this book and the Ministry of Rites to print it and pass it on to eternity. All my progeny may adhere to my orders and not be crafty and confuse the laws which I have fixed forever. Not a single word may be changed. Not only will you not fail to live up to my intentions to pass on the law, but Heaven and Earth and the Ancestors will also bless and protect you without end. Alas. Heed this.

I. FIRST SECTION[8]

1. It has been more than forty years since I first took up arms. I have personally ordered the affairs of the realm. The good and bad, true and false of human nature have all been experienced by me. Those who were wicked and crafty by nature and committed serious crimes obvious beyond doubt have been singled out for heavier punishment than the law provides, with the intention of making people take heed and thus not lightly dare to break the law. However, this is just a provisional measure to punish the wicked; it is not the normal law of the ruler who preserves the accomplishments. From now on, when my descendants become emperors they shall only enforce the Code and the Grand Pronouncements [*Da gao*]. They certainly shall not employ any punishments like tattooing [*qingci*], cutting off the feet [*fei*], cutting off the nose [*yi*], and castration [*yance*]. Why is this so? Because the succeeding rulers will be born and raised in the palace; they cannot have a complete knowledge of human nature's good and evil. I fear that in time something untoward will transpire, harming the innocent by mistake. If there are officials who dare to memorialize requesting the use of these punishments, civil and military officials shall immediately submit accusations. The offenders shall be put to death by slicing and his whole family executed.

2. From ancient times policy was discussed among the three dukes [*san gong*] and the duties of government were divided among the six ministers, but a prime minister was never established. The Qin began the establishment of a prime minister and fell soon thereafter. The Han, Tang, and Song continued the practice. Although there were some virtuous prime ministers, many of them were evil men who monopolized power and confused administration. Now our dynasty has abolished the prime minister and established such offices as the five chief commissions, the six ministries, the Censorate, the Office of Transmission, and the Grand Court of Revision to manage the affairs of the realm.[9] They parallel one another and dare not to seek to dominate each other. It is the court which provides overall control

[8] The contents of this section, in particular the second article which prohibits the reestablishment of the post of prime minister, confirm that this version of the Instruction was issued after 1380, the year when the prime ministership was abolished.

[9] See Hucker (1985), 72.

of government affairs. That is why there is stability. From now on, when my descendants become emperors, they absolutely shall not establish a prime minister. If there are officials who dare to memorialize requesting such establishment, civil and military officials shall immediately submit accusations. The offender shall be put to death by slicing and his whole family executed.

3. In the event of a crime by imperial relatives or in-laws, the case shall be decided by the heir apparent personally. Except for plotting rebellion against the throne, which shall not be pardoned, all minor crimes shall be deliberated collectively by the clansmen in the capital; serious crimes shall be deliberated collectively by the princes outside the capital as well as the clansmen in the capital. All cases shall be submitted to the throne for determination. The families of criminals shall only be reported by the judicial offices, but shall not be interrogated without authority.

The families subject to deliberation are appointed and listed below:

The Empress's family	Imperial consorts' [*huangfei*] families
Heir Apparent's consorts' families	Prince's consorts' [*fuma*] families
Commandery princes's [*junwang*] consorts' families	Imperial princesses consorts' families
Ceremonial companions' [*yibin*] families	Duke of Wei's family[10]
Duke of Cao's family	Duke of Xin's family
Marquis of Xiping's family	Marquis of Wuding's family

4. The barbarians roundabout are hemmed in by the mountains and the sea, isolated in out-of-the-way corners of the world. Although they have land, the land is insufficient; although they have people, the people are difficult to control. If they overestimate their own strength and come to harass our borders, it will be inauspicious for them. As they are not a threat to China, should we rashly send forces to attack them, it will also be inauspicious for us. I fear that later generations of my offspring will rely on the wealth and power of China, and, coveting a momentary martial glory, will rally forces without provocation, at great cost in human life. Always remember that this is forbidden. The barbarians in the northern and northwestern border regions who are next to each other cause continual warfare.

[10] Here reference is made to the nobility of merit, families of close supporters of the first emperor during the dynastic founding. The first Duke of Wei was Xu Da (1332-1385), Zhu Yuanzhang's most senior general (DMB, 602-608). The first Duke of Cao was Li Wenzhong (1339-1384) (DMB, 881-887). The first Duke of Xin was Tang He (1326-1395) (DMB, 1248-1251). The Marquis of Xiping was Mu Ying (1345-1395) (DMB, 1079-1083). The Marquis of Wuding was Guo Ying (1335-1403) (DMB, 780-784).

This necessitates the designation of commanders and the training of troops in time to defend against them.

The following is a list of the foreign countries against which campaigns shall not be launched:

Northeast:

Korea [Chaoxian guo]. (This is Gaoli. Li Renren and his son Li Chenggui are now honored. From Hongwu 6 [1373] until Hongwu 28 [1395] a total of four kings were killed, so for the time being we treat them as barbarians.[11])

East and to the North:

Japan. (Although they sent tribute they were deceitful. They secretly contacted the treacherous official Hu Weiyong and plotted rebellion.[12] Consequently relations were broken off.)

South and to the East:

Greater Ryukyus [Da Liuqiu guo]. (Irregular tribute. The sons of the ruler and his ministers have enrolled in the national university to study and have been shown great hospitality.)

Lesser Ryukyus [Xiao Liuqiu guo]. (No contact, has not sent tribute.)

Southwest:

Annam. (One tribute every three years.)

Cambodia [Zhenla guo]. (Sends tribute at the regular time. This country borders the sea.)

Siam [Xianluo guo]. (Sends tribute at the regular time. This country borders the sea.)

Champa [Zhancheng guo]. (From Champa on, when these countries paid tribute they often included deceitful merchants. Consequently relations were refused. Relations were refused from Hongwu 8 [1375] until Hongwu 12 [1379], when the ban was lifted. This country borders the sea.)

Samudra [Sumendala]. (This country borders the sea.)[13]

Western Ocean Country [Xiyang guo]. (This country borders the sea.)

Java [Zhaowa guo]. (This country is located in the middle of the sea.)

---

[11] Yi Song-gye (1355-1408) founded the Yi Dynasty in 1392, ending Koryo rule and Mongol influence, turning Korea toward the Ming and Neo-Confucianism. The Chinese were confused, however, about Yi Song-gye's father. They thought that he was descended from Yi In-im (also written with a different character im for the third syllable), a pro-Mongol minister. The Koreans protested the mistake which the Chinese side was slow to clear up (DMB, 1598-1603). The next statement may refer to the succession struggles among Yi Song-gye's offspring. See biography of Yi Pang-won (DMB, 1594-1598).

[12] Hu Weiyong (d. 1380) was the senior grand councilor [chengxiang] put to death for plotting to usurp the throne. An added charge was that he had conspired to gain Japanese help with his rebellion (DMB, 638-641).

[13] Semudera was a town on the north coast of Sumatra (Ma Huan [1433] 1970, 218).

Pahang [Penheng guo]. (This country is located in the middle of the sea.)[14]

Baihua [Baihua guo]. (This country is located in the middle of the sea.)[15]

Srivijaya [Sanfoji guo]. (This country is located in the middle of the sea.)[16]

Brunei [Boni guo]. (This country is located in the middle of the sea.)

5. Of the rulers in ancient times, only dynastic founders, rulers who presided over restorations, or virtuous rulers who maintained the heritage were sincerely concerned about the realm. The commonplace rulers looked to the realm for pleasure. This was the beginning of the end of the dynasty. How is this so? When a ruler first gains the realm it is because Heaven has chosen a man of virtue. As for rulers who maintain the heritage, if they are constantly reverential toward Heaven and take to heart their ancestor's concern for the realm they can receive Heaven's blessing forever. If they begin to be negligent disaster will result. Take heed.

6. Every year during the months from spring to fall you must be especially concerned. Only when concern is always on your mind will the people be at peace and the state secure. What you shall be concerned about is that the winds and rain come in the proper season and the fields have a bumper harvest so that the people will be assured of their livelihood. If the wind and rain are out of season the people will be unable to make a living and bandits and robbers will arise. Heroes will then arise to take advantage of the situation and the dynasty's condition will be perilous.[17]

7. In peaceful times, if floods or droughts occur somewhere, you shall take stock of government reserves and excuse the disaster victims' taxes. In bumper harvest years, even though there be no disaster damage, you shall still take stock of the government reserves and if there is a little extra, select an area with bad soil and poor people and excuse their taxes. This shall not become a regular precedent. When an exemption is contemplated it shall be carried out just before the due date so as not to allow unscrupulous people to know about it in advance and seek fame by letting the word out.

8. The ruler, even when living in safety, still shall constantly be on guard. At no time during the day or night may you be careless. Then you will not be spied upon, and the state will not be lost. If you take your safety for granted and forget to take precautions, then evil persons will be able to plot. Neither your life nor your state can be protected. You must be prepared day and night as if you were going into battle with clear orders given. In the day, watch people's speech and actions and at night, patrol to strictly enforce the prohibition on entry so that evil persons will be unable to gain

[14] Pahang is on the east coast of the Malay Peninsula.
[15] Baihua is Pajajaran in western Java (Ma Huan, 210).
[16] Srivajaya was an important kingdom in eastern Sumatra (Ma Huan, 214).
[17] Heroes [*haojie*] in this context are military adventurers.

admission. Though persons be trusted as your own flesh, in meeting with them during the day or night you still shall be alert in your mind. It is better to be prepared even though nothing happens. If you want your retainers to withdraw so as to consult privately with trusted persons on affairs of state, your accompanying eunuchs and armed bodyguards shall only withdraw to a distance of ten *zhang*; they shall not go too far.[18] For example, when in the Yuan dynasty Yingzong was killed in the night it was just because his retainers and eunuchs had withdrawn too far away and the imperial ladies were also not home.[19] Consequently there was this tragedy. You must be highly vigilant.

9. Weapons and armor for emergency use shall never be far from your side. Moreover, select a few good horses which can be trained to run fast and stable them at the doors to the palace. At the four city gates, order the eunuchs each to take a saddled horse to where they are. All these defensive measures are like those which the ancient rulers took.

10. At night you shall always be on guard, always listen for activity within the walls, or even go out of the hall to observe the wind, clouds, and stars. If you do not go out, listen for the calls of peddlers.

11. The ruler who lives in the palace shall get up early and retire late. Little wine shall be drunk. Meals shall be taken on time and not too much shall be eaten after noon. These rules do not apply while travelling outside the capital.

12. It is hard to know if people are good or bad. The way to know that is to give them a charge and test them through it. Only after comparing frequently and investigating circumstances can you know whether they are good or bad. If it is known that one person is good but is not employed or that one is bad but is not dismissed, this is where the destruction of the nation begins. Over the ages indulgence has led to evil persons spreading doubts and dishonor. If you do not know at first and employ such a person, when you know his evil it is no matter to dismiss him. Be careful not to be indulgent.

13. In hearing lawsuits the evidence shall be clear. If it is unclear the punishment will not be properly applied and the guilt will be assigned to the innocent. Eventually Heaven will become angry. In the event of an important case it shall be heard in person. Thus you can prevent the abuse of false charges and mistaken incriminations.

14. Rewards for achievement shall be given out fairly. If they are given unfairly people will not be satisfied. Eventually disaster will necessarily result.

15. Since ancient times, when the princes resided in their fiefs, their happiness must have surpassed that of the emperor. How is this? Their

---

[18] Ten *zhang* would equal thirty-two meters.

[19] The Yuan emperor Yingzong, reign title Zhizhi, reigned 1321-1324.

clothing, palaces, carriages and escorts have all been inferior to those of the emperor. But from their enfeoffment they are treated generously. Their governmental duties are also simple. If they are able to strictly adhere to the rules for vassal states and avoid committing outrages then what great happiness they would have! As for the Son of Heaven, he has constantly to manage the myriad affairs. He retires late and rises early in his worry and concern over the problems of governing the realm. This is why the princes are happier than the emperor.

16. In the past, princes and nobles who have recklessly spied on the throne have all brought about their own destruction. Sometimes the court even got entangled and was also destroyed. The princes and the Son of Heaven are intimate relatives, but sometimes they do not keep their places, or evil persons plot to split them, making the imperial family disharmonious. Thus the outsiders will detect this, and power seekers will seize upon it and achieve their ambitions, thereby subverting the court and undermining the princes themselves. Either a shortcoming in the court or shortcoming on the part of the princes could bring this disaster about. Thus everyone shall uphold the ancestral rules. Do not lose the meaning of the relationships between relatives.

17. What the prince keeps is the ancestral instructions. If the orders of the court are in accord with moral principle then the order shall always be obeyed. If it is not in accord with moral principle see article 12 of the law section.[20]

II. OBSERVANCE

18. My principles of restraint for every day: Do not associate too freely with actors or actresses. Do not sing drunkenly or carry on drinking at night. The empress does not indulge herself. Imperial consorts do not monopolize imperial attention through favor. I have designated the Qianqing Pavilion as the principal sleeping chamber.[21] The empress and consorts each have their own courtyards. Every evening, entry into the imperial presence is according to order. If there is a woman who talks unreliably, the falsity of her statements will be investigated and she will be censured. Thus the palace has no jealous women in it. If in making a court decision the assembled officials all approve, then it will be implemented. The word of a single official is not to be taken as definitive. In a moment of relaxation the word of an individual will be especially examined. Thus the court is not corrupted by prejudice. Tactics and decisions come from myself. Study the trend of events, worry about problems and guard against dangers, like

[20] Reference is made to article 55, below.

[21] The Qianqing Pavilion was part of the imperial palace in Nanjing. The name was also used in the Forbidden City in Beijing.

walking over the abyss on thin ice, and always be anxious. When the evening court is over, retire. Get up when the morning star is out. When you are not sick, never be lazy. This is the way to show respect for Heaven and Man and it is the way to make the nation prosperous.

III. PROPER SACRIFICE

19. In sacrificing to Heaven and Earth, the Gods of Soil and Grain [*sheji*], and the Ancestral Temple [*zongmiao*], be absolutely sincere; then the emotions will be regulated. If you are careless, bad consequences will follow. Thus, when sacrificing always strive to achieve absolute sincerity and not to allow the least bit of carelessness. The spirits of wind, clouds, thunder, rain, mountains, and streams shall also be worshipped respectfully by you yourself. Do not send an official to sacrifice in your place.

20. In sacrificing to Heaven and Earth: five days before the main sacrifice, after noon, bathe, change clothes, and reside in the fasting hall. Early on the second day issue a decree to caution the officials. On the next day announce it to the Temple of Renzu.[22] Fast for three days and then sacrifice.

21. In sacrificing to the Ancestral Temple and the Gods of Soil and Grain: four days before the main sacrifice, after noon bathe, change clothes, and reside in the fasting hall. Fast for three days and then sacrifice.

22. In sacrificing to the Star God [Taisui], wind, clouds, thunder, rain, peaks, Saturn [Zhen], sea, rivers, mountains, streams, city gods, and other spirits: three days before the sacrifice, after noon, bathe, change clothes, and reside in the fasting hall. Beginning on the second day, fast for two days and then sacrifice. (In the spring carry out the sacrifice in the great sacrificial altar [*dasitan*]. In the autumn choose a day and carry out the sacrifice at the appropriate altar.)

23. In ordering officials to be sent to sacrifice on your behalf to rulers of former ages, banners, the Confucian and other temples: one day before the sacrifice, bathe, change clothes, and reside in the fasting hall. On the second day send the official.

Rulers: (Spring sacrifice in the great sacrificial altar. Fall, one day before sacrificing to the mountains and streams, send an official to the appropriate altar to sacrifice.)

Banners: (Fall, when sacrificing to the mountains and streams, send an official to sacrifice at the appropriate altar.)

Confucius: (On the first *ding* day of the middle months of spring and fall, send an official to sacrifice.)[23]

---

[22] Renzu is the temple name of Zhu Yuanzhang's father (Taylor 1975, 57).

[23] *Ding* is the fourth of the ten "heavenly stems" [*tiangan*] which combine with the twelve "earthly branches" [*dizhi*] to make up the cycle of sixty pairs used to number days (and years as

24. In performing the five sacrifices to the household, the kitchen, the gate, and the well, during the first month of the four seasons send a eunuch to sacrifice. Indoors, in the last month of the summer season on the fifth day of earth prosperity, also send a eunuch to sacrifice.

IV. PRECAUTIONS ON COMING AND GOING

25. The divination for all activities can change in an instant; you shall carefully make the judgement by yourself, and not leave it to the occultist. When you are going somewhere, if the chosen horse is suddenly sick, or there is some change in eating, clothing, flags, or armor, or the loss of spoon or chopsticks, dishes overturned, things are not as they ought to be, or if there is a fierce wind or a sudden thunder coming directly against you, or if there is a bird in flight or beast afoot approaching strangely, this is a warning from the spirits and good fortune for the nation. If you are already outside, look about carefully, take precautions, and return. If you have not yet gone out, stop. Celestial phenomena cannot be caused by man; the others are all things that can be caused by man. Perhaps evil persons would take advantage by making it look like there was something when there was not, or like there was not when there was, to hinder your coming and going. Investigate closely. If you do not take heed and proceed, that is defying Heaven and courting disaster. I have been close to the danger point many times; preceding warnings were all accurate. Therefore, whenever I act I scrutinize human affairs, inspect what I eat and use, look up to the way of Heaven and down to the principle of Earth. If they are all unchanged then I proceed. This is how I have achieved safety.

V. PRUDENCE IN AFFAIRS OF STATE

26. Listening and observing broadly and not being biased can enable you to guard against cover-ups and know what is going on at subordinate levels. From now on officials at all levels and artisans of all kinds, if they have something to report, shall report it directly in the emperor's presence. If their report is correct then it shall be turned over to the authorities to handle. The offices shall not impede it. Violators shall be considered the same as treacherous officials. (For example, in the Yuan dynasty the prime minister was ordered to issue a decree saying that if any offices dared to memorialize bypassing the secretariat they would be prosecuted for violation of an edict. Thus the memorials from both inner and outer officials all went through the secretariat. Consequently administration was delayed, making it

---

well). *Ding* would occur six times in every cycle of sixty days and either two or three times in any lunar month.

impossible for the affairs at the lower levels to reach the higher levels, and the state eventually perished.)

27. Whenever government officials, educated men or commoners dare to petition about high officials' talent, virtue and accomplishment in government service, it is essential to investigate the circumstances until they are clearly understood and then decapitate the petitioners. If a high official knew of the circumstances he shall be considered equally guilty. If he did not know, he shall not be punished. (For example, in the Han, [Wang] Mang was prime minister.[24] He manipulated and usurped authority. Emperor Ping gave [Wang] Mang 25,600 *qing*[25] of land in Xingye as a fief. Wang Mang pretended to refuse it. Altogether 487,572 officials and commoners petitioned praising his merit. Consequently power gravitated to Wang Mang and the fortunes of the Han changed. Is this not an admonition?)

VI. CEREMONY

28. Outside the wall of the palace of every prince there shall be erected an ancestral temple, an altar of gods of soil and grain, and other altars.

Ancestral Temple. (To be erected to the left of the prince's palace gate.[26] It should be positioned like the Imperial Ancestral Temple at Court.)

Gods of Soil and Grain. (To be erected to the right of the prince's palace gate. It should be positioned like the National Altar at Court.)

Altars to Spirits of Wind, Clouds, Thunder, Rain, Mountains, and Streams. (To be erected to the west of the Altar to the Gods of Soil and Grain.)

Temple to the Flags. (To be erected to the west of the altars of Wind, Clouds, Thunder, Rain, Mountains, and Streams. The keeper of the flags shall makes sacrifice.)

29. Performing the five sacrifices. (Use one pig, silk, incense, candles, wine, and fruit.)

God of the Impluvium. (Left of the palace gate set up an incense table. On the fourth day of the first month the gate officer shall sacrifice.)

God of the Hearth. (In the kitchen set up an incense table. On the first day of the fourth month the officer in charge of food preparation makes sacrifice.)

Spirit of the Buildings. (In front of the palace, inside the courtyard nearby on the east set up an incense table. On the fifth day of earth prosperity of the sixth month a designated official makes sacrifice.)

---

[24] Wang usurped the throne and formed the Xin dynasty, 8-23 A.D.

[25] A *qing* is 614.4 ares (an are is 100 square meters).

[26] The left is defined from the perspective of the prince (or a ruler) who faces south. Thus the ancestral temple would be to the southeast of the palace gate.

God of the Gate. (Slightly east of the Chengyun Gate set up an incense table. On the first day of the seventh month the gate officer makes sacrifice.)

God of the Well. (Next to the well set up an incense table. On the first day of the tenth month the officer in charge of food preparation makes sacrifice.)

30. On the first day of the year ambassadors are sent to present congratulatory memorials. Princes shall wear their ceremonial robes [*mianfu*] and civil and military officials their court robes [*chaofu*]. After the seals are cleansed and used, the memorial shall be placed in the dragon pavilion.[27] Princes lead the civil and military officials to their places. The princes in front of the hall and upon the terrace and the civil and military officials below the terrace shall carry out the ceremony of the twelve obeisances. Then the princes send their memorials out of the palace gate and stop after five *zhang*. The civil officials escort the memorial out of the state gate. The military officers follow the princes back to the palace.

31. On the Son of Heaven's birthday the princes shall set up an incense table on the terrace in front of the hall. They shall wear ceremonial robes and lead the civil and military officials wearing court robes in worshipping Heaven and Earth. On the first day of the year, after making obeisance to Heaven and Earth, go to the ancestral temple to perform rites, then ascend the central pavilion. Emissaries [*chushiguan*] in ordinary clothing [*bianfu*] perform the four obeisance rite. The civil and military officials in court robes [*jufu*] perform the eight obeisance rite.

32. On the birthdays of previous emperors, sacrifices shall first be carried out at the ancestral temple, then the family rites shall be performed. The various officials shall pay their respects. When that is over, have a banquet.

33. When an edict concerning amnesty reaches the prince's fief, the military officers shall follow the princes to guard him but shall not go beyond the suburbs. The civil officials in court robes shall go out to the suburbs to receive it. The edict of amnesty shall be placed in the dragon pavilion. Lead the way on horseback. The prince in ceremonial robes shall stand about five *zhang* outside the gate to his wall to receive it, and conduct it to the prince's palace where the dragon pavilion is placed in the main hall. The prince shall first perform the five-obeisance rite on the terrace in front of the hall. Then he shall ascend the hall and stand on the east side of the dragon pavilion. The military officers stand guard. The civil officials perform the twelve-obeisance rite from below the terrace, kneeling to hear it read out.

---

[27] The dragon pavillion (*longting*) is a small, portable structure to receive imperial regalia or documents.

34. When court officials are sent by the court to the establishment of a prince as emissaries or pass by in the course of their duties, they shall perform the four-obeisance rite. Even though they be one of the three dukes or a general-in-chief, they still must perform the four obeisances. The prince shall sit to receive them. If an emissary's route passes a prince's establishment, and he deliberately winds around to avoid paying audience to the prince, he shall be decapitated.

35. The civil and military officials of the princely establishment shall go at dawn to the prince's gate to await audience. Provincial administration commissioners, and regional military commissioners together with the officials of guards, prefectures, subprefectures, and districts in the city where the prince resides shall all await audience at the gate of the princely establishment on the first and fifteenth days of the month. If there is business for which they are called to audience it will not be subjected to this limitation.

36. In presenting congratulatory memorials, the heir apparent and the imperial princes shall refer to themselves in the imperial presence as "Senior Son So-and-so" or "Number X Son So-and-so Prince Such-and-such," and address the Son of Heaven as "Your Majesty Father Emperor" [*Fu huang bixia*] and the empress as "Your Majesty Mother Empress" [*Mu hou dianxia*]. Grandsons shall refer to themselves as "Oldest Grandson So-and-so Enfeoffed Such-and-such" or "Number X Grandson So-and-so Enfeoffed Such-and-such," and address the Son of Heaven as "Your Majesty Grandfather Emperor" [*Zufu huangdi bixia*] and the empress as "Your Majesty Grandmother Empress" [*Zumu huanghou dianxia*]. Younger brothers of the emperor shall refer to themselves as "Number X Brother So-and-so Enfeoffed Such-and-such" and address the Son of Heaven as "Your Majesty Big Brother Emperor" [*Daxiong huangdi bixia*] and the empress as "Your Majesty Honorable Elder Sister-in-law Empress" [*Zunsao huanghou dianxia*]. Nephews of the emperor shall refer to themselves as "Number X Nephew So-and-so Enfeoffed Such-and-such" and address the Son of Heaven as "Your Majesty Senior Uncle Emperor" or "Your Majesty Junior Uncle Emperor," and the empress as "Your Majesty Senior Aunt Empress" or "Your Majesty Junior Aunt Empress." Enfeoffed princes who are senior and junior uncles or senior and junior granduncles of the emperor shall refer to themselves as "Subject So-and-so Enfeoffed Such-and such," and address the Son of Heaven as "Your Majesty the Emperor" and the empress as "Your Majesty the Empress." The emperor's great nephews of the second, third and fourth degrees [*congsun*, *zaicongsun*, *sancongsun*, i.e., bss, fbsss, ffbssss] shall refer to themselves as "Second Degree Great Nephew So-and-so Enfeoffed Such-and-such," "Third Degree Great Nephew So-and-so Enfeoffed Such-and-such," "Fourth Degree Great Nephew So-and-so Enfeoffed Such-and-such," and address the emperor as "Your Majesty Senior Great Uncle Emperor" or "Your Majesty Junior Great Uncle Emperor" and

the empress as "Your Majesty Senior Great Aunt Empress" or "Your Majesty Junior Great Aunt Empress."

37. Imperial princes when they pay court on the emperor every year shall not come to court at the same time. The principle is that only one prince comes to court at a time and then returns to his fief. If there is no contingency he shall report to another prince who only then may come to court. The princes, without restriction by year or month, shall come oldest first through the youngest. The sons of the wife shall come first and after they are finished the sons of the concubines, also sequenced from oldest to youngest. When the cycle is finished it shall start again. The sequence shall not be violated.

38. Princes stationed on the border shall come to court on schedule if there is no emergency. If there is an emergency then they shall do what is most practical and not be constrained by the audience period.

39. Although there are differences of age between the emperor and the imperial princes in the court they must observe the etiquette appropriate to ruler and subject. The position of the Son of Heaven is the same as the position of the ancestors. The emperor ought to have a great tablet representing the ancestors engraved with the characters: "Respect Heaven and follow the Ancestors; pass on from generation to generation." When a prince comes to court, even though he be older than the Son of Heaven, the Son of Heaven as holder of the inherited tablet receives reverence. When one sees the tablet it is as if one sees the ancestral spirit.

40. When princes come to court, whether or not they have performed sacrifices, they shall first have audience with the emperor in their normal dress, kowtowing three times without making obeisance. After the audience at the Fengxian Hall is over, irrespective of hall, building, pavilion or gate the Son of Heaven holds the tablet, the prince wears ceremonial robes and performs the rites appropriate to emperor and subject, performing the five-obeisance rite and kowtowing three times. After the audience, if the prince is senior in generation or in age and the Son of Heaven the junior relative, he shall lead the prince to a suitable hall where the prince shall sit on the east facing west. The Son of Heaven in ordinary clothes shall perform the family rites, performing the four-obeisance rite but not kowtowing. The prince will receive this. However, even though carrying out the family rites, the ruler-subject roles must be respected. The Son of Heaven resides in the center and faces south to receive princes senior in generation or age. Next they shall see the heir apparent, performing the four obeisances rite. If the prince is senior in generation or age the heir apparent shall return the obeisance.

41. Imperial princes who are uncles of the Son of Heaven shall not come to court after the age of fifty; their eldest sons can take their places. Junior relatives need not come to court after the age of sixty, when their eldest sons may take their places.

42. When imperial princes come to court and there happens to be a big banquet meeting, the princes shall not enter it. If they are to be feasted, clean food and tea shall be prepared in an appropriate hall, and family rites observed in entertaining them. When the various officials are in a great banquet meeting, the princes are not allowed to take part. This is a precaution.

43. Twenty characters shall be selected to serve as names for following generations of the heir apparent and the imperial princes. From now on when a child or agnatic grandchild is born it shall be reported to the court and turned over to the Imperial Clan Court. In giving a double name, each generation shall take one character as the first character. The second character may be freely chosen at the time in order to make a double name to be entered on the jade [genealogical] tablets. After twenty generations continuations can be made according to precedent, guaranteeing a standard form forever.

Heir Apparent's descendants:

Yun, Wen, Zun, Zu, Xun	Qin, Wu Da, Jun, Sheng
Shun, Dao, Yi, Feng, Ji	Shi, Liang, Shan, Yong, Sheng

Prince of Qin's descendants:

Shang, Zhi, Gong, Cheng, Bing	Wei, Huai, Jing, Yi, Cun
Fu, Si, Zi, Lian, Zhi	Kuang, Shi, Yong, Xin, Dun

Prince of Jin's descendants:

Ji, Mei, Zhong, Qi, Biao	Zhi, Xin, Shen, Min, Qiu
Shen, Xin, Xian, Jing, Mu	Shu, Xue, Ji, Qian, Xiu

Prince of Yan's descendants:

Gao, Zhan, Qi, Jian, You	Hou, Zai, Yi, Chang, You
Ci, He, Yi Bo, Zhong	Jian, Jing, Di, Xian, You

Prince of Zhou's descendants:

You, Zi, Tong, An, Mu	Qin, Chao, Zai, Su, Gong
Shao, Lun, Fu, Hui, Run	Zhao, Ke, Guang, Deng, Yong

Prince of Chu's descendants:

Meng, Ji, Jun, Rong, Xian	Ying, Hua, Yun, Sheng, Rong
Hong, Cai, Sheng, Bo, Yan	Mao, Shi, Li, Chuan, Gong

Prince of Qi's descendants:

Xian, Neng, Chang, Ke, Qing	Rui, Zhi, Shi, Kan, Zong
Yang, Xing, Qi, Yuan, Ya	Yin, Si, Fu, Hui, Tong

Prince of Lu's descendants:

Zhao, Tai, Yang, Dang, Jian	Guan, Yi, Shou, Yi, Hong
Zhen, Ju, Xi, Jian, Da	Kang, Zhuang, Yu, Ben, Ning

Prince of Shu's descendants:

Yue, You, Shen, Bin, Rang	Cheng, Xuan, Feng, Zhi, Ping
Mao, Jin, Shen, Zi, Yi	Duan, Ju, Wu, Mu, Qing

Prince of Xiang's descendants:

Jiu, Zhen, Kai, Fang, Yue	Yang, Wei, Jin, Li, Yi

Gang, Yi Xun, Chao, Zhuo Chuan, Heng, Su, Zi, Chi

Prince of Dai's descendants:

Xun, Shi, Cheng, Cong, Jun Chong, Ting, Nai, Ding, Yi
Chuan, Yi, Lian, Xiu, Yu Bing, Yao, Zhuang, Hong, Ji

Prince of Su's descendants:

Shan, Lu, Gong, Zhen, Bi Jin, Shen, Shi, Lie, Zhong
Xi, Hui, Ji, Fu, Yun Kai, Jian, Chu, Heng, Long

Prince of Liao's descendants:

Gui, Hao, En, Chong, Zhi Xian, Shu, Yan, Zun, Ru
Yun, Reng, Qi, Bao, He Cao, Han, Li, Long, Yu

Prince of Qing's descendants:

Zhi, Sui, Zhi, Tai, Zi Ni, Shen, Shuai, Zhuo, Qi
Shi, Wan, Yin, Ju, Kan Zhi, Juan, Fa, Xu, Pi

Prince of Ning's descendants:

Pan, Dian, Jin, Chen, Gong Duo, Mou, Tong, Yi, Zhong
Zong, Tian, Zhi, Shu, Kuo Zuo, Zhe, Xiang, Qin, Zhong

Prince of Min's descendants:

Hui, Yin, Ying, Yan, Yu Ding, Gan, Qi, Yin, Yong
Chong, Li, Yuan, Zi, Fang Kuan, Rong, Xi, Ben, Cong

Prince of Gu's descendants:

Fu, Zhi, Xi, Xiong, Chang Cong, Xing, Chan, Fu, Chang
Du, Xie, Xun, Yi, You Kuo, Ji, Yu, Zhen, Xiang

Prince of Han's descendants:

Chong, Fan, Zheng, Xie, Xu Rong, Mo, Lang, Jing, Kui
Dan, Shao, Yu, Hao, Cao Ling, Xu, Jie, Fan, Wei

Prince of Shen's descendants:

Ji, You, Quan, Xun, Yin Tian, Cheng, Xiao, Jiong, Huang
Shi, Yuan, Yin, Xi, Wei Kui, Bi, Che, Cheng, Ang

Prince of An's descendants:

Fei, Xu, Bin, Yan, Shang Ning, Tan, Jun, Zhi, Xiang
Hui, Yan, Zhuan, Ji, Ju Zhen, Mi, Guo, Cheng, Gang

Prince of Tang's descendants:

Qiong, Zhi, Mi, Yu, Zhou Shuo, Qi, Yu, Lin, Ju
Qi, Ling, Meng, Song, Ti Jia, Li, Xie, Ming, Tu

Prince of Ying's descendants:

Wei, Wen, Can, Wang, Shi Zhen, Hui, Ji, Gao, Kui
Qi, Lin, Yu, Ji, Zhao Kui, Ying, Ye, Xuan, Ji

Prince of Yi's descendants:

Yong, Mian, Shi, Xu, Dian Bao, Ke, Cai, Feng, Chen
Ying, Chou, Pan, Zhou, Xuan Kun, Yu, Guan, Quan, Jin

Bi, Chu, Si, Jian, Jie[28] Xu, Hao, Bi, Zhen, Chuan

[28] These are extra sets of names.

Zhi, Jun, Fu, Jun, Zheng
Xun, Min, Ru, Li, Qian

Jian, Xu, Yan, Huan, Chang
Zou, Huan, Yuan, Zao, Jiu
Xian, Shi, Sui, Sheng, Ji
Shi, Yi, Ji, Xun, Chi

Hui, Jian, Xin, Yuan, Jue
Xi, Xian, Zeng, Ying, Mi
Jian, Jie, Zhuo, Shen, Zi
Lin, Rao, Yi, Xu, Hui

Prince of Jingjiang's descendants:[29]

Zan, Zuo, Xiang, Gui, Yue
Ruo, Yi, Chun, Yi, Xing
Jing, Bang, Ren, Lü, Heng
Yuan, De, Xi, Fang, Ming

VII. LAW

44. If the heir apparent commits a transgression when he is either at a distant place or only a short way from the capital city, do not send someone to him bearing decrees to investigate. The thing to do is to call him back to directly face his ruler-father's scrutiny and command. If there is someone making an oral transmission, bearing a tally or court documents ordering an investigation, he must be taken into custody and questioned about the circumstances. First take precautions. Urgently send a trusted person to go directly before the emperor to hear the imperial proclamation in person. After clarifying the facts, the emissary will come back and report. The disposition shall be based upon what was proclaimed. This shall be the same for all princes and their descendants.

45. All imperial princes and their heirs who have gone to a distant place, are residing in their fiefs, or are in the capital city, when summoned by the court may only set out to see the emperor when a document bearing the imperial seal and a golden tally is sent to them by a ceremonial companion [*yibin*], imperial princess's consort [*fuma*], or a eunuch.

46. Civil officials in the princely fiefs shall be carefully selected by the court and sent to the princely fiefs to serve. Military officers already have a fixed hereditary system. Should civil or military officers transgress the law, let the prince pass judgement in the case. Legal authorities may not raise obstructions and confusions to alter the prince's decision. If among the civil and military officials there are capable and upright ones who counsel the prince and help him to preserve his fief, they shall not be casually abused. If the court hears of such an official he shall be treated with courtesy.

47. If any of the military or civilian people in the market towns or villages within the city or territory where the prince resides are rude to the prince in any way, the prince shall arrest them at once and send them to the capital. After interrogation to determine the facts they shall be punished. If

[29] The Prince of Jingjiang was Zhu Yuanzhang's grand-nephew Zhu Shouqian (Taylor 1975, 167).

the military or civilian people do nothing rude, but some persons among the prince's entourage feign power and influence to lodge false accusations against good people before the prince, the responsible persons shall be punished.

48. When an imperial prince commits a serious transgression send an imperial relative or a eunuch to summon him. If three times he does not come, again send a regular civil official together with a eunuch to summon him to the capital. The Son of Heaven shall personally proclaim what evils have been committed. If there turns out to be clear proof, he [the prince] shall be taken into custody for ten days by the imperial relatives in the capital and the eunuchs. During that ten days he shall see the Son of Heaven five times. Afterwards he shall be released. Even if the crime is serious physical punishment shall not be used. For a serious crime he shall be reduced to commoner status; for a minor crime he shall come to court and hear the emperor proclaim his wrong, or else send an official to him with an edict in order to tell him the positive and negative consequences of his behavior and cause him to reform. Should a high official treacherously not allow the prince to see the Son of Heaven, or fraudulently incriminate him, causing him to meet with misfortune, it must be such a time when the Son of Heaven will have become a misguided ruler. The prince's administrator's office and his guard shall send a message to the five military commissions demanding that they arrest the treacherous official. The military commissioners shall arrest the treacherous official and memorialize recommending his decapitation and the extermination of his family.

49. Guardians of customs and laws [*fengxian guan*][30] who memorialize about small transgressions of the princes, sowing dissension among imperial relatives, shall be decapitated. Those who memorialize about a serious crime by a prince, based solely on rumor without evidence, shall be considered guilty of the same crime.

50. Princely residences in the capital either are especially fancy or occupy good land. If there are treacherous officials who make improper use of their influence to seize them, the Son of Heaven will have them decapitated and their family members banished to the frontier.

51. Should officials or commoners be guilty of crimes their crimes shall be clearly punished. Do not poison them.

52. When a prince sends an emissary to court it is not necessary for him to go through each of the government offices. He shall go directly to the emperor's presence. Any who dare to block him shall be considered a treacherous official. When a prince's emissary comes to the Meridian Gate [Wumen][31] the gate officer shall send word to the emperor immediately. If

[30] Hucker (1985), item 1982.

[31] The Wumen was the south central, and therefore main, gate of the palace. Since in theory the emperor sat in the center and faced southward a southern gate was the most direct line of approach to his presence.

word is not sent the officer shall be considered to be in league with treacherous officials.

53. In the princely fiefs, in addition to the fixed quota of positions, it is definitely not permissible to recruit eager and clever advisors. It is also impermissible to receive petitioners. If there are such persons, even though the prince tolerates them, the court shall still punish them according to law without causing the prince to be alarmed or suspicious. Should clever advisors be offered to the court do not retain them.

54. If commoners dare to accuse the prince of minor transgressions to accomplish evil ends, they shall be decapitated and their family members banished to the frontier.

55. When an emissary of the court is sent to the princely fief, whether in the princes's presence or among his entourage, shall he say something which is improper, intentionally angering the prince, it is definitely not the Son of Heaven's intention. It must be a treacherous official at court who ordered him to sow discord among our relatives. The prince should swallow the insult and not execute him on the spot. Take him into custody for interrogation in the princely fief to determine the truth. Send someone to make a secret report to the Son of Heaven. The Son of Heaven should then inquire into the facts. The treacherous official and the emissary shall both be decapitated.

56. When a new emperor takes the throne each prince shall send an emissary with a memorial to court to express congratulations. Princes shall guard the border for three years without coming to court. They may order a civil and a military official from their princely establishment to come to the court. If the court is following the fixed ancestral rules and employing upright officials and there is no evil going on, after three years the princes may come to court in succession. If there are no upright officials at the court and evils are taking place then the prince shall train his soldiers and await orders. The Son of Heaven should send a secret edict to the princes to assemble a pacification force to subdue them. After the pacification the troops shall return to their camps. The princes shall pay court to the emperor and then return. If the princes do not come themselves, but send generals to make peace, the generals shall also return their troops to camp. They shall take a number of persons and go to pay court to the Son of Heaven. After no more than five days in the capital they shall return. Their merit should be rewarded later.

57. If there are no imperial sons in the court, the succession shall pass to the younger brother when the elder brother dies, elevating the sons of the wife. Those born of concubines shall not be elevated even though they are older. If there are treacherous officials who advocate abandoning sons of the wife and elevating sons of concubines, the sons of the concubines shall hold fast to their station and not move. They should send a message to the son of the wife who ought to be elevated. The essential of the matter is that

the wife's son occupy the throne. The court shall decapitate the treacherous officials immediately. The audience after three years is the same as that described in the previous article.

58. In the princely fiefs there shall be regular investigations of the military. It is not permitted to conceal defections. If such should occur the responsibility falls upon the two nearest neighbors, those who give them refuge, the responsible officers, and the supervisory leaders. Do not question the prince. The prince also shall not shelter or protect them. If there are treacherous officials who deliberately allow escapes within their jurisdiction and slander the prince, they shall be decapitated and their family members banished to the frontier.

VIII. PALACE REGULATIONS

59. In the supplying of those below the rank of empress including the various grades of ladies and their servants with clothing, food, gold, silver, cash, silk, or any kind of object, the General Palace Service [*shanggong*][32] must first memorialize the throne. Subsequently send the request to the eunuch supervisory official [*neiguan jianguan*].[33] Only after the supervisory official memorializes in reply may he be permitted to go to the warehouses to issue the items. If the General Palace Service does not memorialize the throne, but without authorization sends the request, and the eunuch does not memorialize in reply and makes unauthorized issue, they shall both be executed.

60. If documents are written without authorization to persons outside the palace the writer and the recipient shall both be decapitated. Those who know of the affair shall share the same guilt. Those who do not know about it shall not be tried.

61. There are regulations governing Buddhist and Daoist temples, burning incense, or praying to the stars or the dipper. Those who violate the regulations and those who receive the incense or contribute objects shall all be executed.

62. The empress shall only manage all the ladies of every rank within the palace. In all affairs beyond the palace gate she shall not intervene.

63. In the event that there is sickness within the palace it is not permitted to call in a physician from outside. All that may be done is to describe the symptoms and receive a medicine.

64. Caution shall be taken in the ladies' quarters of the palace; the various officials are not permitted to pay audience to the inner and outer ladies. The honorable ladies in the palace come to court on the Thousand Autumn

[32] Hucker (1985), item 5013.
[33] Hucker (1985), item 835.

Festival [8th month, 5th day],[34] the Winter Solstice, the first day of the year, and the first and fifteenth of every month. In case of extreme cold, extreme heat, rain, or snow they may be excused from paying court.

65. The empress, consorts, and palace women for the Son of Heaven and the princes shall be chosen from among the children of good families in accordance with rituals. There shall be no restriction of location. Do not accept any sent by high officials lest there be treacherous plots. As for prostitutes, intimacy with them is not permitted.

IX. EUNUCHS

66. If the food and drink and other essentials used in the palace are supplied by the government offices at various levels, these things will necessarily be requisitioned from the people, often resulting in unnecessary paperwork and abuses. Therefore, the services for wine, vinegar, and flour and for weaving and dyeing were set up within the palace. After establishing them I unexpectedly saw in the *Rites of Zhou* [*Zhouli*][35] the positions of wine steward [*jiuren*], soup steward [*jiangren*], vinegar steward [*xiren*], and dye steward [*ruanren*][36] which were also filled by eunuchs. Then I knew that this sort of office had been established since ancient times. The purpose is to avoid burdening the people and for convenience of supply. Others, such as the various directorates, offices, bureaus, and storehouses all have eunuchs assigned to manage them. Their activities are easy to carry out. The above office names have been established and are fixed. It is important to honor these arrangements and not alter them lightly.

67. The eunuchs in various offices:

Official Titles for each directorate

- Director [*taijian*] (4A)[37]
  - Left Vice Director [*zuo shaojian*] (4B)
  - Left Supervisor [*zuo jiancheng*] (5A)[38]
  - Right Vice Director (4B)
  - Right Supervisor (5A)
  - Archivist [*dianbu*] (6A)
- Directorate of Grounds [*shengongjian*] (in charge of sprinkling and sweeping)[39]

---

[34] The Thousand Autumn Festival began as a birthday celebration for the Tang Emperor Xuanzong in 729.

[35] The *Zhouli* is a classical text which contains an idealized pattern of government organization. It had a profound effect on Chinese thinking about statecraft throughout the imperial era. For a French translation see Biot (1851).

[36] Hucker (1985) renders these as Eunuch Wine Maker, Eunuch Liquor Maker, Vinegarman, Spiceman and Dyer.

[37] Ranks [*pin*] are numbered starting from one as the highest and subdivided into A [*zheng*] and B [*cong*].

[38] Hucker (1985) does not give this term.

Directorate of Palace Seals [*shangbao jian*] (in charge of imperial seals, tallies, and credentials for military generals)

Xiaoling Directorate of Grounds [*Xiaoling shengong jian*][40] (in charge of sprinkling and sweeping and also growing fruits, vegetables, and other things)

Directorate for Palace Delicacies [*shangshan jian*] (in charge of provisioning and the emperor's food, and the food consumed in the palace; also oversees the Court of Imperial Entertainments [*guanglu si*] in preparing banquets, tea and food in the palace)

Directorate for Imperial Apparel [*shangyi jian*] (In charge of imperial hats, robes, shoes, boots, stockings and other things.)

Directorate of Equippage [*sishe jian*] (In charge of imperial carriages, beds, bedding, curtains and the like)

Directorate of Palace Eunuchs [*neiguan jian*] (In charge of producing marriage trousseaus, crowns, parasols, fans, bedding, curtains, insignia, etc., and eunuch yellow notices [*tiehuang*], as well as utensils, jewelry, grain silos, archives for documents, warehouses for salt, and ice cellars for palace use)

Directorate of Ceremonial [*sili jian*] (In charge of capping, marriage, funerals, and sacrifices as well as all imperial insignia and imperial tallies, rewards, brushes, ink, mounting of calligraphy, and painting; managing the gate-exiting horse placards for palace functionaries sent in the retinue of attendants; overseeing the Court of Imperial Entertainments in preparing all banquets)

Directorate of Imperial Horses [*yuma jian*] (in charge of managing imperial horses and tribute from every region, and overseeing issuing and receiving horses and mules and other items)

Directorate for Credentials [*yinshou jian*] (in charge of patents, yellow notices, seals, account books, books and maps, tallies, counterfoils, documents, memorials, decrees, register of names, credentials, charts and other items)

Directorate for Palace Maintenance [*zhidian jian*] (in charge of sprinkling and sweeping the various structures in the palace)

Attendant [*changsui fengyu*] (6A)[41]

Official titles for officers of the Fengtian and other gates (In charge of opening and closing at dawn and dusk, and regulating entrance and exit):[42]

Gatekeeper (4A)

---

39 Hucker (1985), item 5156, renders this as Directorate for Imperial Temples, which does not fit the duties described here.

40 Xiaoling is the name given to Zhu Yuanzhang's tomb.

41 Hucker (1985) renders this as Palace Groom, indicating that it was a low-ranking (6A) eunuch in the Directorate of the Imperial Horses. Such a function is not clear from this context.

42 To this and the next five items I have assigned separate numbers even though they do not begin with the character *fan* which usually signals a new entry.

Assistant Gatekeeper (4B)
Official titles for each office:
Director [*sizheng*] (5A) Left Vice Director (5B)
Right Vice Director (5B)

Office of Music [*zhonggu si*] (In charge of music for sacrifices at the Fengxian Hall, imperial music, music for palace banquets, the hour glasses and the morning audience bells and gongs)

Office of Fuel [*xixin si*] (in charge of firewood and charcoal for the palace and other such places)

Official titles for services and storehouses:
Commissioner [*dashi*] (5A)
Left Assistant Commissioner (5B)
Right Assistant Commissioner (5B)

Palace Armory [*bingzhang ju*] (in charge of imperial weapons and to superintend the artisans in producing swords, armor, and other items, and combs, toothbrushes, needles, scissors, and other articles used in the palace.)

Palace Weaving and Dyeing Service [*nei zhiran ju*] (In charge of dying and manufacturing all cloth for imperial and palace use)

Sewing Service [*zhengong ju*] (in charge of producing all clothing for wedding ceremonies, supplying them to the Directorate of Palace Eunuchs for disposition. Also manufactures clothing and bedding for the eunuchs)

Kerchief and Cap Service [*jinmao ju*] (in charge of manufacturing silk hats and boots and socks for the eunuchs; also prepares hats and other items to be given as rewards)

Gardening Service [*siyuan ju*] (in charge of vegetables for the palace; also farming)

Condiments Service [*jiucumian ju*] (in charge of the wine, vinegar, flour and sugar used by the eunuchs)

Palace Storehouse [*neichengyun ku*] (in charge of all bolts of cloth, gold, silver, tassles, jade, ivory, and other articles; also jointly manages currency with the Palace Key Storehouse.)

Palace Key Storehouse [*siyao ku*] (In charge of all door locks and keys and issuing and receiving currency and other articles)

Palace Supply Storehouse [*neifu gongyong ku*] (in charge of special rice for imperial use, scented candles, oil and rice for palace use, foodstuffs and fruits for the eunuchs, and other articles)

Officials of the Heir Apparent:[43]
Seal Service [*dianxi ju*] (in charge of seals and writing materials)
Chief [*julang*] (5A) Deputy Chief [*jucheng*] (5B)
Secretary [*jishi fengyu*] (6A)

---

[43] Literally, Eastern Palace [*donggong*], the residence of the heir apparent.

Medicine Service [*dianyao ju*] (in charge of overseeing imperial physicians to make up medicine according to the prescription, decoct and supply it)

Chief (5A) Deputy Chief (5B)

Foods Service [*dianshan ju*] (in charge of preparing and serving food)

Chief (5A) Deputy Chief (5B)

Apparel Service [*dianfu ju*] (in charge of headdresses, hats, garments, gowns, girdles, boots, etc.)

Chief (5A)[44] Deputy Chief (5B)

Weapons Service [*dianbing ju*] (in charge of armor, helmets, spears, bows and arrows, swords, etc.)

Chief (5A) Deputy Chief (5B)

Equippage Service [*diansheng ju*] (in charge of carriages and horses)

Chief (5A) Deputy Chief (5B)

Officials of the Princely Establishment:

Office of Steward [*chengfeng si*] (In charge of managing all the miscellaneous affairs of the princely establishment. If there is a problem it is turned over the Administrator's Office to be disposed of in concert with the guard commander. They shall have no relationship with the eunuch offices in the capital.)

Steward [*chengfeng zheng*] (6A)

Deputy Steward [*chengfeng fu*] (6B)

Seals Office [*dianbao suo*]

Director [*dianbao zheng*] (6A)

Vice Director [*dianbao fu*] (6B)

Foods Office [*dianshan suo*]

Director [*dianshan zheng*] (6A)

Vice Director [*dianshan fu*] (6B)

Apparel Office [*dianfu suo*]

Director [*dianfu zheng*] (6A)

Deputy Director [*dianfu fu*] (6B)

Six eunuchs (one for caps, three for clothing, one for girdles, one for shoes)

Gate Officers

Gate Keeper [*men zheng*] (6A)

Assistant Gate Keeper [*men fu*] (6B)

Household Agents [*neishi*]

Two for medicine [*si yao*]

Two for bows and arrows [*si gongshi*]

Princesses's Households:

Supervisory Office [*zhongshi si*]

---

[44] Hucker (1985), item 6576, renders this Director of the Wardrobe.

Supervisor [*si zheng*] (miscellaneous duties)
Vice Supervisor [*si fu*] (miscellaneous duties)

X. RULES OF OFFICE

68. Enfeoffments:

The Heir Apparent shall be given a gold tablet and a gold seal. (His consort shall be given only the gold tablet, not the seal.)

Imperial princes [*qinwang*] shall be given gold tablets and gold seals. (Their consorts shall be given only gold tablets, not seals.)

Imperial princesses [*gongzhu*] shall be given gold tablets. The sons-in-law are called Commandant-escorts [*fuma duwei*]. They should be given patents.

The oldest son of the wife of the Heir Apparent is called the Imperial Grandson-heir [*huang taisun*]. Younger sons of the wife and sons of concubines shall be invested as commandery princes [*junwang*] when they reach the age of ten. They shall be given gold-plated silver tablets and gold seals. Female offspring shall be invested as princesses and given patents.

The oldest son of the wife of an imperial prince shall, when he reaches the age of ten, be given by the court a gold tablet and a gold seal and named the prince's heir. Should the son of a concubine attempt to usurp the position of the son of the wife, he shall be reduced to commoner status if it is a minor offense, or banished to a distant place if it is a serious offense. If the prince reaches the age of thirty and his wife still has not borne a son the sons of concubines shall only become commandery princes. If the wife reaches the age of fifty without bearing an heir the oldest son of a concubine shall be named heir to the prince.

The younger sons of the wife of an imperial prince and the sons of his concubines shall all be invested as commandery princes when they reach the age of ten. They shall be given gold-plated silver tablets and gold seals. (Sons and agnatic grandsons not yet invested shall be called sons of princes [*wang zi*] and grandsons of princes [*wang sun*]. In speech they shall be called descendants.)

The emperor's agnatic aunt shall be called Princess Supreme [*dazhang gongzhu*].

The emperor's sisters shall be called Grand Princesses [*zhang gongzhu*].

Imperial daughters shall be called Imperial Princesses [*gongzhu*] (from imperial princess on up all shall be given a gold tablet).

Daughters of an imperial prince shall be called Commandery Princesses [*junzhu*] (from commandery princes on down all shall be given patents).

The daughter of a Commandery Prince is called a District Princess [*xianzhu*].

The agnatic granddaughter of a Commandery Prince is called a Commandery Mistress [*junjun*].

The agnatic great granddaughter of a Commandery Prince is called a District Mistress [*xianjun*].

The agnatic great-great granddaughter of a Commandery Prince is called a Township Mistress [*xiangjun*].

In the establishment of the Prince of Jingjiang all the addresses will be lowered one degree in comparison with a Commandery Prince. His daughters shall be invested as District Mistresses.

69. Whenever the heir of an imperial prince inherits the fief the court shall send someone to perform the appointment ceremony and give them the gold tablet and pass on the gold seal.

70. Whenever the heir of an imperial prince or a commandery prince marries, or when a commandery prince is enfeoffed or the oldest son of the wife of a commandery prince succeeds to the title, the court shall first be informed so that someone can be sent to perform the appointment ceremony.

71. For descendants of commandery princes who have civil or military ability and are employable the Imperial Clan Court shall report their names to the court so they can be examined and assigned to posts. Promotion and transfer shall follow the regular rules. If there is a transgression the Imperial Clan Court shall investigate and report the facts to the throne. If it is a minor transgression then they shall be demoted in accordance with the evaluation of their guilt. If it is a serious transgression they shall be dismissed as commoners. Rewards and punishments shall be made clear, but there shall be no actual application of punishment.

72. Descendants of commandery princes are given titles:

Sons shall be made Defender-general of the State [*zhenguo jiangjun*].

Agnatic grandsons shall be made Bulwark-general of the State [*fuguo jiangjun*].

Agnatic great grandsons shall be made Supporter-general of the State [fengguo jiangjun].

Agnatic great-great grandsons shall be made Defender-commandant of the State [*zhenguo zhongwei*].

Fifth generation males shall be made Bulwark-commandant of the State [*fuguo zhongwei*].

Sixth generation males and below shall be made Supporter-commandant of the State [*fengguo zhongwei*].

73. In setting up the Imperial Clan Court the senior imperial prince shall be put in charge of Clan Court business. For secondary positions honored old high officials shall be employed. They shall take charge of the imperial tablets and geneologies, regulate the social distance, and maintain cordiality in the imperial clan. Should there be requests from the imperial family the matter shall be reported to the throne and await the emperor's command.

74. For the civil and military officials in the princely establishment, with the exception of the administrator, the garrison commander, and the guard

commander, who were all originally sent by the court, the guard commanders and the commanders of battalions and companies shall be succeeded by their sons and grandsons. The prince shall first issue a patent giving permission for the succession. Later he shall send someone to carry the patent to the capital for confirmation of the patent and appointment. It shall not be obstructed. Prefectural and district officials are all appointed by the court and are not to be employed by the princely establishment.

75. The military officers, the battalion and company commanders, of the princely establishment shall be chosen and employed by the prince from his military forces. Write down each individual's name and record. The prince shall personally sign the memorial. It shall not pass through the offices but be sent directly to the emperor and reported. The emperor's order shall be announced. Their salaries shall be the same as those for officials at the capital.

76. As to the prince's entourage or officials working in his fief, if the court wants to take them, the prince shall send them immediately, whether they are guilty or not. Delay is not permitted.

77. Officials of the princely establishment:

Administrator's Office [*zhangshi si*]
- 1 Left Administrator [*zuo zhangshi*] (5A)
- 1 Right Administrator [*you zhangshi*] (5A)
- 1 Archivist [*dianbu*] (9A)

Disciplinary Office [*shenli suo*]
- 1 Director [*shenli zheng*] (6A)
- 1 Vice Director [*shenli fu*] (7A)

Foods Office [*dianshan suo*]
- 1 Director [*dianshan zheng*] (8A)
- 1 Vice Director [*dianshan fu*] (8B)

Sacrificial Office [*fengci suo*]
- 1 Director [*fengci zhang*] (8A)
- 1 Vice Director [*fengci fu*] (8A)
- 1 Manager of Music [*dianyue*] (9A)

Seals Office [*dianbao suo*]
- 1 Director [*dianbao zheng*] (8A)
- 1 Vice Director [*dianbao fu*] (8B)

Moral Mentor's Office [*jishan suo*]
- 2 Moral Mentors [*jishan*] (8A)

Medical Office [*liangyi suo*]
- 1 Director [*liangyi zheng*] (8A)
- 1 Vice Director [*liangyi fu*] (8B)

Ceremonies Office [*dianyi suo*]
- 1 Director [*dianyi zheng*] (9A)
- 1 Vice Director [*dianyi fu*] (9B)
- 3 Household Receptionists [*yinli sheren*] (not civil service)

Construction Office [*gongzheng suo*]
1 Director [*gong zheng*] (8A)
1 Vice Director [*gong fu*] (8B)
4 Reader-companions [*bandu*] (9B)
Instructor [*jiaoshou*] (9B)
Storehouse[*ku*]
1 Commissioner [*dashi*] (not civil service)
1 Vice Commissioner [*fushi*] (not civil service)

78. Guard Commands [*zhihui shi si*]. (The officers of these commands and their subordinate officers are established without numerical limitation according to how many troops there are. Rank and salary are all the same as guard units at the capital.)

Guard Commander [*zhihui shi*]
Vice Commander [*tongzhi*]
Assistant Commander [*qianshi*]
Registry [*jingli si*]
Registrar [*jingli*]
Administrative Clerk [*zhishi*]
Guard Prison [*wei zhenfusi*]
Judge [*zhenfu*]
Battalion [*qianhu suo*]
Battalion commander [*zheng qianhu*]
Assistant commander [*fu qianhu*]
Battalion Prison [*suo zhenfu*]
Judge
Company [*baihu suo*]
Commander [*baihu*]
Ceremonial Guard [*yiwei si*]
Director [*yiwei zheng*] (5A)
Deputy Director [*yiwei fu*] (5B)
6 Managers of Ceremonial Regalia [*dianzhang*] (6A)

XI. MILITARY GUARDS

79. The guard for the princely establishments shall have 3 commanders, 6 battalion commanders, 6 company commanders, and 672 regular soldiers. They shall guard the four gates of the prince's compound. Every three days there shall be a rotation back to their camp. The commanders, battalion commanders, company commanders, and soldiers shall be equally divided among the three guard units.

80. When imperial princes come to court their heirs shall govern their fiefs.

81. When imperial princes come to court, the number of their accompanying civil and military officials, cavalry and foot soldiers, is not limited. If

the princes fear that the cost of supplying the retinue is too heavy, they are permitted to reduce them. It is important that their soldiers, body guards, colors, and arms manifest a stern manner in order to make an impression on officials and commoners.

82. Whenever the court moves troops there must be a letter bearing the imperial seal to the prince as well as a letter bearing the imperial seal to the garrison commander. When the garrison commander receives the letter bearing the imperial seal and so also the prince's order, then he may send out his soldiers. If there is no prince's order, he shall not send out his soldiers. If the court has only sent an imperial letter to the garrison commander, but there is no imperial letter to the prince, the garrison commander shall urgently inform the prince. The prince shall speedily send an emissary to the capital who shall report directly to the emperor. If there are any who engage in obfuscation or delay they shall be considered treacherous persons and decapitated without question.

83. Every princely fief has garrison forces and escort guards. The garrison forces are recruited regularly and controlled by their commanders. The escort guards move on order of the prince. If the fief is in a strategic area, and if there is a state of emergency, the garrison forces and the escort guards shall both move on the order of the prince.

84. Princes shall not show favor to garrison soldiers. When the soldiers of their escort guards are worthy of reward the princes may do as they wish.

85. Hunting expeditions and military maneuvers by the princes may be undertaken starting in the tenth month and ending by the third month.

86. Each princely establishment shall be given six sets of boat and horse tallies for the prince's messengers to use in reporting to the throne.

87. Princes shall train their troops ten times a month or seven or eight times or else five or six times. If there is an emergency or the princes have time to spare then there need be no limit.

88. Military equipment for imperial princes:

1 pair command flags [*lingqi*]
2 pair road clearers [*qingdao*][45]
1 ceremonial cross-bow [*xiannu*][46]
1 pair *baize* flags[47]
10 pairs two-pointed lances [*ji*][48]
10 pairs long lances [*shuo*][49]
20 sets bows [*gong*] and arrows [*jian*]
10 pairs swords [*dao*] and shields [*dun*]

---

45 I assume that these are the flags used by those who clear the way for a procession.

46 ZWDCD, 9344.2. In this and following notes an entry number is given rather than a page number.

47 ZWDCD, 23191.1049.

48 ZWDCD, 11883.

49 ZWDCD, 24415.

1 pair red streamers [*jiangyinfan*][50]
2 small drums [*ganggu*]
2 bells [*jinzheng*][51]
2 bell flags [*jinguqi*][52]
24 decorated drums [*huakuanggu*]
12 decorated horns [*huajiao*][53]
1 string of clappers [*ban*][54]
2 flutes [*di*][55]
2 gongs [*luo*][56]
1 time beater [*jie*][57]
1 pair long lances [*jiashuo*]
1 pair stopping streamers [*gaozhifan*][58]
1 pair command streamers [*chuanjiaofan*][59]
1 pair insignia streamers [*xinfan*][60]
1 pair music stoppers [*xizhu*][61]
4 flutes [*di*]
4 horns [*touguan*][62]
12 double drums [*zhanggu*][63]
1 string of clappers [*ban*]
1 big drum [*dagu*]
4 pairs resonant beaters [*xiangjie*]
1 decorated gilt umbrella [*hongxiaojinsan*]
1 red embroidered umbrella [*hongxiusan*]
2 curved parasols [*qugai*][64]
4 square umbrellas [*fangsan*]
1 pair tasseled lances [*jichang*][65]
1 pair spears [*gechang*][66]
1 pair tasseled halberds [*yihuang*][67]

---

50 ZWDCD, 28051.4.
51 ZWDCD, 41049.863.
52 WDCD, 41049.823.
53 ZWDCD, 15829.317.
54 ZWDCD, 14892.
55 ZWDCD, 15829.317.
56 ZWDCD, 15829.317.
57 ZWDCD, 26874.
58 ZWDCD, 3494.6.
59 ZWDCD, 1040.147.
60 ZWDCD, 653.223.
61 ZWDCD, 11960.7.
62 ZWDCD, 44453.62, indicates that this instrument was identified with a non-Han people.
63 ZWDCD, 14804.39.
64 ZWDCD, 14610.227.
65 ZWDCD, 11883.27.
66 ZWDCD, 11800.39.
67 ZWDCD, 1181.114.

1 pair forked spears [*shucha*]
4 pairs ceremonial swords [*yidao*][68]
1 pair dress swords [*banjian*][69]
1 pair wooden staffs [*wuzhang*]
1 pair vertical melon staffs [*ligua*][70]
1 pair horizontal melon staffs [*wogua*]
1 pair round end staffs [*guduo*][71]
1 pair looped staffs [*dengzhang*][72]
1 pair axes [*fu*]
1 pennant [*tong*][73]
1 standard [*hui*][74]
8 ceremonial horses [*danma*]
1 ceremonial stool [*mawu*][75]
1 ceremonial saddle [*anlong*]
1 ceremonial chair [*jiaoyi*][76]
1 foot rest [*jiaota*][77]
1 water jug [*shuiguan*][78]
1 water pan [*shuipen*][79]
1 incense burner [*xianglu*][80]
1 incense box [*xianghe*][81]
2 whisks [*fuzi*][82]
6 pairs ceremonial fans [*shan*]
1 covered pot [*tuohu*][83]
1 covered vessel [*tuoyu*][84]

XII. CONSTRUCTION

89. Princes' palaces shall be built according to the established style. Rules shall not be violated. Yan shall use old Yuan buildings. When sons

---

[68] ZWDCD, 1181.1.
[69] ZWDCD, 21438.89.
[70] ZWDCD, 26299.53.
[71] ZWDCD, 46084.11.
[72] ZWDCD, 41773.2.
[73] ZWDCD, 9276.
[74] ZWDCD, 48878.
[75] ZWDCD, 45550.224.
[76] ZWDCD, 294.192.
[77] ZWDCD, 30379.39.
[78] ZWDCD, 17458.890.
[79] ZWDCD, 17458.339.
[80] ZWDCD, 45496.392.
[81] ZWDCD, 45496.213.
[82] ZWDCD, 12198.2.
[83] ZWDCD, 3937.12.
[84] ZWDCD. 3937.5.

and agnatic grandsons multiply it is permitted to construct small courtyards and palaces for them.

Prince of Qin's establishment	Xi'an
Prince of Jin's establishment	Taiyuan
Prince of Yan's establishment	Beiping[85]
Prince of Zhou's establishment	Kaifeng
Prince of Chu's establishment	Wuchang
Prince of Qi's establishment	Qingzhou
Prince of Lu's establishment	Yanzhou
Prince of Shu's establishment	Chengdu
Prince of Xiang's establishment	Jingzhou
Prince of Dai's establishment	Datong
Prince of Su's establishment	Gansu
Prince of Liao's establishment	Guangning
Prince of Qing's establishment	Ningxia
Prince of Ning's establishment	Daning
Prince of Min's establishment	Yunnan
Prince of Gu's establishment	Xuanfu
Prince of Han's establishment[86]	
Prince of Shen's establishment	
Prince of An's establishment	
Prince of Tang's establishment	
Prince of Ying's establishment	
Prince of Yi's establishment	

90. In princes' palaces it is not permitted to have detached palaces, separate halls, terraces and pavilions, and places of amusement. For the heir apparent who manages the affairs of the empire it is even less permissible to erect detached palaces, separate halls, terraces and pavilions, and places for amusement.

XIII. PROVISIONS

91. When imperial princes come to court each year they shall supply their own food. Their civil and military entourages shall supply their own traveling expenses and fodder for their horses. It is not allowed to make requisitions from the offices for fear it would cause trouble.

92. The total income of the imperial princes shall be counted out and made available at the end of the tenth month. The salaries of the establishment's civil officials and functionaries and the military pay shall all be issued monthly, not later than the fifth of each month. If the soldiers lack ar-

[85] Beiping, "the north pacified," was the name given to Dadu after the defeat of the Yuan (Farmer 1976, 39).

[86] The younger princes listed from here on had not yet been assigned fiefs when this document was written.

mor or weapons, the responsible officials shall pay them according to the number originally stipulated. It is not necessary to memorialize the court every time. Those who dare to refuse requests and cause delays shall be decapitated.

93. The money and grain of the imperial prince shall be paid out by the treasury of the princely establishment on schedule according to established regulations. It is not permitted to send communications to that office and it is not permitted to constantly memorialize. If the court bestows an additional award that is not to be figured in the limits of the fixed regulations.

94. The annual allowance for all imperial princes, commandery princes, sons of princes, agnatic grandsons of princes, imperial princesses and commandery princesses is as follows:

Imperial prince [*qinwang*] (In the Tang system the annual grant was 4,800 piculs of grain, 4,800 rolls of silk, and 450 catties of cotton. In the Song system the annual grant for the Concurrent Supply Commissioner [*lingjiedushi*] was 2,400 piculs of grain, 4,800 strings of cash, 200 rolls of coarse silk, 100 rolls of fine silk, 10 rolls of silk gauze, and 500 ounces of cotton):

Now it is set at 10,000 piculs of rice.

Commandery Prince [*junwang*] (In the Tang system the annual grant was 700 piculs of rice and 60 *qing* of land. In the Song system the annual grant for Concurrent Surveillance Commissioner [*lingquanchashi*] was 1,200 piculs of mi!let, 2,400 strings of cash, 20 rolls of coarse silk, and 50 ounces of cotton):

Now it is set at 2,000 piculs of rice.

Defender-general of the State [*zhenguo jiangjun*] (In the Tang system the annual grant was 600 piculs of rice and 50 *qing* of land. In the Song system sons of commandery princes and below were given offices according to ability. They were paid according to the ranks of their offices):

Now it is set at 1,000 piculs of rice.

Bulwark-general of the State [*fuguo jiangjun*] (In the Tang system the annual grant was 500 piculs of rice and 40 *qing* of land):

Now it is set at 800 piculs of rice.

Supporter-general of the State [*fengguo jiangjun*] (In the Tang system the annual grant was 400 piculs of rice and 25 *qing* of land):

Now it is set at 600 piculs of rice.

Defender-commandant of the State [*zhenguo zhongwei*](In the Tang system the annual grant was 300 piculs of rice and 14 *qing* of land):

Now it is set at 400 piculs of rice.

Bulwark-commandant of the State [*fuguo zhongwei*] (In the Tang system the annual grant was 200 piculs of rice and 8 *qing* of land):

Now it is set at 300 piculs of rice.

Supporter-commandant of the State [*fengguo zhongwei*] (In the Tang system the annual grant was 100 piculs of rice):

Now it is set at 200 piculs of rice.

Imperial Princess [*gongzhu*] and consort [*fuma*]: a stipend of 2,000 piculs of rice.

Commandery Princess [*junzhu*] and consort: a stipend of 800 piculs of rice.

District Princess [*xianzhu*] and consort: a stipend of 600 piculs of rice.

Commandery Mistress [*junjun*] and consort: a stipend of 400 piculs of rice.

District Mistress [*xianjun*] and consort: a stipend of 300 piculs of rice.

Township Mistress [*xiangjun*] and consort: a stipend of 200 piculs of rice.

95. As for the non-senior sons of the heir apparent by his wife and the sons by his concubines, after they have been enfeoffed as princes, they must wait until they have left the palace to be granted an annual stipend the same as that for the sons of imperial princes who have been enfeoffed as commandery princes. As for daughters, they must wait until they marry to be granted an annual stipend the same as that for the daughters of imperial princes who have married.

96. When the oldest son of the wife of a commandery prince inherits the prince's fief, his annual grant shall be reduced by one-half from that of the originally enfeoffed commandery prince.

APPENDIX TWO

THE GREAT MING COMMANDMENT[1] [*DA MING LING*][2]

CONTENTS:[3]

I. PERSONNEL REGULATIONS[4]

---

[1] I have chosen the word "commandment" as a translation for primarily to avoid confusion with the English word "statute," which is reserved for individual articles (*lü*) in the *Ming Code* (*Da Ming lü*) or just "*Code*" in this translation. In the body of the text, however, I often render *ling* as "regulation." Ordinance" is another term that might have been used for *ling*. In the end, commandment seemed better because it suggests the meaning of *ling* as a positive order, a meaning alluded to in the opening lines of the document. Readers should be aware that *ling* in other dynasties might be translated with a word other than commandment. By the same token, one should not assume that the *ling* of the Ming dynasty was a precise equivalent of all other *ling* in Chinese history.

[2] This translation was originally drafted using the text as it appears in the Taibei edition of the HMZS. Later, it was revised using the Tokyo edition of the HMZS. The Tokyo edition has a table of variants at the end of volume 2.

[3] I have assigned a continuous set of numbers to the articles for convenience in referring to the contents. The numbering and names of articles do not agree in all respects with the table of contents printed in the Tokyo edition of HMZS. In trying to devise titles which will suggest the contents of each article I have changed a number of the renderings previously published in "Social Order in Early Ming China: Some Norms Codified in the Hung-wu Period" (Farmer 1987, 28-32).

[4] The contents of the *Commandment* are organized according to the categories of the six ministries. This organization is a prominent feature of Ming legal codification, especially in the *Ming Code*. The ministry names, which are also functional categories, are always ranked in the same order, reflecting their relative standing, i.e., the importance of the functions in the scheme of government. They are Personnel [*li*], followed in descending order by Revenue [*hu*], Rites [*li*], War [*bing*], Justice [*xing*], and Works [*gong*].

12. Redemption of punishment for public crimes
13. Officials in mourning
14. Officials completing term
15. Triennial review of officials
16. Voluntarily confessing public crimes
17. Evaluation and promotion of officials
18. Terms of service for functionaries
19. Upgrading of functionaries in high offices
20. The status of functionaries

II. REVENUE REGULATIONS

21. Surrender by unregistered persons
22. Inheritance
23. Arranged marriage
24. Adopted heirs
25. Widows
26. Sons-in-law marrying in
27. Property without heir
28. Conditions governing divorce
29. Taxation on sale of property
30. Exceptions to corvee obligation
31. Honoring of chaste widows
32. Registering travelers at inns
33. Taxation on brewer's grain
34. Registering households by category
35. Restriction on splitting the family
36. Avoiding land tax
37. Mourning by officials succeeding their grandfathers
38. Official purchases
39. Prohibiting unauthorized taxation
40. Official weights and measures
41. Registration of sales of land and transfer of tax obligation
42. Aid to single persons
43. Betrothal of the unborn
44. Delivery of government supplies

III. RITES REGULATIONS

45. Protocol for court audiences
46. Style of congratulatory memorials
47. Official robes
48. Officials leaving office to care for grandparents
49. Recognition of the virtuous

50. Grades of mourning dress
51. Sumptuary gradations
52. Ordinary dress for ceremonies in rain and snow
53. Marriages of commoners to follow Zhu Xi's *Family Ritual*
54. Students in national university
55. Rewarding children of meritorious officials
56. Sacrifices to three Sage Kings
57. Sacrifices to the Spirits of Nature
58. Sacrifices to Zhou dynasty founders
59. Sacrifices to Confucius
60. Enfeoffment
61. Granting titles to meritorious officers

IV. MILITARY REGULATIONS

62. Guards and jailers
63. Waterway stations' boats and personnel
64. Express stations' equipment and personnel
65. Plunder
66. Impressment and enlistment for military service
67. Military information
68. Retainers and baggage for traveling officials
69. Fortifications and storehouses
70. Traveling rations
71. Issuance of travel passes
72. Issuance of provisions

V. JUSTICE REGULATIONS

73. Five punishments
74. Ten abominations
75. Eight deliberations
76. Redemption
77. Penal instruments
78. Level of jurisdiction
79. Unauthorized investigation of staff supervisor
80. Duties of prefectural judges
81. Administration of prisons
82. Split jurisdiction
83. Accusations
84. Assault and battery
85. Interrogation of prisoners
86. Interrogation of capital cases
87. Jurisdiction over crimes by officials

88. Jurisdiction over crimes by military officers
89. Double crimes
90. Accusations of the old or the disabled
91. Interrogation and punishment for sexual crimes by women
92. Officials on missions prohibited from hearing cases
93. Surveillance of ex-prisoners
94. Rewards for capture of robbers and thieves
95. Voluntary confession
96. Demotion of officials for crimes
97. Autopsy reports
98. Joint robbery or theft by family members
99. Voluntary confession of robbers and thieves
100. Calculating value of ill-gotten goods
101. Evaluating the ill-gotten goods in multiple thefts
102. Accusation of crimes which took place before an amnesty
103. Voluntary return of stolen property
104. Thieves killed by victims
105. Magistrates redeeming minor punishments
106. Confiscation of property
107. Records of accusations
108. Reduction of degree of punishment
109. Penal servitude and life exile under amnesty
110. Shielding crimes of family members
111. Burial money for murder victims
112. Bribe-taking in previous assignment
113. Family members accompanying criminals in life exile
114. Calculating the value of ill-gotten goods
115. Confiscation of ill-gotten goods
116. Requests to waive autopsy
117. Confession by family members
118. Punishment of Buddhist and Daoist clergy
119. Joint crimes by family members
120. Prohibiting confiscation of ancestral tombs
121. Confiscation in the event of an amnesty
122. Amnesty for killing sons and grandsons
123. Thieves exempted from branding
124. Crimes not covered by amnesties
125. Crimes by military personnel
126. Crimes involving ill-gotten goods by military officers
127. Calculating value of bribes
128. Butchering cattle and horses
129. Docking official salaries
130. Testifying against family members
131. Crimes by members of households of high officials

132. Provisional imperial rescripts on crimes
133. Slander
134. Effectiveness of Code and Commandment
135. Prisons
136. Age and health status of criminals
137. Women in legal proceedings
138. False accusations
139. Conversion of punishment for false accusations
140. Avoiding conflict of interest in hearing cases
141. Penal servitude
142. Life exile destinations for officials
143. Penal servitude destinations for village [li] heads

VI. WORKS REGULATIONS

144. Manufacture of military equipment
145. Manufacturing of cloth

THE GREAT MING COMMANDMENT

Hongwu first year, first month, 18th day [February 6, 1368], an imperial decree was received:

I consider the codes and commandments to be devices for ruling the realm.[5] The commandments instruct before the fact, and the codes regulate after the fact.[6] In ancient times the laws were extremely simple, but in later ages they gradually became numerous to the point where there were some laws which no one could understand. How could the people be made to know the intent of the law and not go against it? When it is difficult for people to know, that opens the way to treachery by officials and functionaries who entrap the people with laws. I feel the greatest commiseration with them. The *Code* and *Commandment* fixed today replace multiplicity with simplicity and achieve consistency. The contents will be directly stated so that everyone can easily understand and violations will be prevented. The *Book of Documents* [*Shu jing*] says: "Use punishment so as to do away with punishment."[7] If the whole realm observes the *Commandment* and is not punished by the *Code*, the resultant setting aside of punishments will not be hard to achieve. Be it therefore ordered that they shall be promulgated throughout the realm. Let you subjects realize my intent. Respect this [*qin ci*].

THE GREAT MING COMMANDMENT

I. PERSONNEL REGULATIONS

1. If there are personnel in the official ranks, who have a special talent for civil or military affairs, and who have a thorough knowledge of administration, and who are morally upright, the censors shall report all the facts about such persons to the court.[8]

2. All official personnel, either in the capital or in the provinces, may be allowed to retire when they reach the age of seventy. Those assigned by special imperial decrees shall not be constrained by this limit.

---

[5] The author here is Zhu Yuanzhang, founding emperor of the Ming dynasty.

[6] The distinction is between the *ling* (*Commandment*) and the *lü* (*Code*).

[7] The reference is to the Shujing, "Counsels of the Great Yu" [Da Yu mu], item 11. The passage is translated into English by James Legge (1960, vol. 3, 58-59), and into French and Latin by S. Couvreuer, S.J., (1927, 36-37). In the passage quoted, the minister of justice is being praised for using punishments [*xing*] is such a way as to promote popular virtue and thus to reduce the future need for punishment.

[8] This article directs officials to act in a certain manner, but no punishments are stipulated. The larger part of the *Commandment* has such a character; it more often takes the form of an administrative regulation than of a penal code.

3. As for all the officials and functionaries, in offices at the capital or provincial levels, if there are those who are fathers and sons, brothers, or uncles and nephews the junior must practice avoidance.

4. Regular officials, in the assignment of office, all must practice avoidance of their native places.

5. As for officials of all the prefectures, subprefectures and districts, increasing the population under their jurisdiction and opening up land for farming are the most important duties. Their administrative accomplishments must be thoroughly evaluated by the investigating censors or the provincial surveillance office and the facts reported as a basis for demotion or promotion.[9]

6. In every office a staff foreman [*sili*][10] shall be appointed. Under every staff foreman two writers [*tieshu*] may be assigned.

Yingtian Prefecture:[11] 16 staff foremen
Other prefectures, using autumn grain tax for quota:[12]
200,000-plus piculs, 14
100,000-plus piculs, 10
Less than 100,000 piculs, 8
Subprefectures, using autumn grain tax for quota:
100,000 plus piculs, 10
50,000 plus piculs, 8
Less than 50,000 piculs, 6
Districts, regardless of tax quota, 6

7. Whenever the official in charge of a prefecture, subprefecture or district takes office he must take the total figures for population and land tax handed over by the previous official and first report them to superiors for transmission to the Secretariat to be used as a basis for evaluation.

8. In the public business of all offices both capital and provincial, small matters must be concluded within five days, medium matters within seven days, and large matters within ten days. All must be concluded within the limits. If the matter involves joint consultation with officials in other jurisdictions, or surveying land, then it shall not be constrained by the normal limits.

---

[9] Investigating censor [*jiancha yushi*] and provincial surveillance office [*ancha si*] are standard renderings for office titles suggested by Charles O. Hucker (1985). I have made an effort to follow Hucker's suggestions in most cases.

[10] In this and subsequent entries I will simply indicate the romanization following the translation of an official title. For the Chinese characters see the glossary; for the translation see Hucker (1985).

[11] Yingtian [lit. "Responding to Heaven"] Prefecture was the seat of government at Nanjing. By giving this name to his capital the Ming founder implied that he enjoyed the mandate of heaven. Administratively, Yingtian Prefecture was directly under the control of the central government.

[12] Administrative divisions were classified according to the size of the tax quota they were expected to collect annually. Picul [*shi* or *dan*] is a dry measure of grain equal to 103.55 liters.

9. The public business of all offices both central and provincial shall be checked daily by clerks [*yuanli*] for mistakes and scrutinized by staff supervisors [*shouling guan*] every ten days. In every province the inspectors [*jianjiao guan*] inspect once each season. Tardy matters shall be carried out as circumstances permit. Errors shall be corrected according to precedent.

10. When the officials and functionaries of any office are involved in disputes over such matters as marriage, debts, or land, family members may plead the case. It is not permitted to make an unauthorized official report. Those who disobey ought to be punished according to the article on Improper Conduct.[13]

11. The Rotation Section [*xingzhi ke*] of the Personnel Department [*lifang*] of the Secretariat [*zhongshu sheng*][14] should establish a register with a serial number on each page, with a clerk [*yuandian*] assigned to it and a staff supervisor to oversee it. Concerning assigned officials, record the following information: their ancestors for three generations, their examination year and ranking, their native place, their career history, arrival in office, completion of term, replacement, reassignment dates, and rank; each shall be recorded in detail for reference purposes. Those who make omissions shall be punished according to the *Code*.

12. When a review of files reveals that an official of any office has committed a public crime [*gongzui*][15] through delay or mismanagement, and the official has been relieved or transferred before punishment has been carried out, he may be permitted to redeem his punishment by paying a fine. Those who are in mourning for parents, retired or cashiered shall not be prosecuted.

13. Officials who are in mourning for parents and commit crimes involving ill-gotten goods [*zangzui*][16] and government money and grain shall be arrested and prosecuted according to the *Code*, but those who commit public crimes shall be exempted from prosecution.

14. When officials in any place have completed their terms of office they must promptly remove their families from their official residences, and personally report to the Secretariat. On the second day he will be escorted to

[13] "Improper Conduct" [*buyingwei*] is a catchall term for actions not covered by a specific statute but which, on principle, ought not to be done. See *Code*, article 410.

[14] The Secretariat was a central administrative organ in the early Ming. It was abolished in 1380 when the highest executive offices were eliminated. See Hucker (1985, 72).

[15] A distinction is made between "public crimes" [*gongzui*] committed in the course of performing official duties and "private crimes" [*sizui*] committed outside the round of official duties. See *Code*, articles 7 and 8.

[16] The Chinese term *zangzui* refers to crimes involving ill-gotten goods [*zang*] of which there are six classes: embezzlement of government money and grain by those responsible [*jianshoudao*], making unjust decisions in exchange for bribes [*wangfa*], embezzlement of money and grain by those not having responsibility [*changrendao*], bribe taking without making an unjust decision [buwangfa], theft [*qiedao*], and various other manners of receiving ill-gotten goods [*zuozang*]. See "Table of the Six Categories of Ill-gotten Goods," *Code*, 1623-1626.

an audience. If he comes, but the responsible department fails to escort him to an audience, the department shall be punished.

15. The responsible officials in each prefecture, subprefecture and district, after serving for three years, shall not be relieved without cause before the term is up. After three years in office they may personally carry the records of their administrations to the capital for an imperial audience. If there are no shortcomings or transgressions they may continue to serve. Assistant magistrates [*zuoerguan*] and staff supervisors should all come together to the capital every three years. If there is urgent business, then they can rotate their coming.

16. Those who discover and report mistakes in public business shall be exempt from punishment. When colleagues are implicated together and one person discovers and reports the matter, the others shall be exempt from punishment. If the case is wrongly judged and the punishment carried out, this article does not apply.

17. All civil officials in the capital shall undergo evaluation once every thirty months. At every evaluation they shall be raised one step. For officials outside the capital, three years constitutes a term of duty. After every term they should be raised one step. First, from those who have completed their service and been certified, appoint all those selected. Next come those recommended for their talent. Rank four officials at step A or step B will not be differentiated on the basis of capital or provincial posting and will be raised after sixty months to rank three. Those rank three officials of step A or step B who, without decision by the authorities, receive promotion and appointment from the emperor to the second rank or above, shall be assigned prestige titles in accord with their rank. As for the others, even though the post is nominally higher, the prestige title shall remain at their original rank.

18. As for the Secretariat, the Chief Military Commission [*da dudu fu*], the Tribunal of Censors [*yushi tai*], and all the offices at the capital and, in the provinces, the branch secretariats and provincial surveillance offices, all the clerks [*yuan, lingli, shuli*], seal keepers [*zhiyin*], couriers [*xuanshi*], agents [*zouchai*], clerks [*dianli*], writers [*tieshu*][17] and the subordinate office functionaries shall be employed for a term of thirty months.

19. In the Secretariat, the Chief Military Commission, the Tribunal of Censors, and the branch secretariats in the provinces, government functionaries who have held the position of staff supervisor [*shouling*] without transgression for ninety months are qualified for appointment as a probationary official.

[17] Despite the fact that more than one term is rendered as clerk I have followed Hucker's translations in preference to introducing new terms. I assume that the term *lingli* is a scribal error for *lingshi* (Hucker 1985, 315), which occurs below in article 51.

20. In all offices the seal keeper, courier, and agent are considered as functionaries [*li*]. Functioning officials assigned as functionaries and staff supervisors [*shouling guan*] in each office who have not attained regular ranks shall all be considered the same.

II. REVENUE REGULATIONS

21. Those households and persons omitted from the records may proceed to the local official office to surrender. Their crimes shall be pardoned and they shall be registered and assume labor service duties.

22. The family's property and land is divided equally among sons of the wife or others according to their numbers without regard to whether they were born of the wife, a concubine, or a slave, with the exception of beneficiaries of official protection, in which case preference shall be given to the eldest son and grandson of the wife. Bastard sons shall get half the portion of a son. In other cases, if there is no other son, an appropriate successor shall be designated heir, to share equally with the bastard sons. If there is no appropriate successor they may inherit the entire amount.

23. All marriages shall be arranged by the paternal grandparents or parents. If there are neither paternal grandparents nor parents, another relative shall do the arranging. If after her husband dies the wife remarries and takes her daughter with her, the mother alone shall arrange the daughter's marriage. If the boy or girl dies after an engagement but before the wedding takes place, the gifts need not be returned. If the betrothed boy is a robber or commits crimes punishable by penal servitude [*tu*], life exile [*liu*], or relocation [*yixiang*][18] so that the girl's family wishes to break the engagement, they may return the betrothal gifts. If a betrothed girl commits fornication, once the punishment is carried out, and the boy's family wishes to break the engagement, the betrothal gifts must be returned. If after five years for no reason the boy does not marry the girl, or if the husband disappears and does not return for three years, it is permitted to go to the officials, to request and receive approval, and to marry someone else. In such cases, the betrothal gifts need not be returned.

24. Those who have no sons may designate a nephew from the same lineage [*zong*] and the appropriate generation [*zhaomu*][19] to become their heir. First exhaust the closest relatives with a common father and next the circle of nine-month [*dagong*], five month [*xiaogong*] and three month [*sima*] mourning relatives.[20] If there is none among all of these, then it is permitted to select from among distant relatives anyone with the same sur-

---

[18] Relocation was to be used as a substitute for other punishments following an amnesty.

[19] *Zhaomu* refers to the order of tablets in the ancestral temple and thus connotes proper generational sequence.

[20] For definitions of the grades of mourning see article 50, below.

name to name an heir. If, after designating an heir, a natural son is born, the family property shall be evenly divided with the originally designated heir. In no case is it allowed to raise someone of a different surname as an heir. To do so would disrupt the clan system. When someone of the same surname is designated, the generational hierarchy may not be violated in a way which would disrupt the generational sequence.

25. In the event that a wife whose husband dies, leaving her without a son, wants to hold to her vows, and her husband's status ought to be continued, an heir of appropriate ancestry shall be selected by the clan head. When the wife is married a second time, the first husband's property and the original dowry shall both be disposed of by the former husband's family.

26. Marrying a son-in-law in to take the family surname must be done by a matchmaker. A marriage contract shall be drawn up, clearly stating the time limit for taking care of the parents-in-law or returning home. Those with only one son may not marry him out. Even if the son-in-law is contracted to take care of the parents in old age, there still should be someone designated from his wife's lineage to continue the rites. The family property shall be evenly divided. If he dies before a successor is designated it is up to the clan head to designate a successor according to the *Code*.

27. When a family is cut off, and there is no appropriate heir in the same lineage, the surviving daughters may inherit the property. If there are no daughters, the property shall go to the government.

28. Even though a wife meets one of the Seven Grounds for being divorced, she may not be discarded lightly if she meets one of the Three Restrictions precluding divorce. Adulterers are not covered by these limitations.

Seven Grounds for divorce:

no sons, lewdness, not serving parents-in-law,
talking too much, theft, jealousy,
incurable disease.

Three Restrictions on divorce:

the wife having done three years' mourning
the husband married poor, became rich
the wife no longer having a family to return to

29. In transactions involving land, houses, and livestock, taxes must be paid to relevant government offices.[21] In addition to the regular tax, a fee of forty *wen* cash shall be paid for every contract. Beyond this it is not permitted to make additional exactions.

30. Any subject who is beyond the age of eighty and has only one son, if he has property and owes labor service, is permitted to hire someone to take

[21] The phrase *wufutoushui* is apparently a transposition of *fuwutoushui* which occurs in article 33.

his place. Those without property may retain a supportive son and be excused from miscellaneous labor service.

31. If among the people there is a woman who was widowed before the age of thirty, who held to her vows and preserved her purity until she was past fifty, a commemorative gateway shall be erected for her family or neighborhood. Her household shall be excused from labor service.

32. Every month hostels shall submit a copy of their registers to the warden's office [*bingma si*] in the capital or the local official in the provinces for affixing seals. Each day write down the names, numbers, and dates of departure of merchants coming to the hostel. At the end of the month this shall be delivered to the officials for inspection. Should a merchant die at a hostel unaccompanied by a relative or personal subordinate, the officials [shall be] notified of the items of property. The official shall send notice to the father, brother, son, or wife of the deceased so as to identify and return the property. If, after a year, no one identifies the property, it shall be turned over to the government.

33. All persons who manufacture grain liquor for sale must pay taxes to government offices before they will be permitted to sell the goods. Violators will be punished for tax evasion. Those who make fermented rice for home consumption are not covered by this tax requirement. If a liquor-selling family does not have its own fermented rice and must buy fermented rice which has already been taxed, it will be taxed again according to the regulations when it is made into liquor and sold. If the fermented rice is produced by the wine maker himself, he must also pay tax to government offices on the fermented rice.

34. All military [*jun*], civilian [*min*], physician [*yi*], craftsman [*jiang*], geomancer [*yinyang*], and other categories of household shall permanently register according to what they originally reported. This may not be casually altered or confused. Violators will be punished. They must remain in their original registration.

35. Those sons and paternal grandsons whose grandparents or parents are living may not divide the wealth and reside separately. If father or grandfather permit the division then it is permissible.

36. All taxes among the people have regular quotas. It is not permitted to improperly present land, mountain groves, and kilns to princes, imperial in-laws, title holders, great officials, or government offices, which results in harm to the people. Offenders will be prosecuted.

37. All senior grandsons [*disun*][22] who have succeeded the grandfather and entered officialdom due to the protection privilege [*yin*] must observe

---

[22] The senior grandson [*disun*] denotes the senior son of ego's [the deceased's] senior son [*zhangzi*]. In both cases these sons are born of wives, not of concubines. This is a manifestation of the descent-line system (Ebrey 1991, xx-xxii).

three years mourning upon the grandfather's death. Those holding office must return home and observe full mourning. Violations shall be punished.

38. Civil and military officials in the capital and the provinces shall not harm the people in the name of mutually beneficial hiring or purchase [*hegu hemai*]. If there is something which an official lacks it may be purchased at a price appropriate to the season and fair to both sides. If a merchant comes selling goods, the price must be paid at once. If the price is improperly reduced or not immediately paid, let the investigating censor and the provincial surveillance office investigate, or the merchant may make a complaint to higher authorities. The transgressor should be punished according to the article on Improper Conduct.

39. Superior and inferior offices in the capital and the provinces may not levy taxes without written authorization from the Secretariat. The Secretariat also may not levy taxes without having received an imperial rescript.

40. In the matter of dry measures, scales, and linear measures, the Agricultural Propagation Office [*sinong si*][23] should manufacture them just like the iron peck [*dou*] and iron pint [*sheng*] sent down from the Secretariat, and issue them to the prefectures and subprefectures in the capital and present them to the Secretariat for distribution to the branch secretariats, which can manufacture similar ones according to these models and, after inspecting them for accuracy, distribute them to subordinate prefectures and subprefectures. The official [*zhengguan*] of every prefecture shall supervise the manufacture and inspection according to the model. These will then be issued to the granaries and storehouses of every subprefecture and district for use in receiving and paying. Brokers and shopkeepers must take them to the government office to have them branded with a seal. If the dry measures, scales, and linear measures of rural villagers are the same as the official prototypes, they may be used.

41. In the mortgage or sale of land which transfers tax obligation, each subprefecture and district should establish a register to record the transactions. The principal official should supervise keeping the register and recording the transactions promptly. At the end of the year they are combined into a master register and transmitted to the prefecture. Do not allow property to be sold and the tax obligation to remain with the original owner, thus harming the people.

42. Every month the officials shall issue a grain allowance of three pecks of rice to widowers, widows, orphans, and childless persons. Every year they shall be given a bolt of cotton cloth. It is essential is to care for them. Investigating censors and officials of the provincial surveillance office must constantly give close scrutiny to these matters.

---

[23] Hucker gives several renderings for *sinong si*, none of which quite fits here. I suggest Agricultural Propagation Office.

43. In the matter of marriage, men and women each have their appropriate age. The arrangement of marriage by the practice of pointing to the belly and cutting the front of the woman's garment is prohibited.[24]

44. In each locality officially requisitioned goods are to be delivered to the government, except for textiles which must be personally delivered by the head of the producing agency. For items such as military supplies and cloth, the people of the locality shall only be ordered to deliver to the district office. If the goods are numerous, seven days is the limit for the district office to inspect and receive the goods. The people shall be sent home promptly. It is not permitted to cause trouble and harass them. The government office supplies the labor and assigns official transport personnel to oversee delivery to the prefectural offices. Each prefecture should follow the same limitations to inspect, receive and forward to the branch secretariat. The branch secretariat should assign its official personnel to go together with the delivery personnel from the prefecture to transmit the entire amount to the Secretariat. The agencies concerned in each locality shall establish tallies and registers. In the event of a delivery, the authorized number of porters and boats shall be recorded and dispatched according to the amount of goods. Do not assign the community heads [*lizhang*] and taxpayers originally making the delivery to do the transporting. All violations shall be punished according to the article on Improper Conduct.

III. RITES REGULATIONS

45. In court audiences, officials shall be arranged according to rank and grade. Mistakes are not allowed. Those who disobey will be reprimanded by the censor in charge of deportment [*jiuyi guan*].

46. All congratulatory memorials must be written with elegant style and fine characters, signed, and sealed. It is not permitted to transgress by using taboo words. The wrapping, case, sealing, and presentation of the memorial should follow current ceremonial practice.

47. Civil and military officials must wear official robes corresponding to their own ranks and may not assume the robes of a higher rank.

a. All official robes button on the right.

Rank one: purple silk robe with large *duke* flowers[25] five inches across

Rank two: purple silk robe with small *duke* flowers three inches across

Rank three: purple silk robe with *sanda*[26] flowers two inches across

---

[24] On this expression for arranged marriage, *zhifu keshanjin*, see *Ciyuan*, 1: 363.

[25] *Dukehua* is identified in the ZWDZD, 21209.135, as a designation used for official gowns of the Yuan period.

[26] I have not found a definition for *sandahua*.

Ranks four and five: purple silk robes with small assorted flowers (one and a half inches across)

Ranks six and seven: dark red silk robe with small assorted flowers (one inch across)

Ranks eight and nine: green silk robe without flower pattern

Unranked officials: reddish-brown with green narrow body

b. All belts shall be made of red leather

Rank one: belt set with jade

Rank two: belt set with flowered rhinoceros hide

Ranks three and four: belt set with golden lichee pattern

Ranks five to nine: belt set with black horn

Unranked officials: girdles set with black horn

(all of the above shall use a ceremonial cap)

48. When officials request to leave office to care for agnatic grandparents who have reached the age of seventy, if there are no other able-bodied family members, the request shall be granted. Only after the relatives have died and the period of mourning has been fulfilled is it permitted to request reassignment.

49. The chief officials shall nominate for recognition filial sons and grandsons, righteous men and chaste wives [widows] who are outstanding in both resolve and action. The investigating censors and provincial surveillance officials shall personally review each case and report to their superiors. The magistrate shall erect a commemorative gateway for the family or neighborhood.

50. Gradations of mourning dress must follow the old system.[27]

a. Unhemmed sackcloth for three years (For the *zhancui* garment use the coarsest hemp cloth without a hem—that is called *zhancui*.)

A son for his father

The senior agnatic grandson who is the heir to the grandfather, for the grandfather (also applies to the heirs of great-grandfather or great-great-grandfather)

An unmarried daughter for her father (the same for engaged daughter)

A married daughter living in her father's home for her father (i.e., those who have been divorced within one year of the father's death)

A father for the oldest son of his wife [*dizi*][28]

[27] The mourning grades are defined in terms of the prescribed time period and dress required. Longer periods and coarser dress were required in observing the death of closer relatives in the male line of descent to which one was attached. The degree of mourning required of an individual for a potentially deceased relative was used in the law codes to determine the closeness of their relationship. This proximity, in turn, was used in calculating the severity of crimes and punishments. For a short account see Bodde and Morris (1973, 35-38); for a longer account see DeGroot (1894, 2: 493-566). Diagrams of kinship terminology can be found at the beginning of the *Code*; HMZS (Taibei edition), 4:1628-36.

A wife [*qi*][29] for her husband

A concubine [*qie*] for her master

For the husband's father

An adopted heir for his adopted father (i.e., one adopted as a son by a branch of the family for his adopted father)

b. Hemmed sackcloth for three years (The *zicui* garment is made of slightly finer hemp cloth with a hem on the lower border. This is called *zicui*.)

A son for his mother (even if the father survives)

An unmarried daughter for her mother (also applies to engaged daughter)

The heir of a deceased agnatic grandfather for the grandmother (the same applies to the heir of great-grandfather and great-great-grandfather)

A mother for her senior son [*zhangzi*][30]

A daughter, who has been married and returned home, for her mother (i.e., one who had been divorced within one year of the mother's death)

A wife for her husband's mother

A stepmother [*jimu*][31] is considered the same as a mother

A concubine acting as foster mother [*cimu*] is considered the same as the mother

A stepmother for the senior son

A concubine for her master's senior son

An adopted heir for his adopted mother (one adopted as a son by a branch of the family for the adopted mother)

c. Hemmed sackcloth and staff for a year

A son for a mother remarried after the death of the father or for a mother who has been divorced (the mourning clothes of a mother mourning her son would be the same)

An agnatic grandson and heir for his grandmother when the grandfather is still alive (the same applies to heirs of great-grandfather and great-great-grandfather)

A son after his father's death wears this garment for his father's wife, the stepmother, the concubine acting as foster mother, or the adoptive mother [*yangmu*][32] who has returned to her natal family. A son who has

---

[28] The term *dizi* denotes the eldest son born of ego's wife, not a concubine. I assume that the term *dizi* is here restricted to the eldest son and thus corresponds to the term *zhangzi* used below in section (b).

[29] The term *qi* is translated as wife, in contrast to *qie*, which is rendered concubine. In most cases kinship terms denote the offspring of wives and exclude those of concubines.

[30] The term *zhangzi* here designates the wife's oldest son. I assume that it designates the same person as the term *dizi* in section (a), above. See note 28.

[31] The term *jimu* is translated as stepmother, *cimu* as foster mother, and *yangmu* as adopted mother. These and other terms appear in the *Code*, 4: 1636

[32] See note 31.

followed his remarried mother to her new family wears this garment (the garment for such a mother mourning her son would be the same)

A husband for his wife

d. Hemmed sackcloth for a year

For agnatic grandparents (the same for the father's mother if she was a concubine)

For agnatic uncles and their wives

For brothers

For sons other than the senior one [*zhongzi*][33]

For the sons of brothers (the same for their unmarried daughters)

For the senior agnatic grandson

For the unmarried daughters of agnatic aunts and sisters (the same for those who have been married but are left without husband or son)

An unmarried daughter for her elder and younger brothers (an unmarried niece is the same)

A childless widow for her brothers and their sons (the same for their unmarried nieces and sisters)

A daughter for her agnatic grandparents (the same if she is married)

A concubine for her son

A concubine for her parents

The son of a concubine for his mother (i.e., the wife is still alive)

A married woman for her brother who is her father's heir

An adopted heir for his natural parents (the reciprocal mourning dress is the same)

A married woman for her parents

A concubine for her master's wife

[A stepson] for the stepfather if they reside together

A concubine for her master's sons other than the senior son

A husband's parents for their daughters-in-law

A woman for the children of her husband's brothers (male and female are the same)

e. Hemmed sackcloth for five months

For agnatic great-grandparents

A woman for her agnatic great-grandparents (the same if she is married)

f. Hemmed sackcloth for three months

For agnatic great-great-grandparents

A woman for her agnatic great-great-grandparents (the same if she is married)

For the stepfather when residing apart (i.e., formerly lived together but now are no longer living together)

---

[33] The term *zhongzi* denotes sons other than the senior son, *zhangzi* or *dizi*. It is not entirely clear whether *zhongzi* can include sons of concubines [*shuzi*], hence the formulation used here.

g. Greater coarseness for nine months (*Dagong* uses coarse cloth for the garment. For a death in late teens [*zhangshang*] it is nine months; for death in early teens [*zhongshang*] it is seven months.)[34]

For male cousins on the father's side (the same for unmarried female cousins)

For agnatic grandsons other than the senior one [*zhongsun*][35] (the same for unmarried granddaughters)

For married daughters

For married agnatic aunts and sisters

A married woman for her brothers and their sons (the same for unmarried agnatic aunts, sisters, or nieces)

A divorced mother for her daughters

An adopted heir for his natural brothers (reciprocal mourning dress the same)

A married woman for her agnatic uncles and their wives (reciprocal mourning dress the same)

An adopted heir for his natural unmarried agnatic aunts and sisters (reciprocal mourning dress the same)

For husband's agnatic grandparents

For husband's agnatic uncles and their wives

For the wives of brothers' sons

For the wives of husband's brothers' sons

When the husband is an adopted heir, his wife for his natural parents

For the wives of sons other than the senior one

For sons who die in late [*zhangshang*][36] or early [*zhongshang*] teens (male and female the same)

For father's younger brothers who die in late or early teens

For agnatic aunts and sisters who die in late or early teens

For brothers who die in late or early teens

For senior agnatic grandson who dies in late or early teens (same for great-grandson or great-great-grandson)

For brother's sons who die in late or early teens

For the sons of husband's brothers who die in late or early teens (males and females the same)

h. Lesser coarseness for five months (*Xiaogong* uses slightly coarse cloth. Death in youth [*shang*].)

For agnatic great uncles and their wives [ffb, ffbw]

For brother's agnatic grandson [bss][37]

---

[34] For definitions of terms referring to childhood and the teens see the end of article 50, below.

[35] The term *zhongsun* designates grandchildren through the male line born of wives and excluding the senior grandson.

[36] The following terms denote degrees of maturity. See explanatory text at the end of article 50.

[37] The Chinese terms often imply that a relative is connected through the male line of descent. Since the English terms are not specific on this point the modifier "agnatic" is added in a number

For brother's unmarried agnatic granddaughters [bsud]
For father's male agnatic cousins and their wives [ffbs, ffbsw]
For the sons of male agnatic cousins [fbss]
For the unmarried daughter of male agnatic cousins [fbsud]
For unmarried daughters and granddaughters of agnatic grandfather's brothers [ffbud, ffbsud] (reciprocal mourning dress the same)
For unmarried agnatic great aunts [ffusi] (reciprocal mourning dress the same)
For male agnatic second cousins[38]
For maternal grandparents [mf, mm]
For married agnatic female cousins [fbmad] (reciprocal mourning clothes the same)
For mother's brothers and sisters (reciprocal mourning dress the same)
An adopted heir for his married agnatic aunts and sisters [fmasi, masi] (reciprocal mourning dress the same)
For married agnatic granddaughters [smad]
For sons of husband's male agnatic cousins [hfbs]
For grandsons of husband's brothers [hbss]
Husband's brother's wives for each other
For husband's unmarried paternal aunts and sisters [hfsi, hsi] (a married one the same; mourning dress the same)
For father's wife's parents and siblings [fwf, fwm, fwb, fwsi]
For father's concubine who acted as one's foster mother
For the wife of the senior agnatic grandson [wswsw]
The son of a divorced mother for his stepmother's parents and siblings
For brother's wives (reciprocal mourning dress the same)
For sons and daughters dying in childhood [*xiashang*]
For father's younger brothers or any of his sisters, or one's own siblings dying in childhood
For senior agnatic grandsons dying in childhood [weswes]
For a non-senior agnatic grandsons dying in late teens (male and female the same)
For a brother's sons dying in childhood (male and female the same)
For agnatic cousins dying in late teens [fbs, fbd]
An adopted heir for his father's sisters and his own siblings dying in late teens
A married woman for her brother's sons dying in late teens (male and female the same)

---

of cases. Where more clarity is needed the relationship is represented in brackets by standard abbreviations [e.g., b=brother or brother's, c= concubine or concubine's, e=elder, f=father or father's, h=husband or husband's, m=mother or mother's, ma=married, s=son or son's, si=sister or sister's, u=unmarried, w=wife or wife's]. For a listing of such abbreviations see Feng (1948, 2).

[38] Those having a common paternal great-grandfather.

For husband's brother's sons dying in childhood (male and female the same)

For husband's father's younger brothers dying in late teens

i. Coarse hemp for three months (*sima* used is somewhat finer woven cloth)

For agnatic male third cousins [fffbsss]

For agnatic great-grandfather's brothers [fffb] and their wives

For brother's agnatic great-grandsons [bsss]

For grandfather's agnatic male first cousins [fffbs] and their wives

For brother's unmarried agnatic great granddaughters [bssud]

For daughter's sons (male and female the same)

For agnatic male cousin's grandsons [ffbss] (for agnatic male cousin's unmarried granddaughters [ffbsud] the same; if married no mourning)

For the sons of agnatic male second cousins [ffbss] (the same for the unmarried daughters of agnatic male second cousins; if married no mourning)

For agnatic great-grandsons or great-great-grandsons

For all children of mother's sisters

For sons of maternal uncles [mbs]

For sons of agnatic aunts [fsis]

For agnatic great-grandfather's unmarried sisters [fffusi] (reciprocal mourning dress the same)

For agnatic great-grandfather's brothers' unmarried daughters [fffbud] (reciprocal mourning dress the same)

For father's unmarried agnatic female second cousins [fffbsud] (reciprocal mourning dress the same)

For father's married agnatic female first cousins [ffbmd] and one's married agnatic female second cousins [ffbsmd] (reciprocal mourning dress the same)

A married woman for her father's agnatic first cousins [ffbs] and their wives (reciprocal mourning dress the same)

A son born of a concubine [*shuzi*] who has become his father's heir, for his mother

For married sisters of agnatic grandfather [ffmsi]

An adopted heir for his maternal grandparents

For brother's married agnatic granddaughters (reciprocal mourning dress the same)

For husband's brother's agnatic great-grandsons [hbss]

For husband's agnatic male first cousin's agnatic grandsons [hfbsss]

For husband's agnatic male second cousin's [hffbss] sons (male and female the same)

For wives of non-senior agnatic grandsons

For the father's concubines [*shumu*][39] (i.e., father's concubines who have sons)

For father's concubine who acted as one's wet nurse [*rumu*][40]

For wife's parents (reciprocal mourning dress is the same)

For husband's agnatic great-grandparents

For husband's agnatic grandfather's brothers [hffb] and their wives

For brother's agnatic grandsons' wives [bssw]

For husband's brother's agnatic grandsons' wives [hbssw]

For husband's grandfather's agnatic male first cousins [hfffbs] and their wives

For agnatic male first cousins' sons' wives [fbssw]

For sisters' sons' wives

For husband's maternal grandparents

For daughters' sons' wives

For agnatic male first cousins' wives [fbsw]

For husband's mother's brothers and sisters

For husband's agnatic male cousins' sons' wives [hfbssw]

For husband's agnatic male first cousins' wives [hfbsw]

For husband's agnatic female first cousins [hfbd], unmarried and married

For sisters' sons' wives

Son for parents; wife and concubine for husband while the body is being reburied; when it is finally buried this ends

For agnatic male or female first cousins who die in early teens or childhood

For non-senior grandsons dying in early teens or childhood (male and female the same)

For father's agnatic male cousins [ffbs] dying in late teens

For maternal uncles and aunts dying in late teens[41]

For agnatic male second cousins [ffbss] dying in late teens

For agnatic male cousins' sons [fbss] dying in late teens [bss]

For brothers' agnatic grandsons dying in late teens

For father's agnatic female first cousins [ffbd] and one's agnatic female second cousins [ffbsd] dying in late teens

An adopted heir for his natural brothers dying in early teens or childhood

A married woman for her brothers' sons dying in early teens or childhood (male and female the same)

---

[39] The term *shumu* denotes a concubine who has borne a child.

[40] The term *rumu* literally means wet nurse, but the chart "*Sanfu bamu*" in the *Code* (HMZSb, 4: 1636) makes it clear that a concubine status is implied.

[41] Here I assume that the character *zi*, sister, is a misprint for *yi*, aunt.

An adopted heir for his agnatic aunts and his own sisters dying in early teens or childhood

An adopted heir for his father's brothers or his own agnatic male first cousins [fbs] dying in late teens

For husband's father's younger brothers dying in early teens or childhood

For husband's agnatic aunts and sisters dying in late teens

According to the *Rituals* there are three [grades of] dying in youth. From age nineteen down to sixteen is called dying in late teens [*zhangshang*]. From fifteen down to twelve is called dying in early teens [*zhongshang*]. From eleven down to eight is called dying in childhood [*xiashang*]. For death in late or early teens, reduce the mourning garb from the formal requirement by one grade. For death in childhood,reduce the mourning garb from death in late or early teens, by one degree. As for the child of three to seven years, this is infant death, which does not require mourning clothes. Should a child have already taken a wife or been given in marriage then the mourning dress is the same as for an adult.

51. The clothing colors, hats, belts, houses, and saddles of the officials and commoners all have gradations. Superiors may also use that which is appropriate to an inferior; but inferiors may not usurp that which is appropriate to a superior. Official personnel who have completed their service and retired are subject to the same regulations as those still in service. If the father or agnatic grandfather was an official who died without committing a crime punishable by removal and exclusion from official service, the sons and grandsons may reside in the homes of their fathers and grandfathers.[42] Their clothing, horses and carriages shall be the same as their father's and grandfather's. Those who are officials shall follow the style appropriate to their rank. Imperial grants and the clothing color for military officers and military personnel are not bound by these restrictions.

a. Houses are not permitted to employ double brackets and double eaves. Multistory houses are not included in the double eaves limit. For officials of the first and second ranks, the main hall may have seven bays and nine trusses. In the ridges of the house it is permitted to use animal heads. The pillars, beams, posts, and rafters may be painted and decorated in green. The main gate may have three bays and five trusses; on the gate, use green paint and an animal-faced door knocker in brass. For the third to the fifth ranks the main hall may have five bays and seven trusses. It is permitted to use animal heads. Pillars, beams, posts, and rafters shall be jade green with decorations. The main gate is allowed three bays and three trusses; the gate shall be painted black with an animal-faced, tin knocker. For the sixth to the ninth ranks, the main hall may have three bays and seven trusses. The beams shall be painted brown. The main gate may have one bay and three

---

[42] For removal and exclusion from official service [*chumingbuxu*] see *Code*, article 14.

trusses, a black door with an iron knocker. The houses of commoners may not exceed three bays and five trusses. They may not use fancy brackets, variegated color, or carved ornamentation.

b. Clothing absolutely may not use the gold embroidered five-clawed dragon motif. Officials of the first and second ranks may have gowns covered with gold flowers. Third and fourth ranks, the gown shall have gold decorations. Fifth rank: gold sleeves on a knee gown. Sixth rank and above are permitted four-clawed dragons on their gowns. For the seventh rank and below, the civil officials are not permitted to use the dragon and phoenix motif. They are only permitted six gold flowers. For eighth and ninth ranks, the gown may have four gold flowers.

c. Caps and Belts.

For officials from the first to the fourth ranks, the top of the cap, the cap button, and the girdle shall generally have gold, jade, and precious stones for adornment. For the fifth and sixth ranks, on the top of the cap it is permitted to use gold and jade; for the button, coral or amber. The girdle employs gold, silver, and rhinoceros horn. Seventh to ninth ranks: on the top of the cap silver may be used, or gold plate; the cap button is of crystal or amber. The girdle uses silver mixed with iron. On the above caps the cap flowers may use prescribed patterns and dragon phoenix motifs. Boots should all use gold thread flower patterns.

Official's wives and daughters. From the first to the third ranks, the robe should all be gold cloth, and the headdress, ornaments and bracelets should use gold, jade, and precious stones. Wives and daughters of fourth- and fifth-rank officials should dress in garments of gold-decorated cloth. Their headdresses should use gold and jade beads. For the sixth to the ninth ranks, the gowns should use gold-washed cloth and small gold decorations. The headdresses should use gold beads. Only the earrings may use jade beads. All of the above should employ colored embroidery.

The gowns of commoners, male and female. It is absolutely not permitted to usurp the use of gold embroidery. They are permitted to use linen, silk gauze, and silken and hempen cloth. Only one gold hair ornament and one pair of gold earrings are allowed; for additional items only silver and green jade are allowed. On the top of the hat it is absolutely not allowed to use gold, jade, coral, or amber for the cap ornament. The boots may not have flowers in gold thread decoration.

d. Carriages absolutely may not be decorated with a dragon and phoenix motif.

Officials of the first to the third ranks may use a reduced gold decoration, and silver dragon pattern on embroidered sashes with dark curtains. Fourth and fifth ranks: white lion-head pattern on embroidered sashes with dark curtains. Sixth to ninth ranks: use a white cloud pattern on plain sashes with dark curtains. Sedan chairs should follow the same regulations as carriages.

Commoner's carriages should use black paint and have a plain front and flat top and black curtains. Sedan chairs should follow the same regulations as carriages. It is absolutely not permitted to use the cloud motif.

e. Bed curtains absolutely must not make use of the yellow dragon and phoenix motif.

Officials of first to third ranks may use gold-patterned embroidered gauze. Fourth rank and fifth rank: embroidered gauze. Sixth rank and below may use plain gauze.

Commoners use a cheap gauze.

f. Parasols.

Officials of the first and second ranks: silver gourd pattern, brown silk outside with red lining. Third and fourth ranks: red gourd pattern, brown silk outside with red lining. The above all have triple rims. Fifth rank: red gourd pattern, parasol dark green on the outside and red lining. Sixth rank and below: only use dark green cheap silk, two rims. All rain umbrellas should use oiled silk.

Commoners absolutely may not use silk or cheap silk umbrellas. They may use oiled paper rain umbrellas.

g. Saddles and bridles absolutely may not make use of decorations with the dragon and phoenix motif.

Officials of the first and second ranks use gold decoration. Third through fifth ranks use silver. Sixth rank and below may use only stone and reduced iron.

Commoners are not allowed to use gilt: they may use only brass and iron decorations.

h. Utensils may not be manufactured with a dragon and phoenix pattern.

Officials of the first and second ranks may use gold and jade. Third to fifth ranks: only the wine cup may use gold. Sixth rank and below, the wine cup may use silver.

Commoners may use only silver on the wine cup. More than this is prohibited.

i. Tombs, burial plots, stone animals.

Officials of the first rank: plot ninety paces [*bu*], tomb height one *zhang* and eight feet.[43] Second rank: plot eighty paces, tomb height one *zhang* and four feet. Third rank: plot seventy paces, tomb height one *zhang* and two feet. The above all have six stone animals. Fourth rank: plot sixty paces. Fifth rank: plot fifty paces. Tomb height eight feet. The above all have four stone animals. Sixth rank: plot forty paces. Seventh rank and below: twenty paces, tomb height six feet. The above paces are all from the center of the plot and counted to the edge. Fifth rank and above may use a stone stele [*bei*] with tortoise base and hornless dragon top [*guifu chishou*]. Sixth rank

---

[43] A pace is the equivalent of five Chinese feet; a *zhang* is ten such feet or 3.2 meters.

and below may use a stone stele [*jie*] with square base and round top [*fangfu yuanshou*].

Commoners: plot of nine paces, through the center eighteen paces. Only a tombstone may be used.

j. For official gowns, saddles, and bridles and other objects for ranked officials, only the government and households which are authorized to use them may manufacture them. When they are privately manufactured, or manufactured by households not authorized to use them, the artisans and craftsmen shall be punished according to the *Code*.

k. Commoner houses must all conform to the styles prescribed in this *Commandment*. Those which usurp carved decoration must be scraped away; those with colored decorations or green and blue must be blotted out with earth brown. If the brackets and beams were built many years ago, they need not be torn down. From now on, those who build in violation of these prohibitions will be punished according to the *Code*.

l. Palace eunuchs' official caps already have a prescribed style. The gown color should follow that of the seventh rank.

m. When bodyguards are on duty, gold-plated girdles and ivory sashes are already prescribed. Their gown color should follow that of the eighth rank.

n. The clothing colors of the clerks [*yuan, lingshi, shuli*], couriers [*xuanshi*],[44] and agents employed by the various offices shall be in accordance with their ranks and appropriate to their backgrounds.

52. Should it rain or snow during congratulatory audiences at court, the receiving of rescripts, the presenting of memorials, or routine audiences, officials are permitted to wear ordinary clothes while performing the ceremony.

53. Marriages among the people must follow the *Family Ritual* of Master Zhu [i.e., Zhu Xi].[45]

54. National University [*guoxue*] students [*shengyuan*]. The places shall be filled by sons, grandsons, younger brothers, and nephews of civil and military officials from ranks one through nine who are over the age of twelve. The quota will be one hundred. If there are outstanding commoners above the age of fifteen who have a general knowledge of the *Four Books* [*Si shu*][46] and who want to enter the National University, the Secretariat may memorialize and recommend their admission. The quota will be fifty.

[44] I assume that this is an error for *xuanshi*, rendered by Hucker (1985, 251) as courier. The term occurs as *xuanshi* in article 18.

[45] The reference is to *Zhuzi jiali* by the Song philosopher Zhu Xi (1130-1200). For a complete translation with annotations see Ebrey (1991).

[46] The *Four Books* are *The Great Learning* [*Daxue*], *The Doctrine of the Mean* [*Zhongyong*], *The Analects* [of Confucius, *Lunyu*], and *Mencius* [*Mengzi*]. In the Southern Song period Zhu Xi extracted the first two texts from longer works and wrote commentaries on all four which came to

55. When a loyal and hard-working civil or military official dies in the service of his ruler, he should be posthumously promoted two levels above the rank and grade he then held. His son may succeed him at one level lower than the father's actual rank and grade. Those killed in battle should be given a posthumous rank three levels higher. Their sons may succeed at their actual rank. For those without sons, a selection should be made from those qualified to inherit, and an appointment made at a lower rank. The local office should erect a shrine and periodically offer sacrifice.

56. For the sacrifice at the Temple of the Three Sage Kings [*San huang miao*]: the spring sacrifice shall be in the third month, third day; the autumn sacrifice shall be in the ninth month, ninth day. Accompanying rituals and ceremonies must all be according to prescribed form. In the Capital, oxen, sheep, and other objects, and in each prefecture, subprefecture, and district, the sacrificial objects should be provided for by an official grant of three piculs of rice.

57. For the sacrifice to the Altar of Soil and Grain [*sheji*] and others: the spring sacrifice is the first *wu* day of the second month;[47] the fall sacrifice is the first *wu* day of the eighth month. The Sacrifice to the Altar of Soil and Grain is in the southwestern suburb. On the *chou* day following the solar season Spring Begins [*lichun*][48] sacrifice to the Wind Spirit in the northeast suburb. On the *shen* day following the solar season of Autumn Begins [*liqiu*] sacrifice to the Thunder Spirit and the Rain Spirit in the southwestern suburb. The altars and headstones must be according to the old forms. In the Capital the officials shall provide the sacrificial objects. In the prefectures, subprefectures, and districts the officials shall provide three piculs of rice for the Soil and Grain sacrifice. The officials shall provide two piculs of rice for the Wind, Thunder, and Rain spirit sacrifices.

58. For the sacrifice at the Temple to King Wu and King Cheng:[49] in the Capital the sacrifice is on the first *wu* day of the second month in the spring and the first *wu* day of the eighth month in the fall. Oxen, sheep, and other objects should be used for the sacrifice.

---

be known as the *Four Books*. In Yuan times the *Four Books* with Zhu Xi's commentaries became the core texts for the civil service examinations.

[47] The Chinese lunar calendar designated days (and years) with pairs of cyclical characters. Ten "heavenly stems"[*tiangan*] were combined with twelve "earthly branches" [*dizhi*] to form sixty pairs which made up a cycle. *Wu* is the name of the fifth of the branches, thus it occurs six times in the cycle on the 5th, 15th, 25th, 35th, 45th, and 55th days. It would occur two or three times in a lunar month of twenty-nine or thirty days. For a listing of the stems and branches see Mathews (1960, 1176).

[48] The solar seasons are twenty-four divisions of the year into periods of fourteen or fifteen days according to the position of the sun. The terms assigned to these seasons imply changes in the weather (or flora and fauna) appropriate to the northern hemisphere. For this reason the solar seasons provided guidance to Chinese farmers in their agricultural pursuits. *Lichun* is approximately February 5-19; *liqiu*, August 7-22. For a complete listing of the seasons see Mathews (1178).

[49] Wu and Cheng were the first rulers of the Zhou dynasty, conventionally dated from 1122 B.C.

59. For the sacrifice at the Confucian Temple [Kongzi *miao*]: In the spring use the first *ding* day of the second month; in the fall the first *ding* day of the eighth month. Tablets of those admitted to the temple,[50] ritual and music shall follow the prescribed forms. In the Capital, use oxen, sheep, and other objects for sacrifice. The sacrificial objects in the prefectures, subprefectures, and districts should be provided for by an official grant of three piculs of rice.

60. Gradations of enfeoffment and posthumous enfeoffment.

Rank 1, A and B: enfeoffment and posthumous enfeoffment for three generations

Noble Rank [*jue*]: Duke of State [*guogong*]

Merit Title: (A: Supreme Pillar of State [*shang zhuguo*]; B: Pillar of State)

Mother and wife become Consort of State [*guo furen*]

Rank 2, A and B: enfeoffment and posthumous enfeoffment for two generations

Noble Rank: Commandery Duke [*jungong*]

Merit Title: (A: Senior Military Protector [*shang hujun*]; B: Military Protector)

Mother and wife become Commandery Mistress [*jun furen*]

Rank 3, A and B: enfeoffment and posthumous enfeoffment for two generations

Noble Rank: Commandery Marquis [*jun hou*]

Merit Title: (A: Senior Commander of Light Chariots [*shang qingche duwei*]; B: Commander of Light Chariots)

Mother and wife become Commandery Mistress [*jun furen*]

Rank 4, A and B: enfeoffment and posthumous enfeoffment of parents

Noble Rank: Commandery Earl [*jun bo*]

Merit Title: (A: Senior Commander of Cavalry [*shang qi duwei*]; B: Commander of Cavalry [*qi duwei*])

Mother and wife become Commandery Mistress [*junjun*]

Rank 5A: enfeoffment and posthumous enfeoffment of parents

Noble Rank: District Viscount [*xianzi*]

Merit Title: (Commandant of the Fleet-as-Clouds Cavalry [*yunqi wei*])

Mother and wife become District Mistress [*xianjun*]

Rank 5B: enfeoffment and posthumous enfeoffment of parents

Noble Rank: District Baron [*xiannan*]

Merit Title: (Commandant of Militant Cavalry [*wuqi wei*])

Mother and wife become District Mistress [*xianjun*]

Rank 6, A and B: enfeoffment and posthumous enfeoffment of parents

Father use only the prestige title

---

[50] The term *peixiang* refers to those Confucian worthies throughout the ages whose tablets have been installed in the Confucian Temple.

Mother and wife become Respectful Lady [*gongren*]
Rank 7, A and B: enfeoffment and posthumous enfeoffment of parents
Father use only the prestige title
Mother and wife become Manifest Lady [*yiren*]

61. In enfeoffment of the five ranks to Duke [*gong*], Marquis [*hou*], Earl [*bo*], Viscount [*zi*], and Baron [*nan*], meritorious great officials may only be enfeoffed as high as Duke. Only after death may enfeoffments be made at the rank of Marquis [*hou*].[51]

IV. MILITARY REGULATIONS

62. Prefectures, subprefectures, and districts shall appoint ushers [*zhihou*], jailers [*jinzi*], and constables [*gongbing*] from households with a tax obligation of less than three piculs of grain and more than two piculs. Except for the obligation to pay grain tax they are exempted from other labor service duties. It is not permitted to appoint persons from households with a large grain tax quota.

Yingtian Prefecture:
20 ushers 30 jailers
Other prefectures, based on the autumn grain tax quota:
200,000 piculs and above:
20 ushers 15 jailers
above 100,000 piculs
18 ushers 13 jailers
below 100,000 piculs
15 ushers 12 jailers
Subprefectures and districts, based on the autumn grain tax quota:
100,000 piculs and above
15 ushers 10 jailers
30 constables
above 50,000 piculs
13 ushers 8 jailers
30 constables
below 50,000 piculs
10 ushers 7 jailers
30 constables

Police Offices attached to subprefectures and districts shall each appoint thirty constables.

Police Offices along waterways shall appoint one hundred constables.

63. At the waterway stations along the main routes traversed by official messengers, each station shall provide ten boats. Along side routes traversed by messengers, each station shall provide five boats. For every boat

[51] The text says marquis [*hou*] but prince [*wang*] would make more sense in this context.

there should be ten sailors. The station households whose grain tax was specified in the old quota are to fill the positions. With the exception of the grain tax, those households are exempted from performing all other labor service. If the households meeting the old quota are insufficient, the officials should fill the positions with appropriate persons from households paying grain tax of more than five piculs but less than ten piculs. Regardless of whether one or two households are lacking, calculate the amount of their grain tax and ask them to serve an appropriate number of days.

64. Express stations should be set up every fifteen *li*. Each station should have four station soldiers and one station chief. Their numbers should be provided from the manpower of nearby households with a grain tax of more than one picul five pecks and less than two piculs. They should be young, able-bodied, and in person. They should be exempted from other labor service.

Each station should be supplied with the following items of equipment:

One twelve-watch [*shichen*] wheel [*lunzi*][52]

One *hongchuoxie* with sign board[53]

Two station calendars (one volume for communication coming down from higher offices, one volume for each office's communications to higher authorities)

An ever-bright lantern for night use

Each station soldier should maintain the following items:

One foot shackle	One bronze bell
One spear	Three feet of oil cloth
One soft cloth wrapper	Bamboo hat and hemp raincoat, one each
One red stick [*mengun*]	One Muslim calendar (See *Zhusi zhizhang*, Ministry of War section)[54]

65. In the newly submitted cities, towns and villages military officers and soldiers may not use the submission as an excuse to harbor the civilian populace, rob their possessions, occupy their houses by force, or force their wives and daughters into marriage. Violations will be investigated and punished.

66. The classification of military and civil households should be based upon registration. Military officers may not invent pretexts and without authority grab hold of common folk to fill the ranks. Commoner families are likewise not allowed to trick officials by claiming attachment to military households so as to escape from labor service. Should there be a military deserter, a warrant should be requested, in the Capital from the Chief Mili-

---

[52] The day was divided into twelve watches [*shichen*] of two hours each. Presumably the wheel [*lunzi*] referred to here is some device for keeping track of time.

[53] I am unable to identify a *hongchuoxie*.

[54] The *Zhusi zhizhang* was issued in 1393. The passage alluded to appears in HMZS (Taibei edition) 2:940-41.

tary Commission or in the provinces from the branch secretariat. Then the soldier may be impressed into service.

67. Whenever there is military information, in the provinces, in every prefecture the military and civilian offices should report it to the branch secretariat and the circuit attendants of the provincial surveillance office. The branch secretariat shall report it to the Secretariat and the Chief Military Commission respectively. The provincial surveillance office shall report it to the Tribunal of Censors. In the Capital the directly attached military and civilian offices will report to the Secretariat, the Chief Military Commission, and the Tribunal of Censors. The Secretariat, the Commission, and the Tribunal shall each memorialize the throne. If the Chief Military Commission, the Tribunal of Censors, and the Secretariat all communicate among themselves but keep the matter secret and delay memorializing the throne, they shall be punished as traitorous officials. The minor offenders will be exiled to a malarial region. Severe offenders will receive capital punishment.

68. Regulation on the allowances for personnel sent out on missions. From now on the retainers [*cong*] shall number as follows: for the first rank, ten; second rank, eight; third and fourth ranks, six; fifth rank, four; sixth and seventh ranks, three; eighth and ninth ranks, two retainers. Administrative aids [*yuanshi*], clerks [*lingshi, shuli*], seal keepers [*zhiyin*], couriers [*xuanshi*], and agents [*zouchai*] may have two retainers. Military officers are not bound by this limit. As for using boats at the water stations, each regular official is entitled to bring 200 catties of luggage. Each retainer may bring 50 catties of luggage. As for the mounts of the horse stations, each horse is not to exceed 10 catties of luggage. Pack horses are not to exceed 60 catties each. Those who try to smuggle in more ought to be punished according to the article on Improper Conduct.

69. The walls, towers, and guard stations of various places. In the interior, at walled cities, there should be established every twenty *zhang* one guard station. On the frontier, walled cities should have one guard station established every ten *zhang*. If the military commanders increase the numbers in response to changing conditions, it is not limited by this regulation. In jurisdictions without a military command the officials should take the initiative to establish guard stations and frequently inspect them. Do not be careless or allow them to run down. When the assigned official finishes his term of service he must turn them over to his successor. Violations will be punished.

70. Of those passing by on an official mission, the regular official shall be apportioned three pecks of rice; retainers, two pecks of rice per person. When lodging during an official mission, the regular official shall be apportioned five pecks of rice and retainers three pecks. On a water route the allowance shall be paid out at the transient rate. On a land route, when they spend the night, the allowance shall be paid out at the lodging rate.

71. When miliary or civilians have public or private business requiring travel, the military commanders will issue the permits in the Capital. In the provinces, military persons should request issuance of permits from the provincial military officers and the commanders. Civilians should request permits from the responsible subprefecture or district. The checkpoint officers in each locality should investigate thoroughly before letting them go. Military personnel who go more than 100 *li* beyond their stations without permits will be prosecuted the same as for desertion.

72. In every station which issues provisions, the officials will retain a portion of grain from the commercial taxes and the various taxes and assign responsible persons to manage it. If someone arrives on official business, grain should be issued to him in accordance with the precedents without delay. Subsequently, the amount issued should be reported to the relevant higher authorities.

V. JUSTICE REGULATIONS

73. The Five Punishments [*wu xing*]:

i. Light stick [*chi*], five degrees:

10 20 30 40 50

ii. Heavy stick [*zhang*], five degrees:

60 70 80 90 100

iii. Penal servitude [*tu*], five degrees:

Heavy stick 120 strokes. Convert to heavy stick 100 strokes and one-year penal servitude.

Heavy stick 140 strokes. Convert to heavy stick 100 strokes and one-and-one-half-year penal servitude.

Heavy stick 160 strokes. Convert to heavy stick 100 strokes and two-year penal servitude.

Heavy stick 180 strokes. Convert to heavy stick 100 strokes and two-and-one-half-year penal servitude.

Heavy stick 200 strokes. Convert to heavy stick 100 strokes plus three-year penal servitude.

iv. Life Exile [*liu*], three degrees:

2,000 *li* 2,500 *li* 3,000 *li*

v. Death Penalty, two degrees:

Strangulation [*jiao*] Decapitation [*zhan*]

74. The Ten Abominations [*shi e*]

1. Plotting rebellion
2. Plotting great sedition
3. Plotting treason
4. Contumacy
5. Depravity
6. Great irreverence

7. Lack of filial piety
8. Discord
9. Unrighteousness
10. Incest

75. The Eight Deliberations [*ba yi*]

1. Imperial relatives
2. Old retainers of the emperor
3. Heroic achievement
4. The morally worthy
5. Ability
6. Diligence
7. High position
8. Guests of the state

When persons in the above categories commit crimes a memorial should be sent up for Imperial decision. In cases involving one of the Ten Abominations this article is not applicable.

76. Redemption of punishment [*shu xing*]

Light stick, 10 strokes. Redemption for one half catty copper.

Heavy stick, 10 strokes. Redemption for one catty copper.

Penal servitude, 1 year. Redemption for 120 catties copper.

Penal servitude, 1 and a half years. Redemption for 140 catties copper.

Penal servitude, 2 years. Redemption for 160 catties copper.

Penal servitude, 2 and a half years. Redemption for 180 catties copper.

Penal servitude, 3 years. Redemption for 200 catties copper.

Life exile, 2,000 *li*. Redemption for 220 catties copper.

Life exile, 2,500 *li*. Redemption for 240 catties copper.

Life exile, 3,000 *li*. Redemption for 260 catties copper.

Those who are beyond the age of seventy or below the age of fifteen, and those who are incapacitated, disabled, or maimed, if they have committed offenses punishable with the light or heavy stick, or penal servitude or life exile, are permitted to redeem the punishment by payment of copper. If a person was instigated to commit a crime the instigator shall be punished. For sexual crimes, theft and robbery, capital offenses, or one of the Ten Abominations, this provision shall not apply. In cases punishable by penal servitude or life exile, when there are paternal grandparents or parents eighty or more years of age and no adult male to care for them, the case may be decided and punished according to the General Principles of the

Code,[55] which allow for the convicted person to stay home and care for the aged relatives.

77. Penal Instruments

Cangue. Length, 5 feet 5 inches; width, 1 foot 5 inches. For capital crimes, weight 25 catties; for life exile, 20 catties; for heavy stick, 15 catties. All of these shall be made of seasoned wood with the length and weight carved upon it.

Cangue. Length, 1 foot 6 inches; width, 3 inches; thickness, 1 inch.

Chain. Length, 10 feet. Weight of fetters, 3 catties.

Light stick. At the large end, .27 inches in diameter; at the small end, .17 inches in diameter. Length, 3 feet 5 inches.

Heavy stick. Large end, .32 inches in diameter; small end, .22 inches in diameter. Length, 3 feet 5 inches.

Interrogation stick. Large end, .45 inches in diameter; small end, .35 inches in diameter. Length, 3 feet 5 inches.

The above mentioned heavy and light sticks must have all knots removed and a measuring stick should be employed to bring it in line with the regulations. It is not permitted to use resin or other materials to bind it. When imposing punishments use the small end. The light and heavy stick should be applied to the buttocks. During interrogation by flogging the beating should be divided between the buttocks and the legs. For those who commit a serious crime where the ill-gotten goods and evidence are clear, but refuse to confess, a group of officials should sit on the case and investigate it clearly. Then it is permitted to interrogate with torture.

78. Crimes punishable by sixty strokes or less should be decided and the punishment administered at the district level; eighty strokes or less should be decided and the punishment administered at the subprefecture level; one hundred strokes or less should be decided and the punishment administered at the prefectural level. Penal servitude and life exile should be reported to the Court for disposition.

79. In any office, should there be a crime by the staff supervisor [*shouling guan*], there are preexisting laws to investigate and punish.[56] The ordinary officials of the office should not make unauthorized investigation.

80. In every prefecture there are judges [*tuiguan*] whose sole duty is to hear criminal cases and handle documents concerning them. They are not allowed to manage other matters. When prisoners accused of crimes are handed over to them they must first carefully ascertain the facts and then convene the officials for judgement. Other offices are not permitted to encroach upon their function.

---

[55] This refers to the Terms and General Principles [*mingli*] section of the *Code*, specifically to article 18, "Offenders remaining with parents to care for them," which provides for the conversion of penal servitude to 100 blows of the heavy stick and redemption in copper cash.

[56] The term *shoulingguan* denotes the official in charge of an office. See Hucker (1985, 433).

81. Every prefecture has a warder [*siyu*] who is solely in charge of the confinement of prisoners. If someone is falsely accused they are permitted to make a petition. If it is disapproved by the prefectural office it should be directly sent up to the provincial surveillance commission [*xiansi*]. Other offices are not permitted to encroach upon their functions. For prefectural, subprefectural ,and district jails appoint one assistant official to supervise. Male and female prisoners must be confined separately. Warders must frequently and carefully inspect them. In subprefectures and districts which lack a warder the jail officer [*tilao guan*] shall inspect. If a prisoner becomes ill, it should be reported to the jail officer, who will investigate the situation and provide medicine to cure the illness. Except in the case of fettered capital offenders, prisoners whose crimes are punishable by penal servitude, life exile, or beating with the heavy stick, and who are seriously ill, may be released from their fetters. Relatives may enter to see them. For crimes punishable by light stick or less, they may, with a guarantor, be given medical treatment outside the jail. When the prisoner is cured, he should be tried and punished according to the *Code*. If the case is not concluded, he shall be returned to jail and the case heard.

82. In litigation which involves the affairs of two subprefectures or districts the officials where the complaint was first lodged should make request to the prefecture of the accused to allocate the jurisdiction.

83. Litigations should proceed from lower to higher. Clearly indicate year and month. State the facts of the case. Do not state what is doubtful. Those making false accusations shall suffer the penalty for the crime alleged. Those guilty of overstepping their jurisdiction shall be punished for violation of the article on Improper Conduct in the *Code*. When officials who should hear cases refuse to hear them, it is permitted to appeal directly to higher authorities.

84. In cases involving assault and battery the transgressors should be conditionally sentenced [*baogu*] according to the *Code*.[57] If they confess to a serious offense they shall be imprisoned according to the law. If they confessed to a minor offense they may be released in charge of a guarantor. The accuser, the witnesses and others involved are not allowed to hang around the offices and neglect their occupations. Violations will be investigated and punished.

85. Interrogations of prisoners must be conducted according to the law, detailing the facts and developing the logic. Do not illegally inflict pain to forge a case. Violations will be investigated and punished.

---

[57] The term *baogu* refers to article 326 of the *Code*, "Time limit on responsibility for wounds caused," which provides for a period of medical treatment of the victim at the offender's expense to see if the victim will die or recover from injuries received in the beating, the outcome to determine the crime for which the offender should be punished.

86. In cases of capital punishment it is necessary to investigate everything completely. In the capital it is sent to the Tribunal of Censors. In the provinces it goes through the investigating censor and the provincial surveillance office for thorough review free of injustice. Officials deciding the case must wait for disposition from above. If the offender retracts his testimony, or if the family members claim that there is injustice, it is permitted to transfer the case.

87. In the case of officials of the sixth rank and below guilty of a crime involving ill-gotten goods with a punishment of penal servitude or life exile, the Tribunal of Censors shall decide the punishment at its discretion. However, in other cases involving more serious crimes, or officials of the fifth rank and above, make a thorough examination until it is well understood, and then memorialize the throne for disposition. Miscellaneous crimes by officials of the sixth rank and below shall be judged by the provincial surveillance office. For fifth rank and above, circulate it for joint deliberation and request the Tribunal of Censors to memorialize the throne.

88. When military officers commit the crime of taking or receiving bribes in the capital, with the exception of officials of the Chief Military Commission, all the commanders of guards and battalions should be memorialized to the throne by the Tribunal of Censors. In cases of officials of the sixth rank and below, deliberate, decide, and carry out a punishment. In the provinces, in the area through which the investigating censors periodically circulate, if there are military officers guilty of taking or receiving, secretly send a sealed report to the Tribunal of Censors, which will memorialize the throne, asking for disposition and action.

89. When a criminal commits two crimes at once, punish him according to the more serious one. If the crimes are of equivalent severity, sentence according to one of them.

90. As for old persons, the incapacitated, the disabled, and maimed, only when they are making accusations concerning plotting rebellion, treason, sedition, or unfilial sons or grandsons must they go before the authorities pleading the case. In other public business the above categories of persons may send to plead in their stead a family member living with them who is conversant with the facts of the matter under litigation. If there are false accusations the guilt shall fall on the representative.

91. When a woman commits a sexual crime, her clothing shall be taken off when the case is heard and the punishment of beating is administered. For other crimes the undergarments may be allowed when the punishment of beating is administered, and in cases of penal servitude or life exile tattooing is waived.

92. Official personnel on detached service [*chaishi renyuan*] are not permitted to receive complaints or judge prisoners. Violations will be punished for violating the article on Improper Conduct in the *Code*.

93. Thieves who served out their sentence or completed their years of penal servitude, should be assigned by the officials of their native places to be patrolmen [*jingji*].[58] First offenders who have been tattooed on the arm, after two years without transgression and through official investigation, may be taken off the register of patrolmen, and the tattoo marks removed. A repeated offender with tattoo marks on the arm must wait three years without transgression for the investigation as above. Those able to capture three robbers or five thieves, without limit of years and months, may be taken off the register and have their tattoos removed immediately. If many are captured the captors should all be rewarded like ordinary persons.

94. When an ordinary person captures one robber or two thieves, the reward is twenty ounces of silver. For five or more robbers, ten or more thieves, give one official position. For lesser numbers, reward with silver according to the number captured. Those who are obligated by profession to catch criminals are excluded from this regulation. The ill-gotten goods captured with the apprehension of robbers and thieves should be returned to the owner. If there is no owner then it should be confiscated. As for those who make advances against or buy stolen goods from robbers or thieves, if they do it without knowledge of the circumstances, do not prosecute them; just recover the stolen goods. The value is given to the owner at the expense of the criminal.

95. When a person commits a crime and then voluntarily confesses before it has been discovered, his guilt shall be excused. If a minor crime has come to light, and confession is made to a serious crime, the offender shall only be charged with the minor crime. Those making voluntary confession which is incomplete or untruthful shall be punished for the crime which is incompletely or untruthfully confessed. Capital punishment shall be reduced one degree. Crimes in which people are injured, in which goods cannot be recompensed, from which the offender runs away when the matter comes to light, and sexual crimes are not covered by the provision for voluntary confession.

96. When officials commit crimes requiring forty strokes of the light stick or less a record of transgression shall be made [and the official] returned to office. At fifty blows of the light stick they shall be removed from office. At sixty strokes of the heavy stick, demote one degree; at seventy blows, demote two degrees; at eighty blows, demote three degrees; at ninety blows, demote four degrees. They shall all be removed from their current appointments. The regular officials shall be employed as miscellaneous officials; miscellaneous officials will be employed on the distant frontiers. Officials committing "public crimes" up to the punishment of ninety strokes are not bound by the requirement of removal from their current appointment. Just add a record of the transgression. For punishments of one hun-

[58] The meaning of *jingji* is obscure.

dred strokes of the heavy stick, regardless of whether it is a public crime or private crime, do not reappoint.

97. Autopsy forms shall be printed in every prefecture. Each page will be made in three copies with a registration number and half seal for identification by matching. These are sent down to the subprefecture and district. Whenever there is an initial or repeat inquest into the injuries to a corpse, fix a time and appoint an official to lead the staff supervisor [*shouling guan*], functionaries [*li*], coroner [*wuzuo*], and messengers [*xingren*] to personally go to the site. Call together those persons who ought to take part in the inquiry and jointly make a careful investigation and ascertain the deceased's condition in life and the cause of death. Note it down in the proper form, signed and stamped with a seal. One copy goes to the survivors, one copy is pasted to the file, and one copy submitted to higher authorities. The official documentary form of initial and repeat inquests shall follow the old system.

98. When family members engage in robbery or theft together they shall all be judged according to the rules for ordinary robbers and thieves in determining principal and accessories (i.e., when a father, sons, and brothers together carry out robbery or theft).

99. A robber or thief who confesses before his crime has become known, or confesses to the victims, shall be exempted from punishment. If he is able to round up his companions, he shall be rewarded as would an ordinary person. Those with repeated violations and those who have harmed people shall not be permitted to confess.

100. In calculating the value of ill-gotten goods figure 400 *wen* of copper cash as one *guan*.[59]

101. In the matter of theft, if a group of thieves steal the possessions of one household, sentence each of them as if each had stolen all the ill-gotten goods.[60] If they steal from two or more households, sentence each of them on the basis of the household from which the most ill-gotten goods were stolen.

102. Those who make accusation of a crime committed before a general amnesty shall be punished for the crime of which the accusation is made. In the event that the crime involves money or grain, marriage, or land matters requiring investigation, and although the violations have already been pardoned and matters still must be set straight and collections made, this article does not apply.

103. In a case where something is taken or received illegally by an official but has not yet been discovered and the person repents and returns it to the owner, it is judged the same as voluntary confession.

---

[59] The term *guan*, literally a string of copper cash, here is an abstract measure of monetary value.

[60] The term in the Chinese text is *bingzang*, referring to the assessment of punishment according to the total value of the goods stolen.

104. When a thief has left the scene of the crime and the owner of the goods pursues him, and the thief is killed while resisting arrest, there must be an investigation to determine if the owner has a wound on his body in which case by law he shall not be prosecuted. If he has no wound, the authorities must personally determine whether or not the criminal is a former thief assigned to patrol duty,[61] or bears a grudge against the owner. When these issues are settled terminate the case.

105. Public crimes of the local prefects, subprefects, and district magistrates rated at forty or less strokes of the light stick may be redeemed with copper.

106. In crimes entailing confiscation of the household by the state, with the exception of rebellion and treason, only confiscate land, property, and livestock.[62]

107. In the case of persons lodging accusations, the responsible officials shall establish an oral accusation file and designate an accusation writing clerk [*shuzhuang renli*]. If the accusation shall be accepted for hearing, immediately record the case, issue the charge, and enforce it. If the accusation should not be heard, the reasons for not accepting it must also be written down and clearly recorded in the file. Officials and functionaries shall sign and seal the document for further review.

108. As to the rules for the reduction of punishments, the two death penalties and three life exiles shall all be reduced uniformly. (For example, if the death penalty is reduced one degree it becomes life exile at 3,000 *li*. Reduced two degrees it becomes penal servitude for three years. The crime meriting life exile at 3,000 *li* reduced one degree would likewise become penal servitude for three years.)

109. From now on if there is a national amnesty, with the exception that those prisoners presently in confinement whose cases have not yet been decided and those who ought to be pardoned all shall be released, the cases in which the prisoners have already been sentenced to penal servitude or life exile, or banished to malarial regions to settle, shall be considered closed. Except for those who shall be released from penal servitude when their term is up, no other life exiles sent to settle distant places shall be allowed to return.

110. When relatives living together of the mourning grade of *dagong* or higher, and mother's parents, daughter's sons, or agnatic grandsons' wives, husband's brothers, and brothers' wives are guilty of crimes, it is permissible to shield them. Slaves shielding their masters likewise shall not be charged. Those shielding relatives within the mourning grade circle of *xiaogong* shall have their punishment reduced by three degrees from that of

---

[61] See article 93, above.

[62] The text implies that in cases of rebellion and treason, confiscation of the household would extend to some members of the household, who would become slaves.

ordinary persons. For those guilty of plotting rebellion or contumacy do not apply this provision.

111. Murderers who forfeit their lives [i.e., are sentenced to death] shall pay burial money to the family of their victims of ten ounces of silver. Those not forfeiting their lives shall pay twenty ounces of silver. Those who ought to have forfeited their lives but did not by reason of amnesty also shall be forced to pay twenty ounces. Where there are coconspirators, determine the number and apportion the levy evenly. Send it to the family of the deceased.

112. If those receiving bribes in office have left office when the matter comes to light, or if they received the bribe in their former assignment and have been reassigned when it comes to light, they shall in all cases be prosecuted and punished according to their present assignment.

113. In the case of one sentenced to life exile, if the wife, concubines, household members, parents, sons, and agnatic grandsons want to accompany him they may. Those who are relocated [*yixiangren*] shall follow this provision. If the person being exiled dies, then, even though the register has been attached to the new location, if they want to return they may. If the criminal was under sentence for plotting rebellion, making insect poison [*gu*],[63] witchcraft, or a grudge killing, then the household members are not covered by the provision allowing return.

114. In calculating the value of ill-gotten goods account shall be taken of prices prevailing at the place and time of the crime. If ill-gotten goods are leased objects, their value shall also be assessed according to the price at the time of the crime. Even if the leased value is greater it shall not exceed the price of the objects themselves.

115. In all cases of illicit goods, goods that involve both parties in offenses shall be confiscated by the state; the goods extorted by force or the threat of force shall be returned to the owner.[64]

116. When persons hang themselves or drown themselves in water, if there are no complications and the family wishes to have a normal burial, then the officials, having carefully inquired thoroughly, shall grant requests for waiving of the autopsy. If the deceased was killed by robbers, and if the survivors request waiving of autopsy, the official shall personally inspect the injuries and turn the body over to the relatives for burial. When prisoners have a serious illness and are released to guarantors for treatment, should they then die under circumstances which are not suspicious, it is likewise permitted for their relatives to request waiving the autopsy. On the

[63] The term *gu* refers to article 312 in the *Code*, "Rearing venomous animals and preparing poisons," a heinous crime.

[64] The phrase *bicizhuzui* implies culpability of both parties, as when a bribe is offered to an official even though no illegal favor is done in response. See article 23 of the *Code*.

other hand, if they die from wounds, even though the relatives request it, the autopsy shall not be waived.

117. In all cases of voluntary confession by the criminal, if the law permits sheltering, a relative confessing on behalf of the criminal is the same as a voluntary confession. If the criminal does not voluntarily confess but a father confesses for a son, a younger brother for the elder brother, a person senior in generation or age [*zunzhang*] for one junior in generation or age [*biyou*], it is as if the criminal had voluntarily confessed in person.[65] If a person junior in generation or age levies a charge against a person senior in generation or age it is the same as if the criminal had voluntarily confessed; still, the junior person shall be charged with the crime of violating the principles of family hierarchy.[66]

118. When Buddhist monks and nuns and Daoist priests commit crimes and are sentenced, they shall be returned to the secular world to perform labor.

119. When family members commit crime together, just prosecute the senior member. If they cause damage or injury to others, they shall all be punished as a common principal and accessories without regard to family status.

120. When the property and land of criminals is confiscated, if ancestral tombs are contained in it, they shall not be included in the inventory.

121. For a crime entailing confiscation of the criminal's property, with the exception of plotting rebellion, treason, and great sedition, in case there is an amnesty, if the seizure has not taken place before the amnesty, it shall be cancelled. If the seizure has taken place before the amnesty the property shall be retained by the state.

122. The intentional killing of a son or agnatic grandson, even though an amnesty occurs which does not pardon plotting to kill or intentional killing, still shall be punished according to the *Code*. If the killer makes false accusations of others, and if there is an amnesty according to which the falsely accused person shall be pardoned for the alleged crime, the criminal shall be punished according to the article on intentional killing of a son or agnatic grandson. If the crime of which he accused others shall not be pardoned, he still shall be punished severely.[67]

123. When thieves are granted amnesty they shall all be exempted from tattooing.

---

[65] In the context of this sentence, which concerns those senior in the hierarchy of mourning grades confessing on behalf of their juniors, the phrase "the younger brother for the elder brother" appears to be inconsistent.

[66] Violating the principles of family hierarchy (*ganmingfanyi*) is an offense against the Confucian notion of an ideal ordering of family members by right principles (*mingyi*) of generation and age. Bodde and Morris (1973, 405) render this "accusations by junior against senior relatives."

[67] The phrase in Chinese is *congzhonglun*, which implies levying the heaviest penalty.

124. Robbery, plotting to kill, or intentionally killing shall not be pardoned even though there is an amnesty. If among the accessories there are those who have committed crimes punishable by the heavy stick, they shall be sentenced according to the *Code*. Those who are not coconspirators with the robbers shall be released.

125. When military officers or soldiers commit crimes deserving of penal servitude, life exile, or tattooing, just administer the number of strokes of the heavy stick, and in place of penal servitude, life exile, or tattooing, sentence them to military exile according to the old practice. If they have committed capital crimes, deliberate and memorialize the throne requesting an imperial determination.

126. A military officer who commits a crime involving ill-gotten goods punishable by the heavy stick shall be reduced in rank according to precedent. Subsequently he shall be employed according to his status. Those deserving penal servitude or life exile shall be sentenced to military exile. After they have established their merit, they shall be promoted according to precedent. For those deserving death, deliberate and memorialize the throne requesting an imperial determination.

127. Officials and functionaries taking or receiving bribes, in an affair in which bribes were received from several households, shall be punished according to the largest bribe from one household.

128. When horses and oxen are old or sick and no longer useful, report to the authorities requesting a determination. Only then is it permitted to butcher them. The horns and sinews shall be given to the authorities. Failure to report to the authorities shall be punished the same as the crime of private butchering. If the animal dies of sickness, report to the authorities before butchering it. Violations shall be punished.

129. The monthly salary of civil officials is a combination of cash and rice. When deduction is made from the salary only deduct the cash. Military officers are paid monthly entirely in rice. If their salary is to be deducted, calculate it on the same basis as the civil official and deduct the amount equivalent to the cash.

130. In an accusation against an agnatic grandfather or father, such a person's son or agnatic grandson shall not be called as a witness. In an accusation against an elder brother, the younger brother shall not be called as a witness. In an accusation against a husband, the wife shall not be called as a witness. In an accusation against a master, his male or female slave shall not be called as a witness. Violations shall be punished.

131. When servants and retainers of the household of imperial relatives, meritorious nobles, or high civil or military officials commit crimes, just punish the offender. All government offices shall prosecute according to the *Code*. If there is unwillingness to give them up, one degree will be added to the offender's punishment. If it involves a serious offense and they are not given up, memorialize the throne.

132. When a special imperial rescript temporarily designates a crime which is not included in the *Code* or *Commandment*, all the offices are not allowed to cite it as a precedent. If it is cited by analogy to the *Code*, thus making punishment lighter or heavier, the official shall be punished as if he had intentionally incriminated someone.

133. Even though there is a great amnesty, evil persons who put forward malicious whispers to the throne to cause others to die by execution shall not be pardoned.

134. The *Code* and *Commandment* have force from the day they are promulgated. If a crime took place before then, it still shall be decided according to the new *Code*.

135. Prisoners confined in jails who are seventy or older, fifteen or younger, or disabled, shall be unshackled. Minor and serious offenders shall not be mixed together. The cangues and shackles shall be washed frequently. The bedding shall be arranged frequently. In winter a brazier and in summer cooling drinks shall be provided. Those who have no family shall daily be given a rice ration of one peck. In winter give them one quilted garment, in the evening give them lamp oil. When they are sick give them medicine. This is all disbursed from the government cash and grain of the local officials. The warden should regularly request issuance. Do not allow deficiency or neglect. Among officials guilty of private crimes, except for capital punishment, those sentenced to penal servitude and life exile shall remain in shackles; the others sentenced to heavy stick and below shall be unshackled. For public crimes, those from life exile down shall all be unshackled. The warder [*siyu guan*] shall constantly and carefully enforce this.[68] Jail guards [*yuzu*] shall not torture prisoners. Jail officers [*tilao guan*] shall inspect frequently. If there are violations the jailer [*jinzi*] shall suffer severe punishment. If jail officials make violations, report to higher authorities for investigation and punishment.

136. One who is not aged, disabled, maimed, or incapacitated at the time a crime is committed but is so by the time it is discovered shall be judged as one who is aged, disabled, maimed, or incapacitated. One who is underage when a crime is committed but grown up at the time it is discovered shall be judged as one who is underage.

137. A woman shall be confined for contumacy, sexual crime, robbery, and murder; for miscellaneous crimes she shall be assigned to the custody of clan relatives within the circle of mourning grades pending decision. Invariably, matters concerning marriage, land, family property, and such things shall not be reported to the officials by a woman. They must be brought by a representative. If the husband is dead and there is no son, then

---

[68] The meaning of the phrase *juling* in this sentence is unclear. The Tokyo edition renders it *juqian*.

it is permitted for the woman to come before the officials. If she has been injured and there is no one to represent her, she is permitted to lodge an accusation.

138. Those who make false accusations shall themselves be punished for the crime. When two or more persons are accused but only one accusation is false, the guilt shall be apportioned according to the relative severity of the charge. If two or more charges are made, and the more serious charge is true while the lesser charge is without basis, or if there are multiple charges, then one charge being true shall void guilt for all of them. If two or more charges are made and the lesser is true, but the more serious charge is without basis, or if one charge is made that a less serious crime is more serious, then the punishment of light or heavy stick, penal servitude, or life exile shall all be applied as retribution against the accuser according to the excessive level of the charge.

139. In cases of false accusation of a crime punishable by heavy stick as a crime punishable by penal servitude, or false accusation of a crime punishable by penal servitude with heavy stick as a crime punishable by life exile, or false accusation of a crime punishable by near exile as a crime deserving distant exile, the excess of punishment determines the retribution for false accusation. Penal servitude for one year can be commuted to heavy stick twenty strokes; for a half-year add one degree. Three degrees of life exile, likewise, each commute to twenty strokes of the heavy stick. When a false accusation is made of a crime deserving the heavy stick, penal servitude, or life exile as a crime deserving the death penalty, the retribution shall be death.

140. When officials hear a case involving litigants to whom they are related in the mourning grades, are connected to the family by marriage, have a master or teacher relationship, or have an old grudge, they shall remove themselves from the case.

141. Penal servitude for labor service:

Under Huguang province:

For prefectures, subprefectures, and districts south of the Yangzi, send them to Huangmei to work in the iron smelters.

Under Jiangxi province:

For prefectures, subprefectures ,and districts east of the Yangzi, send them to Xinyu to work in the iron smelters.

For prefectures, subprefectures, and districts west of the Yangzi, send them to Jinxian to work in the iron smelters.

Under Zhejiang province:

Those undergoing penal servitude shall be sent to work on the salt farms under the jurisdiction of the Lianghuai Salt Distribution Commission [*yanyun si*].

Under Jianghuai province:

Those undergoing penal servitude shall be sent to work on the salt farms under the jurisdiction of the Liangzhe Salt Distribution Commission.

Under the Metropolitan prefectures and subprefectures:

For prefectures, subprefectures, and districts north of the Yangzi, send them to work on the salt farms under the jurisdiction of the Liangzhe Salt Distribution Commission.

For prefectures, subprefectures, and districts south of the Yangzi, send them to work on salt farms under the jurisdiction of the Lianghuai Salt Distribution Commission.

142. When officials and functionaries are guilty of crimes of accepting ill-gotten goods punishable by up to life exile, regardless of whether they are from north or south of the Yangzi, send them to prefectures under Liangguang or Fujian, including the malarial regions of Longnan, Anyuan, Tingzhou, and Zhangzhou to settle. Persons from subprefectures and counties close to the malarial regions specified and who commit the crime of accepting ill-gotten goods shall be sent to outposts on the northern frontier.

143. In jurisdictions south of the Yangzi, for *li* heads guilty of accepting ill-gotten goods and whose punishment is penal servitude, those from prefectures under Huguang branch secretariat and Jiujiang, Nankang, and Chizhou prefectures shall be sentenced to penal servitude according to the *Code*. Those from other places shall be sentenced according to the *Code*: the land which they are presently cultivating shall be confiscated, and together with the household members with whom they are living, they shall be transferred to take up residence on land north of the Yangzi. Grant them uncultivated land to farm according to the number of *qing* and *mu* of land confiscated.

VI. WORKS REGULATIONS

144. In every locality government offices variously manufacture military weapons, military clothing, and other articles. It is essential that the products be sharp and sturdy, and fit for use. Officials in charge of the manufactory shall constantly examine the work. The materials used in the work shall be requested realistically and records kept in a register for future review. The principal supervising official [*tidiao zhengguan*] shall inspect carefully. Should there be unsuitable items, investigate and take action to make up the deficiencies.

145. When offices are manufacturing fabrics it is important that they be tightly woven, the colors bright, and the dimensions and weight not fall short of the sample. Officials in charge of the manufactory shall constantly examine the work. Materials used in the work shall be requested realistically. The principal supervising official shall supervise strictly. Should

there be unsuitable items, investigate and take action to make up the deficiencies.

APPENDIX THREE

THE PLACARD OF PEOPLE'S INSTRUCTIONS[1]
(*JIAO MIN BANG WEN*)[2]

CONTENTS[3]

---

[1] The *Placard of People's Instructions* was originally translated by George Jerlang Chang and published in *Ming Studies* 7:63-72 (1978). This is a substantial revision by Edward L. Farmer with the assistance of Jiang Yonglin.

[2] The translation was made from the Tokyo edition of HMZS, vol. 1, 467-476. It also occurs in the Taibei edition of HMZS, vol. 3, 1405-1444.

[3] The contents were given serial numbering by the translator to facilitate reference.

28. Community sacrifices
29. Promotion of agriculture
30. Water conservation
31. Corruption of tax collection
32. Abolishing community schools
33. Encouraging family solidarity
34. Prohibiting heterodox instruction
35. Harmony in the village
36. Sale of land
37. Military conscription
38. Appeals through channels
39. Obey these instructions
40. Enforcing the placard
41. Elders may report to capital

THE PLACARD OF PEOPLE'S INSTRUCTIONS

In order to instruct the people, Minister Yu Xin[4] and others of the Ministry of Revenue, together with civil and military officials, on the nineteenth day, of the third month of the year Hongwu 31,[5] attended the morning audience at the Fengtian Gate and respectfully received the sacred edict.[6]

Since ancient times, rulers have represented Heaven in managing human affairs by setting up separate offices to order the various affairs and bring peace to the lives of the people. Worthies and gentlemen of bygone times feared only that they would not be employed by their rulers. All who were employed exerted the utmost diligence to serve the rulers, thus bringing glory to their parents, wives and children, and to establish fine reputations in the world. How could there have been any lawbreaking conduct? Therefore, the officials were competent for their posts and the people were content in their livelihoods. Since the world was unified I have set up the cardinal principles, promulgated laws and established offices according to ancient rules: in the capital, the six ministries and the Censorate; in the provinces, the provincial administration commissions, the provincial surveillance commissions, prefectures, subprefectures, and districts.[7] Although the titles are different from previous dynasties the system of government is the same.

That most of the appointed officials are from among the common people could not be helped. For some time it has been difficult to tell whether they were virtuous or wicked. Scholars are not real scholars and the officials are all cunning ones. They often take bribes and break the law, turn benevolence and righteousness upside down, and injure the good people, so that the common people bring all of their complaints to the capital. So it has been for years without cease. Now this order is promulgated to declare to the people of the realm that all minor matters concerning households and marriage, land, and disputes involving assault and battery shall shall be judged by the elders [*laoren*] and the *lijia* of their communities [*li*].[8] Seri-

---

[4] Yu Xin was Minister of Revenue from 1393 to 1402. See *Ming shi, juan* 111, "Qiqingbiao" [Table of ministers], 3401-4.

[5] The date is April 6, 1398. See Keith Hazelton, *A Synchronic Chinese-Western Daily Calendar 1341-1661 A.D.*(Minneapolis: Ming Studies, 1984), 58.

[6] What follows this introductory paragraph has the form of an imperial edict.

[7] I have attempted to adjust the translation to conform to the usage suggested in Hucker's *Dictionary*.

[8] The term *lijia* refers to the administrative structure imposed upon the rural population by the Ming government. Groups of 110 households were constituted into a "community" [*li*] which was divided into "tithings" [*jia*] of ten households each. Both the community and the tithing had headmen, *lizhang* and *jiashou* respectively, who are collectively referred to here by the term *lijia*. *Lijia* has been left untranslated both because it is so central to this document and to avoid confusion with less technical terms such as "village." Hucker's "Community Self-monitoring System" is too long for frequent repetition.

ous matters involving sexual crime, robbery, fraud ,or homicide shall be reported to the officials. After this order is promulgated, any officials or functionaries who dare to confound it shall be sentenced to the death penalty. For those commoners who dare to confound it, their entire families shall be banished to the frontiers. These regulations have been declared before. You in the Ministry of Revenue shall once again proclaim them.

1. In all minor matters involving household and marriage, land, assault and battery, and disputes among the people, it is not permitted to bring lawsuits directly to government offices. These matters must go through the local *lijia* and elders for judgement. Those who do not go to the *lijia* and elders, regardless of the merits of the cases, shall be sentenced to sixty strokes of the heavy stick and the case sent back to the *lijia* and elders for judgement.

2. The elders and the *lijia* live close to and have fields side by side with the common people of the village and *li* so that matters of right and wrong, good and evil, are all known to them. Whenever there is an accusation from the people, a meeting shall immediately be held and the case judged fairly. The bamboo or thorn stick may be used for appropriate torture. If the case cannot be settled, causing the people to go bother the government offices, the *lijia* and elders shall each be sentenced to sixty strokes of the heavy stick. Those who are over seventy years of age shall not be beaten, but redeem the punishment according to the *Code*. They shall still make an appropriate judgement in the case. If they act wrongly out of personal consideration, and confound right and wrong, the *lijia* and elders shall be punished for the crime of judges implicating the innocent and exonerating the guilty.[9]

The litigations[10] which shall be judged by the elders and *lijia* are as follows:

household and marriage, land, assault and battery, suits over ownership, fires, theft, abusive language, money lending, gambling, eating fruits of gardens and orchards without permission, illegal killing of plowing oxen,

---

[9] Reference is made here to article 433 of the *Code*, *churu ren zui*.

[10] In most instances the matters specified are references to articles or groups of articles in the Code: household and marriage [*huhun*], articles 81-95 and 107-124; land [*tiantu*], articles 96-106; assault and battery [*douou*], articles 325-346;
disputes over ownership [*zhengzhan*]; fires [*shihuo*], article 406; theft [*qiedao*], article 292; abusive language [*mali*], articles 347-354; money lending [*qianzhai*], articles 168-170; gambling [*dubo*], article 402; eating fruits of gardens and orchards without permission [*shanshi tianyuan guaguo deng*], article 105; illegal killing of plowing oxen [*sizai gengniu*], article 254; discarding or destroying utensils or crops [*qihui qiwu jiase deng*], article 104; animals biting and killing people [*chuchan yaosha ren*], article 255; unauthorized use of property by younger or subordinate members of the family [*biyou sishan yongcai*], article 94; dishonoring the spirits [*xiedu shanming*], article 180; son or grandson violating instructions [*zisun weifan jiaoling*], article 361; teaching witches and heterodoxy [*shi wu xiejiao*], article 181; domestic animals trampling or eating crops [*liuchu jianshi hejia deng*]; equally dividing irrigation water [*junfen shuili*].

discarding or destroying utensils or crops, animals biting and killing people, unauthorized use of property by junior or younger members of the family, dishonoring the spirits, son or grandson violating instructions, witchcraft and heterodoxy, domestic animals trampling or eating crops, equally dividing irrigation water.

3. When the elders and *lijia* judge suits among the common people they shall convene in each *li's*[11] exhibition pavilion [*shenming ting*]. Three, five, or ten elders shall be selected by the people of the *li* from those who are upright and well respected. After their names have been reported to the officials, they shall judge the suits. If the case involves more than one *li*, the elders and the *lijia* of the several *li* shall meet together for a joint judgement. The seating order is as follows: first the elders, next the *lizhang*,[12] then the *jiashou*.[13] The seating order shall take account of age. If the *lizhang* is older than the elder, he shall be seated above the elder. If the suits among the common people are so judged that the precedence between elder and younger is maintained, the aged will naturally be respected and honored.

4. Elders judging suits, regardless of whether they have had court audiences or not, as long as they are over fifty years of age, act virtuously in the village, have wide experience and are respected by the people, may judge cases and distinguish between right and wrong. Those who, although old, are deficient in experience and are not able to distinguish right and wrong, shall also be ranked as elders, but shall not judge cases.

5. Whenever encountering difficult cases or cases involving their own children and relatives, the elders of a *li* shall meet with all the elders and *lijia* of the four neighboring *li* to the east, west, south, and north or of three or five *li* for settlement. If the suits are so judged that many experienced people are involved, right and wrong will naturally be made clear.

6. The elders and the *lijia* judge suits primarily for the convenience of the officials. Any incompetent officials who dare to cause trouble so as to implicate innocent persons shall be punished.

7. If an elder commits a crime, all elders and *lijia* shall hold a joint meeting and inquire into the facts of the case. He who commits a minor crime shall be judged at once and no longer be permitted to sit with the elders to judge suits. If he commits a serious crime, the elders and *lijia* shall meet together to make a complete inquiry and send the report to the local officials. The criminal shall be sent to the capital. The officials shall not make the arrest or do the interrogation without authority. If officials do

---

[11] *Li* in this case must refer to an administrative unit or community, i.e., the collectivity making up the *lijia* unit, rather than a natural village.

[12] Hucker, *Dictionary*, renders *lizhang* as community head. The community head was an annually rotated leadership position in the local administrative grouping of 110 households.

[13] Hucker, *Dictionary*, renders *jiashou* as tithing chief. The tithing chief was the leader in the lowest-level self-governing grouping of ten households.

make the arrest and interrogation without authority, the elders may come to report to the throne. The officials shall be punished.

8. Elders who act improperly, take advantage of the law to perpetrate wickedness, ignore public opinion, or cause trouble, shall be arrested by the other elders and sent to the capital.

9. Elders shall not use the judging of cases as a pretext to intimidate the *lijia*, control the officials, or evade corvee obligations. In the event of such a crime the offender's family shall be banished to the frontier.

10. In the villages all serious matters involving sexual crime, robbery, fraud or homicide shall be reported to the local officials. If the officials and functionaries clearly know that these matters shall not be judged by the *lijia* and elders, but refuse to take responsibility, they shall be severely punished. If the matters shall be judged by the *lijia* and elders, and crafty persons deliberately disobey the order and directly report to the officials, but the officials and functionaries do not immediately send them back to the elders for judgement, but instead delay them, and practice corruption and fraud for profit, they shall also be severely punished.

11. In the preceding article the officials are ordered to judge serious matters involving sexual crime, robbery, fraud, and homicide. From now on, with the exception of such cases among the people as the Ten Abominations,[14] armed robbery, and murder, which shall not be judged by the elders, should there occur cases of sexual crime, robbery, fraud or homicide which does not entail one of the Ten Abominations, armed robbery, or murder, and in the village if the victims want to restrain themselves and save trouble by not reporting to the officials for fear that they will be implicated and suffer, while the accused admit their guilt in hopes of avoiding punishment, it is permitted for them to go to the elders for judgement. The elders in the local community shall not refuse to judge the suits. If the elders of the *li* have already settled the case, but crafty persons not involved in the case cause trouble by reporting the case and thus bothering the officials, and the officials cause trouble by incriminating the innocent for bribes, they shall all be punished.

12. After a case among the common people has been settled by the elders and *lijia*, if crafty persons disagree with the judgement and repeatedly appeal to the officials by fabricating evidence and making false accusations, they shall be sentenced to capital punishment and their families banished to the frontier. If the officials fail to check the reasons for accepting appeals, thereby taking bribes and practicing fraud, they shall all be punished.

13. Elders and *lijia*, when judging suits, shall not establish a jail. Regardless of whether men or women commit, they shall not be imprisoned. The interrogation takes place during the day and the accused shall be re-

---

[14] The Ten Abominations is a group of crimes given special attention in the law codes. For a listing see *Commandment*, article 74, in appendix 2.

leased at night. If the case is not settled they shall return the next day for questioning. Those who dare to cause trouble by practicing imprisonment shall be severely punished.

14. The *lijia* and elders are allowed to judge the suits only when the people under their jurisdiction voluntarily report their disputes. When suits among the common people are rather minor and the persons involved want to restrain themselves and not report the matters, but the *lijia* and elders, when hearing about it, seek to take advantage of the opportunity and cause trouble, they shall be sentenced to sixty strokes of the heavy stick. When ill-gotten goods are involved they shall be punished according to the article on ill-gotten goods.[15]

15. In every *li*, if there are armed robbers, military deserters, escaped prisoners or troublemakers among the common people, and if one person cannot make the arrest alone, the *lijia* and elders shall immediately gather people to arrest them and send them to the officials. Violation shall be punished for the same crime as the criminals themselves.

16. The elders and the *lijia* shall not only make judgements about right and wrong among the people, but also urge them to do good. Among the common people in each village and *li* every adult male must work. Whenever someone goes or comes it shall be noted. The articles of the *Grand Pronouncements*[16] must be proclaimed and observed. Violation shall be punished.

17. The elders of each village and *li* shall send reports of the facts of good conduct of filial sons, obedient grandsons, virtuous husbands, chaste widows, or even persons having only a single praiseworthy virtue to the Imperial Court, and to the officials who shall then forward them to the Court. If the *li* elders have memorialized and the officials fail to do so, the officials shall be punished. Whenever the investigating censor [*jiancha yushi*] or the surveillance commissioner [*ancha si*] come for inspection, the *li* elders shall also report these virtuous people to them to verify the facts for their memorials.

18. In each village and *li*, if there are unregistered rowdies causing trouble and committing crimes day after day, refusing to mend their ways and dominating and coercing people, then these are not good subjects. The elders shall discipline them severely. If they go on as before and do not change, the elders shall arrest them and send them to the officials, who shall transport them to the capital. If the officials out of favoritism do not transport them, but set them free, the elders may memorialize.

---

[15] Reference is made to article 368 of the *Code*.

[16] The *Grand Pronouncements*, also rendered *Great Warnings*, are the *Yuzhi dagao* and its sequels, didactic instructions by the Ming founder to his subjects consisting of 236 items in four collections issued between 1385 and 1387. The complete text of the *Grand Pronouncements* is contained in HMZS (Tokyo edition vol. 1, 33-169.

19. In each village and *li* a bell with a wooden clapper shall be prepared. Old persons, disabled persons unable to function normally, or blind persons shall be selected and guided by children to walk through the *li* holding the bell. If there are no such persons in the *li*, then they shall be selected from other *li*. Let them shout loudly so that everyone can hear, urging people to do good and not violate the law. Their message is: "Be filial to your parents, respect superiors, maintain harmony with neighbors, instruct and discipline sons and grandsons, live and work in peace and contentment, do no wrongful acts." This shall be done six times each month. At the time of the autumn harvest, the people of the village and *li* shall give food to the bell carriers in accordance with their ability to pay. If the residents of the village are scattered and remote, each *jia* shall prepare a bell, and it will be easy to deliver the message. The style of the bell: it shall be made of copper with a wooden clapper hanging in the middle.

20. Those crafty persons in the villages and the *li* who, because of having been reprimanded by the elders, hold grudges and try to incriminate them by making false accusations, shall be punished severely when the matter comes to light.

21. In the *li*, year after year there are lawbreaking officials, deserters from corvee or military who have come back home, or fugitives from other places. The elders shall go to each family and every household reminding and warning the people of the *li* not to shelter them. These military fugitives shall be sent to the authorities lest they cause disturbance year after year, harming neighbors and relatives. Those who shelter them in the village will be implicated when the matter comes to light.

22. The Imperial Court establishes offices and divides their responsibilities essentially in order to bring peace to the people. When appointments are made it is hard to know whether officials are virtuous or not. Only when they take office and assume their duties can we see if they are good or evil. If an official who in fact is fair, diligent, honest, and creates happiness for the people is falsely accused, then the *li* elders may, in accordance with the *Grand Pronouncements*, gather a large number of people and send a memorial on his behalf. Account will be taken of it in judging the case. If there are officials who take bribes and harm the people, the elders may repeatedly remonstrate with them in accordance with the previous regulations of this placard. If the officials disregard the advice, the elders shall make the facts known, arrest them, and send them to the capital so as to spare the people further injury. Officials on whose behalf memorials are sent must be acknowledged by everyone to be good. Those who are arrested shall be known by everyone to be evil. It is essential that many people be involved, for only then can public opinion be known. If only three, five, or ten or so people declare the officials are good or evil, then because of their subjective bias it is difficult for the Imperial Court to trust the judgement. There are persons who know their superior officials to be upright, but make plans to

trick them into taking bribes or use the bribes to frame them, and even arrest them without authority. There are also cases in which the officials are incompetent, but persons who regularly consorted with them and gave them bribes falsely declare that they are good and improperly memorialize on their behalf. These are serious crimes which confuse right and wrong, disrupt the government and subvert the laws. How can the criminals save themselves and their families?

23. In Liangzhe[17] and Jiangxi many people are prone to litigation. They cannot endure even minor matters, and go directly to the capital to bring suits. Even when judicial officials are capable, judge cases fairly, and deal with them promptly it still entails traveling expenses. If judicial officials hold too many prisoners, are unable to deal with them promptly, or fail to judge cases fairly, imprisonment will drag on for months, causing many to die. Of those who are involved, quite a few innocent ones will die. Examining the causes of this, it is simply because they are usually unable to advise and counsel one another, and cannot endure petty resentments that they frequently bring the suits to the officials and so get themselves killed and their families ruined. Year after year they ignore our warnings and do not change. From now on, the elders shall earnestly exhort the people of their own *li* that minor matters involving household and marriage, land, assault and battery, or disputes should be mutually endured. If anyone is humiliated beyond what he could reasonably be expected to bear, he still must take the case to the elders, who shall weigh the seriousness of the matter, judge the case, and carry out the punishment. Thus they can redress the grievance and avoid entanglement with the officials. If crafty persons do not respect the instructions of the placard, do not listen to the exhortation of the elders, and readily bring suits to the officials or bypass the immediate jurisdiction to bring the suit directly to the capital, the elders may arrest and try them.

24. Among the peasants in Henan and Shandong some are lazy and do not work hard at farming, thereby causing shortages of clothing and food. Previously the Imperial Court sent out officials to oversee farming. Today an order is issued: henceforth only the elders of each *li* shall oversee farming. Each village shall set up a drum. During the months of cultivation, the drum shall be beaten at the fifth watch.[18] When they hear the drum everyone shall go to the fields. The elders in charge shall keep surveillance. If there are any who are lazy and do not go to the fields, the elders may discipline them. The elders shall strictly oversee the adult males doing their work and not allow loafers to eat without working. If the elders do not oversee the farmers, causing impoverishment and wrongdoing, so that crimes are reported to the officials, the elders of the village shall be found guilty.

---

[17] Liangzhe refers to Zhedong and Zhexi, east and west of the Qiantang River, i.e., Zhejiang.

[18] The fifth watch corresponds to the two-hour period from four to six a.m.

25. Villagers are not equal in wealth. No family is without the happy and sad events of marriages and funerals. From now on, the households of the *li* shall help one another whenever these events occur. For example, in case the marriage of the child of a certain poor family cannot be managed temporarily, if every household of the *li* contributes one *guan* of paper currency[19] and there are a hundred households, there will be one hundred *guan*; if every household contributes five *guan*, there will be five hundred *guan*. With help like this, could it not be accomplished? From now on when a family has a marriage this rule shall be used to take turns giving help. If the father or the mother of a family dies and has to be buried, each family shall contribute some amount of money or some rice to help the family with the inner and outer coffins, or rites performed by Buddhist or Daoist priests to secure a good destiny for the deceased. All this can be accomplished. From now on if a family has this kind of problem the previous rule should be followed to provide for mutual help and even poor families will then be able to furnish a small amount of money and rice. In this way, with united efforts, the required sum is easily raised. When this is done over a long period of time, friendliness will naturally prevail in the village.

26. At seven and eight or even at twelve and thirteen, children's desires have not yet awakened nor have they lost their innocence. They shall be instructed at an early age to study the three editions of the *Grand Pronouncements*, so they will truly take these first teachings most seriously, enabling them to know how to avoid evil and pursue good fortune. In the future, they will turn into virtuous persons and gentlemen, becoming good subjects. In this way they will not cause their parents concern and will not violate any law, thus preserving themselves and their families.

27. The purpose of the community wine drinking ceremony is to rank the elder and younger, and distinguish the worthy from the unworthy. This is a good way to improve customs. The people have already been ordered to carry it out. Now it is declared again: it must be carried out in accordance with the regulations previously issued; elder and younger are to be seated in ranked order, the worthy and unworthy are to be seated separately. When this is done for a long time, will not the people pursue good and avoid evil? The customs will be pure and honest and every individual will become a good subject.

28. Although humans cannot see the *yin* and *yang*, the inner and outer of the way of the ghosts [*gui*] and gods [*shen*][20], there in the nether world the

---

[19] A *guan*, literally string of copper cash, here represents the face value of a paper note.

[20] This passage refers to the traditional Chinese belief in the duality of the soul. The *yin* element [*po*] was coarser and associated with the earth, while the *yang* element [*hun*] was more refined and associated with heaven. After death the *po* could become a ghost [*gui*] while the *hun* could become a spirit or god [*shen*]. Ghosts were the source of many problems in the world of the living while spirits could become the subjects of sustained religious worship. The distinction between *yin* and *yang* elements in the soul is made in the *Liji* [*Book of Rites* or *Record of Rituals*]. For a

ghosts and gods are always watching. Whether one does good or evil, every deed will be requited. Previously, villages were ordered to sacrifice to their own gods of earth and grain, and to the abandoned ghosts and gods of their local area. Now it is declared again: at the appropriate seasons the common people shall offer the sacrifices according to the regulations, causing blessings to fall on the good and calamities on the bad. When the people are in fear of the warning they will not dare to do evil. When this is done, the good will constantly increase and the evil constantly decrease. Does this not improve the way of the world?

29. Now the realm is at peace. Except for paying taxes and performing corvee service, the people do not have other obligations. Everyone shall be attentive to his livelihood so as to have sufficient clothing and food. It is essential that every household follow the regulations in planting mulberries, dates, persimmons, and cotton. Every year silkworms shall be reared. The production of silk and cotton will be sufficient to provide clothing. The dates and persimmons during the prosperous years can be exchanged for currency and during the lean years they can be used for food. Such activity is beneficial to you people. The *lijia* and the elders shall oversee and inspect as usual. If any dare to disobey, their families shall be banished to the frontier.

30. In the countryside, if there is water which can be used to irrigate growing rice, harmful water which must be guarded against, or an obstructed river which must be dredged, the elders of the local *li* shall gather to investigate, make measurements, calculate the need for labor, and make plans and drawings with notes attached explaining how to construct and dredge. Come to the capital to memorialize. Based on these plans the people's welfare will be promoted and harm prevented.

31. From the ancient times, the purpose of the people_s paying taxes and performing corvee service is essentially to secure peace. In recent years, those in office are incompetent; officials and functionaries are unable to teach people to do good and are bent solely on taking bribes. When the time comes for tax collection and corvee service, they always receive money in return for extending the time limit, exempting the duties of the rich and sending the poor to perform them instead. This causes the ignorant people [*yumin*] to follow their example: to refuse to pay their allocated taxes punctually, to claim to have sold grain which they actually still have, to refuse to perform their share of corvee service. From now on, when paying taxes and performing corvee service, the people shall not bribe the officials. The allocated taxes shall be payed punctually and their corvee service shall be performed on time. If the taxes have already been paid and the corvee service performed, but the officials, functionaries, tax captains

brief account see Paul Chao, *Chinese Kinship* (London: Kegan Paul International, 1983), 102-103.

and *lizhang* collect them again the suffering families may gather a number of people to tie up the offenders and send them to the capital for severe punishment.

32. In the Yuan dynasty, many village children attended school. In the early years of the Hongwu period, villages everywhere were ordered to establish community schools [*shexue*] to instruct the children in good conduct. Incompetent officials and *lijia* took advantage of this to indulge in corrupt practices. The children of families with adult males obviously had the spare time to attend school but the officials took bribes and excused them from attending school. Nevertheless the children of families without adult males who had no spare time to attend school, were forced to go to school. This caused hardship for the people. Therefore, the community schools were abolished. From now on, the children of the common people, regardless of their location and number, shall be instructed by virtuous persons. The schools shall open early in the tenth month and close at the end of the twelfth month each year. If families with many adult males have enough spare time, they may have their children continually engaged in study. Those officials, functionaries and *lijia* who dare to interfere with them shall be punished severely.

33. The favor which our parents bestow in giving us birth is extremely great. Their toilsome labors of nurture are recorded in detail in the *Grand Pronouncements*. Now it is declared again that among the people those who have living agnatic grandparents and parents shall unstintingly support them in accordance with their families' means. Those whose agnatic grandparents and parents are dead shall sacrifice to them at the appointed times to show their filial respects. Parents shall instruct their children; children shall be filial to their agnatic uncles; wives shall encourage their husbands to do good. In this way the clans will become harmonious, no one will break the law and parents, wives and children will care for one another day and night. Will this not lead naturally to the enjoyment of peace?

STANDARD PRAYER TEXT

In Hongwu year ___ with cyclical characters [*jiazi*] ___, month ___ with starting day [*suo*] ___, on day ___ such-and-such filial grandson with the entire family declares to the spirits of his great-great-grandfather and grandmother, great-grandfather and grandmother, grandfather and grandmother, saying:

In times past from generation to generation our ancestors nurtured their children, sheltered them in their arms, and took infinite pains on their behalf. At the start of every season, according to the heat or cold, they dressed their children in more or fewer clothes and adjusted what they ate and drank. They worried lest their children go too close to fire or water, suffer from mosquitoes or other insects, or become ill. They cared for them by every possible means, for fear they would be upset. Their anxiety was without a moment's rest. That we grew up and got to where we are today is thanks to the favor of our ancestors' unremitting toil. Though we want to repay them, we know not how to do so. In this present season of (spring, summer, fall, or winter), as the weather is about to become (warm, cool, hot, or cold), when we recall times gone by, we cannot but think of them with longing. Respectfully now we make ready the wine, the grain, the soup, and the rice and, accompanied by the whole family of this household, we make this offering. May it be accepted.

34. Year after year, educational officials [*jiaoguan*] and teachers [*xundao*] in every place sent up memorials slandering the throne. They were rebellious and disloyal. When cases came to light, the teacher Jing Dehui and a number of others from Hangzhou and other schools were executed. From now on, it is essential that the education officials throughout the realm follow the maxims of former sages and worthies to instruct youths and, by developing their abilities, prepare them to hold office. Those who dare to not follow the maxims of the sages and worthies, recklessly encourage unorthodox ideas, confuse and mislead youths, and pervert their consciences shall be executed and their families banished to the frontier.

35. In the villages and the *li* the common people live close together and their fields are side by side. From fathers and agnatic grandfathers on down, they are either related or they know one another. Among the older ones, some are of the fathers' or agnatic grandfathers' generations, some are of the agnatic uncles' generation, and some are of the elder brothers' generation. Although they are not relatives, they are fellow villagers. They see one another from morning to night just as if they were relatives. Young children shall be respectful and polite. Those who dare to be frivolous and disrespectful and do not follow instructions shall be appropriately punished by the *li* elders. Aged persons who do not use the rites to guide the youth, but rely on their seniority to create disturbances involving innocent persons in criminal charges, shall also be punished. It is essential that neighborhoods be harmonious and that seniors and juniors love one another. When this is the case for a long time there will be no litigation. Then will it not be possible to stroll among the fields and villages and enjoy peace?

36. When the common people in the villages and *li* are not able to earn a living and their family fortunes are declining, and if they encounter unusual and unexpected calamities, are short of money, and have no alternative but to sell their ancestor's land and property, they may make a clear deed to sell the property at their convenience. Neighbors and relatives shall each sign their names. There shall be no coercion, no obstruction, and no blackmail for valuables, drink, or food. Violation shall be punished.

37. The duty of the soldiers, the guards, and battalions in every place is just to resist invasion and guard against rebellion so as to protect the people. Year after year, some of them deserted during campaigns, some ran away from their garrisons, and some escaped from military exile [*chongjun*]. The guards and battalions often sent people out to seize male adults to fill the vacancies and to arrest the actual deserters. The good *lijia* and elders dared not hide them and immediately seized them and sent them on their way. Some ignorant persons, however, not knowing what is good and what is bad, covered up for one another, bribed officials, and then made false reports that there were no draftees or that the households had been extinguished. When the guards and battalions sent people out to check again, they discovered that there were indeed some adult males. Many people have been punished for such abuses. From now on, whenever there is a draft, the elders and the *lijia* shall immediately send draftees on their way so as not to cause the officials to disturb the peaceful countryside by sending people back and forth. If there are those whose names are erroneously listed, or whose names are falsely used for the draft, it shall be reported to the elders and the *lijia*. The elders and the *lijia* shall immediately investigate and examine thoroughly, and send along the correct names of suitable draftees and the draftees themselves, so as to avoid reports being brought to the capital thus bothering the officials by making them go back and forth checking and rechecking. As for those who are obliged to be drafted as soldiers but obstinately refuse to go to their posts, cheating the officials and making false accusations, the elders may point out the facts and send them to the officials for punishment. If the elders fail to take charge, they shall also be punished.

38. It has already been decreed that lawsuits among the common people may only be brought from below to above. Those who bypass the immediate jurisdiction shall be found guilty. The designated officials often fail to observe this regulation and thereby cause too much bypassing of jurisdiction. From now on, those who still dare not to observe this regulation shall be punished for the crime of violating an imperial edict.[21]

39. The principles of right and wrong that are expressed in this placard are all to teach people the duties of filial piety, brotherly subordination, loyalty, fidelity, propriety, righteousness, honesty, and the sense of shame. The designated officials, elders, and *lijia* shall understand the purpose of the Imperial Court's instructions to the people. Everyone shall pursue good and avoid evil to protect himself and his family, to obey and preserve these instructions like a constant stream of water. Do not regard this as an empty document but strive to make it effective. Violation of this decree shall be punished according to the crime committed.

40. It should be frequently declared, to independent prefectures, subprefectures, and districts by the investigating censor [*jiancha yushi*] and to the

---

[21] This is a reference to article 64 of the *Code*.

prefectures, subprefectures, and districts of the provinces by the provincial surveillance office [*ancha si*] of each unit that it is essential to observe the principles in this placard forever. Those who dare to regard this placard as unimportant and do not declare it shall be punished.

41. When elders judging lawsuits have matters to memorialize, they may bear this placard and come to the capital without any official transit pass. They shall not be hindered at the passes. Other people shall not have such a privilege. Those who falsely use elders' names, and bearing this placard, come to the capital to report matters shall be severely punished.

Respect this. The ministry shall now print the details of the imperial decree and clearly publish it throughout the realm for respectful obedience and enforcement. The thirty-first year of Hongwu, fourth month, ___ day.[22]

[22] The fourth month of Hongwu 31 corresponds to the period from April 17 to May 16, 1398. The day is left blank.

APPENDIX FOUR

CONTENTS OF THE GREAT MING CODE[1]
(*DA MING LÜ*)[2]

CONTENTS:[3]

I. TERMS AND GENERAL PRINCIPLES

1. The Five Punishments
2. The Ten Abominations
3. The Eight Deliberations
4. Crimes by persons entitled to Eight Deliberations
5. Crimes by civil officials
6. Crimes by military officers
7. Public crimes by civil officials and military officers
8. Private crimes by civil officials and military officers
9. Crimes by parents and agnatic grandparents of those entitled to Eight Deliberations
10. Substitution for penal servitude and life exile for crimes by military officers and soldiers
12. Officials removed from office for legitimate reasons
13. Crimes committed by officials prior to appointment
14. Loss of status and imposition of labor obligation
15. Family members of life exiles
16. Exclusions to general amnesty
17. Ingrate to penal servitude or life exile when amnesty proclaimed
18. Crimes for which criminals are permitted to remain at home to care for relatives
19. Crimes by government artisans, musicians and by women
20. Crimes by those already under penal servitude or life exile
21. Redemption of punishments for the aged, the young, or the disabled
22. Crimes by those not yet old or disabled when their crimes were committed
23. Restitution and confiscation of ill-gotten goods
24. Voluntary confession of crimes

---

[1] In the text this has been referred to as the *Ming Code* or simply the *Code*.
[2] The text of the *Code* in its 1397 form can be found in HMZS (Taibei edition), vol. 4, 1605-2206.
[3] I have numbered the articles to facilitate reference to the text.

25. In multiple crimes the most serious is punished
26. All the parties to a crime escaping
27. Public crimes by members of the same office
28. Errors in public administration
29. Principals and accessories in joint crimes
30. Criminals fleeing when crimes are discovered
31. Concealment by relatives
32. Capital crimes by clerks and bailiffs
33. Execution of rebellious soldiers
34. Murder of military personnel
35. Crimes by civil and military persons residing in the capital
36. Crimes by naturalized persons
37. Specific articles with different regulations
38. Principles for the increase and decrease of punishments
39. References to "sedan chairs" and "carriages"
40. References to "relatives in the second degree of mourning" and "agnatic grandparents"
41. References to "the punishments are the same"
42. References to "supervisory officials" and "custodial officials"
43. References to "a day" as being one hundred units (*ke*)
44. References to "Daoist priests" and "Daoist nuns"
45. Judgement of crimes following the newly promulgated law
46. Judgement of crimes that have no specific articles
47. Places for penal servitude, life exile, and banishment

II. ADMINISTRATIVE LAW

A. *Administrative Regulations*

48. Selection for military posts
49. Unauthorized selection of officials by high officials
50. Prohibition on designating civil officials as dukes or marquises
51. Appointment privilege for sons of officials
52. Appointment of supernumerary officials
53. Inappropriate recommendation of officials
54. Recommendation of officials who have transgressed
55. Leaving post without authorization
56. Late arrival at official duty station
57. Unexcused failure to attend the emperor or to hold court in the morning
58. Unauthorized selection of subordinate officials
59. Certificate of completed official service
60. Treacherous clique
61. Developing ties with officials close to the Emperor

62. Memorializing in praise of the virtue and achievements of high officials

B. *Regulation of Official Documents*

63. Familiarity with the laws
64. Violations in carrying out imperial edicts
65. Destruction of imperial edicts or seals
66. Accidental loss of imperial edicts or seals
67. Violations of name taboos in memorials or statements to the throne
68. Not memorializing matters that ought to be memorialized
69. Not returning after being sent on a mission with an imperial edict
70. Divulging important military information
71. Delay in transmitting official documents
72. Arranging government files
73. Reviewing government files
74. Colleagues substituting signatures and endorsements on government documents
75. Adding to or deleting from official documents
76. Custody and use of seals
77. Omission of seals
78. Omission of seal on paper currency
79. Unauthorized use of seals to despatch troops
80. Travel passes

III. CIVIL LAW

A. *Households and Labor Service*

81. Omitting to file a household register
82. Households to be registered according to occupations
83. Unauthorized founding of temples and unauthorized ordination of Buddhist and Daoist priests
84. Illegal designation of heir
85. Taking in stray children
86. Unequal levying of tax and labor service
87. Unequal assignment of office service
88. Protecting official family members from office or labor service
89. Prohibition on removal of local head or village head
90. Evasion of office of labor service
91. Appointment of prison guards
92. Illegal use of commoners and government artisans under an official's jurisdiction
93. Separating household register and property

94. Unauthorized use of property by junior or younger members of the family
95. Support of the orphaned and elderly

B. *Landed Property*

96. Evasion of land tax
97. Inspection of crop lands damaged by natural calamity
98. Land of nobility of merit
99. Fraudulent sale of land and dwellings
100. Purchase of land and dwellings in location of an official's service
101. Mortgage and sale of lands and dwellings
102. Illegal cultivation of government or private land
103. Allowing crop land to go uncultivated
104. Discarding or destroying utensils or crops
105. Eating fruits of gardens or orchards without permission
106. Unauthorized loan of government vehicles or boats

C. *Marriage*

107. Marriage
108. Pawning and renting wives and daughters
109. Violations of status of wives and concubines
110. Expelling son-in-law and remarrying daughter
111. Marriage during mourning period
112. Marriage during imprisonment of parents
113. Marriage between persons with the same surname
114. Marriage between different generations
115. Marriage to relative's wife or concubine
116. Marriage to a woman as wife or concubine from among those under an official's jurisdiction
117. Marriage to runaway women
118. Coerced marriage to a woman from a good family
119. Taking a musician as wife or concubine
120. Marriage by Buddhist or Daoist priests
121. Marriage between commoners and inferior classes
122. Marriage by Mongols and Semu
123. Dismissal of wife
124. The punishment for contracting parties or go-betweens in illegal marriages

D. *Government Granaries and Treasuries*

125. Paper currency

126. Coinage
127. Late payment of grain tax
128. Over collection of grain tax
129. Concealment or expenditure of grain or other levies
130. Monopolizing payment of grain tax
131. False issuance of tax receipts
132. Misapplication of excess tax receipts to make up other quotas
133. Unauthorized loan of government money or grain
134. Unauthorized loan of government property
135. Improper transfer of expenditures or receipts
136. Embezzlement by granary or warehouse employees
137. Embezzlement of military pay
138. Mutual surveillance by officials and the employees of granaries and warehouses
139. Theft from government granaries and warehouses as a result of laxness
140. Holding and paying money and grain and unauthorized removing of official sealing strips
141. Improper disposal of government property
142. Harassment of receipt or payment
143. Purity of gold and silver payable to the government
144. Damage to property in government granaries
145. Transmission of government property
146. Improper decisions on forfeitures and restitutions
147. Custody of government property
148. Concealment of property confiscated by government

E. *Taxes and Tariffs*

149. Salt: Unlicensed trade in salt[4]
150. Salt: Salt workers trading privately on the side
151. Salt: Women trading privately in salt
152. Salt: Purchase of unlicensed salt
153. Salt: Authority to prosecute private salt trade
154. Salt: Anti-smuggling patrols
155. Salt: Private salt trade by military personnel
156. Salt: Verification of salt in transit
157. Salt: Misuse of salt certificates
158. Salt: Prohibiting weapons and private boats in transport of salt
159. Salt: Adulteration of salt
160. Salt: Territorial restriction of salt certificates

[4] I have added extended titles to the twelve articles on salt.

161. Supervisory personnel and powerful persons trading in salt
162. Obstruction of salt administration
163. Smuggling of tea
164. Smuggling of alum
165. Tax evasion
166. Shippers concealing cargo
167. Those failing to meet tax quota

F. *Money Lending*

168. Usury
169. Depletion of property held in trust
170. Obtaining lost property

G. *Markets*

171. Illegitimate brokers
172. Price appraisal by market authorities
173. Monopolizing markets
174. Illegitimate manufacture of volume measures, weights and linear measures
175. Utensils and textiles not up to standard

IV. RITUAL LAW

A. *State Sacrifice*

176. Imperial sacrifices
177. Destruction of tumuli and altars
178. Provincial rites for various spirits
179. Tombs of previous rulers
180. Dishonoring spirits
181. Prohibition of witchcraft and heterodoxy

B. *Ceremonial Regulations*

182. Preparation of imperial medicine
183. Imperial clothing and objects
184. Keeping prohibited books and private practice of astronomy
185. Imperial presents of clothing and other items
186. Errors relating to imperial audiences
187. Violation of ceremonial procedures
188. Violation of procedure in imperial audiences
189. Obstructing access to emperor

190. Memorials and statements to throne
191. Incumbent official raising stele praising himself
192. Prohibitions on the reception and send off of higher officials
193. Official messengers treating local officials contemptuously
194. Violations of sumptuary regulations
195. Buddhist and Daoist clergy honoring parents
196. Failure to report heavenly portents
197. Soothsayers wildly predicting fortune and disaster
198. Concealment of parent's or husband's death
199. Abandoning parents to assume office
200. Funeral and burial ceremonies
201. Community wine drinking ceremonies

V. MILITARY LAW

A. *Imperial Palaces and Guards*

202. Unauthorized entry into the imperial ancestral temple
203. Unauthorized entry into the imperial palaces
204. Unauthorized substitution for imperial guards
205. Tardiness or irregularity by imperial escort guards
206. Walking directly on imperial pathway
207. Substitution for craftsmen working in the inner palace
208. Failure to leave the palace compound at the end of the day's construction work
209. Unauthorized exit and entry through palace gates
210. Identification measures for exit and entry of eunuchs
211. Shooting arrows at palaces
212. Weapons of imperial guards
213. Prohibition on those with criminal records being imperial guards
214. Intrusion into imperial procession: Avoidance of processions
215. Intrusion into imperial procession: Presentation of petitions
216. Intrusion into imperial procession: Intrusion by domestic animals
217. Gates of imperial camps
218. Climbing over city walls
219. Locking of city gates
220. Carrying identification tags

B. *Administration of Armed Forces*

221. Unauthorized dispatch of government forces
222. Reporting military matters
223. Emergency report of military matters
224. Requests for frontier supplies

225. Errors and failures in military operations
226. Tardiness in military campaigns
227. Unauthorized substitution of soldiers
228. Military commander abandoning position
229. Allowing troops to pillage and ravage
230. Failure to train and discipline soldiers
231. Provoking commoners to revolt
232. Unauthorized sale of captured horses
233. Unauthorized sale of weapons and equipment
234. Destruction and abandonment of weapons and equipment
235. Private possession of prohibited military weapons and equipment
236. Allowing soldiers to neglect military duties
237. Unauthorized employment of military personnel by dukes and marquises
238. Desertion by officers or men on campaigns or in garrison
239. Preferential treatment of military dependents
240. Curfew

C. *Guard Posts and Forts*

241. Passing a checkpoint without authorization, by circumvention or through deception
242. Granting passes under false pretenses
243. Harassment of travelers at checkpoints
244. Smuggling wives and daughters of military deserters out of the city
245. Interrogation of spies
246. Illicit export of goods and defiance of maritime prohibition
247. Unauthorized employment of local police

D. *Horses and Cattle*

248. Improper care of government livestock
249. Breeding horses
250. Inaccurate counting and grading of animals purchased
251. Improper care of sick animals
252. Abuse of animals
253. Failure to break and train government horses
254. Unauthorized butchering of horses and cattle
255. Animals causing bodily harm
256. Concealment of issue of government livestock
257. Unauthorized use of government livestock
258. Government messengers demanding use of government horses

E. *Postal Service and Transport*

259. Delivery of government documents: Speed requirements
260. Delivery of government documents: Damage, tampering or concealment
261. Delivery of government documents: Inspection of post houses
262. Interception of sealed government documents
263. Failure to maintain post houses
264. Unauthorized employment of post house attendants
265. Delay of government messengers
266. Excessive use of postal horses
267. Excessive issuance of supplies
268. Failure to provide transport for express post
269. Transport delays hindering government missions
270. Occupation of the best rooms of the hostel
271. Using government horses to transport private goods
272. Unauthorized ordering of commoners to carry sedan chairs
273. Families of deceased officials to be sent home at government expense
274. Hiring substitutes to do transport work
275. Carrying private goods while riding on government animals or boats
276. Unauthorized lending of transport horses

VI. PENAL LAW

A. *Robbery and Theft*

277. Plotting rebellion and great sedition
278. Plotting treason
279. Making magical inscriptions and magical incantations
280. Theft of ritual items
281. Theft of imperial edicts
282. Theft of official seals
283. Theft of property from imperial palaces
284. Theft of keys to city gates
285. Theft of military equipment
286. Stealing wood from imperial estates and tombs
287. Theft by supervisory and custodial officials from granaries and treasuries
288. Theft by commoners from granaries and treasuries
289. Armed robbery
290. Rescuing prisoners by force
291. Snatching in daytime
292. Theft

293. Theft of horses, cattle and other livestock
294. Theft of grain from the field
295. Theft from relatives
296. Extorting property by threats
297. Obtaining public or private property by fraud
298. Seizure or sale of free persons into slavery
299. Opening of graves
300. Unauthorized entering of a house at night
301. Harboring of thieves and robbers
302. Conspiracy to commit robbery
303. Taking property publicly or stealthily are both theft
304. Removal of tatoos

B. *Homicide*

305. Murder
306. Murder of imperial agents or of immediate superior officers
307. Murder of grandparents and parents
308. Killing an adulterer
309. Murder of parents of deceased husband
310. Killing three or more persons in one family
311. Mutilating a living person
312. Killing a person by making or keeping *gu* poison
313. Killing in a fight and intentional killing
314. Depriving persons of clothing and food
315. Killing or injuring in play, by error, or by negligence
316. Husband beating to death transgressing wife or concubines
317. Killing a son, grandson, or slave and attributing the crime to another
318. Injuring another with bow and arrow
319. Killing or injuring others with horses and carriages
320. Incompetent doctors killing or injuring patients
321. Killing or wounding by means of traps
322. Causing the death of an individual by oppressive threats
323. Private settlement and concealment of killing of a superior
324. Knowledge of crime contemplated by an acquaintance

C. *Assault and Battery*

325. Assault and battery
326. Time limit on responsibility for wounds caused
327. Quarreling in imperial palace
328. Assaulting member of the imperial relatives
329. Assaulting imperial emissaries or one's immediate superior authorities

330. Subordinate official assaulting his superior
331. Superior and subordinate officials assaulting each other
332. Officials of rank nine or above assaulting superiors
333. Resisting and assaulting a pursuer
334. Assaulting one's teacher
335. Illegitimate detention by force
336. Commoners and inferior persons assaulting each other
337. Male and female slaves assaulting their masters
338. Wife or concubines assaulting husband
339. Relatives of the same surname assaulting each other
340. Assaulting a superior relative of the third degree of mourning or higher
341. Assaulting a senior or elder relative of the second degree of mourning
342. Assaulting grandparents or parents
343. Wife or concubines and husband's relatives assaulting each other
344. Assaulting sons of wife's former husband
345. Wife or concubines assaulting deceased husband's parents
346. Protecting father or grandfather from blows

D. *Abusive Language*

347. Cursing
348. Cursing imperial emissaries or one's immediate superior authorities
349. Subordinate officials cursing superiors
350. Male or female slaves cursing their masters
351. Cursing senior or elder relatives
352. Cursing grandparents or parents
353. Wife or concubines cursing husband's relatives of second degree of mourning
354. Wife or concubines cursing deceased husband's parents

E. *Accusations and Suits*

355. Litigation bypassing appropriate jurisdiction
356. Making accusations through anonymous letters
357. Refusal to accept an accusation
358. Avoidance in presiding over litigations
359. False accusations
360. Improper charges which violate social order
361. Son or grandson violating instruction
362. Prohibition of prisoners from bringing accusations
363. Instigation of litigation
364. Coordination of litigation involving both military and civilians

365. Family members lodging accusations on behalf of officials
366. False accusation of crime punishable by military exile or banishment

F. *Bribery*

367. Acceptance of valuables by government personnel
368. Crimes involving ill-gotten goods
369. Receiving valuables after litigation
370. Offering valuables to influence litigation
371. Officials requesting or borrowing people's property
372. Family members of officials making requests from commoners
373. Surveillance officials accepting bribes
374. Levying unauthorized exactions for public benefit
375. Unauthorized acceptance of property from dukes and marquises
376. Retention of stolen goods
377. Government personnel tolerating promises of property

G. *Deception and Fraud*

378. Forgery of imperial edicts
379. False transmission of verbal imperial order
380. Memorializing or responding to imperial inquiry untruthfully
381. Illegitimate manufacture of seals or calendar
382. Counterfeiting paper currency
383. Illegitimate minting of coinage
384. Posing as a government official
385. Posing as a eunuch or other official
386. Close attendants of emperor falsely claiming to be on secret mission for emperor
387. Falsification of portents
388. Avoiding duty by feigning illness, death or injury
389. Instigating others to break the law

H. *Sexual Violations*

390. Illegitimate sexual intercourse
391. Conniving in adultery committed by wife or concubines
392. Adultery between relatives
393. Falsely accusing senior male relatives of illegitimate intercourse
394. Slaves or employees having illegitimate sexual intercourse with master's wife
395. Illegitimate sexual intercourse with wives and daughters of subordinates

396. Illegitimate sexual intercourse during period of mourning or by Buddhist and Daoist clergy
397. Illegitimate sexual intercourse between commoners and inferior persons
398. Government personnel patronizing entertainers
399. Purchase of free persons to be entertainers

I. *Miscellaneous Offenses*

400. Destroying exhibition pavilion
401. Giving medicine to corvee workers, artisans, and soldiers when ill
402. Gambling
403. Castration of eunuchs
404. Asking favors in public matters
405. Illegitimate settlement of public matters
406. Causing fire by negligence
407. Arson
408. Theatrical performance
409. Violation of the *Commandment*
410. Improper conduct

J. *Arrests and Escapes*

411. Apprehension of criminals by police
412. Criminals resisting arrest
413. Escape from confinement, prison riots, and flight
414. Escape of those under penal servitude or life exile
415. Delaying the execution of a sentence of penal servitude
416. Custodial officials who are not aware of prisoner's escape
417. Knowingly concealing criminals
418. Time limit for arrest of thieves and robbers

K. *Trial and Imprisonment*

419. Failure to imprison persons who should be confined
420. Intentionally imprisoning or interrogating innocent persons
421. Prolongation of imprisonment
422. Mistreatment of prisoners
423. Giving prisoners edged tools that they can use to free themselves and escape
424. Instructing prisoners to change their testimony
425. Prisoners' clothing and food
426. Meritorious officials under confinement allowed visits by relatives

427. Prisoners under sentence of death soliciting aid in committing suicide
428. The aged or children exempt from torture in questioning
429. Joint trial of accomplices when held separately
430. Conducting trial in accordance with specifications in the charge
431. Plaintiff not to be detained after trial is completed
432. Prisoners falsely accusing innocent persons
433. Officials implicating the innocent and exonerating the guilty
434. Reversing false judgements
435. Authorities deciding degree of punishment
436. Autopsy or inspection of injuries not according to facts
437. Illegitimate execution of punishment
438. Crimes by senior officials or their messengers
439. Citation of *Code* and *Commandment* in judging crimes
440. Getting prisoners to accept their sentences after conviction
441. Incorrect judgement of crimes before an amnesty
442. Deliberately committing crimes in anticipation of amnesty
443. Failure to require criminals under penal servitude to perform labor service
444. Crimes by women
445. Memorials concerning death penalty needing responses
446. Incorrect judgement of crimes
447. Clerks writing statements for suspects

VII. LAWS ON PUBLIC WORKS

A. *Construction and Manufacture*

448. Unauthorized construction and manufacture
449. Wasting manpower and selecting unsuitable material
450. Construction and manufacture not in accord with regulations
451. Taking home government materiel
452. Manufacture of private cloth by government looms
453. Illegitimate weaving of cloth with dragon and phoenix patterns
454. Manufacture exceeding time limit
455. Repair of granaries and storehouses
456. Government personnel not residing in official residences

B. *River Conservancy*

457. Breeching of dikes
458. Failure to maintain embankments
459. Encroaching on public streets
460. Maintaining bridges and roadways

REFERENCES

Note: References in the text generally follow the author-date system. Exceptions have been made in the cases of Chinese texts which are referred to by key words or abbreviations. Codes translated as appendixes are referred to by article or item number as they appear in the translations. In some cases, dictionaries are cited by entry number. Chinese characters for authors and titles are listed in the Glossary.

ABBREVIATIONS:

Code:	*Da Ming Lü* (*Great Ming Code*). Cited by article number in appendix 4.
Commandment:	*Da Ming ling* (*Great Ming Commandment*). Cited by article number in appendix 2.
DG:	*Yuzhi da gao* (*Grand Pronouncement*). Cited by article number in HMZS (Tokyo edition).
DGSB:	*Yuzhi da gao sanbian* (*Grand Pronouncement, Part Three*). Cited by article number.
DGXB:	*Yuzhi da gao xubian* (*Supplementary Grand Pronouncement*). Cited by article number in HMZS (Tokyo edition).
DMB:	*Dictionary of Ming Biography.*
ECCP:	*Eminent Chinese of the Ch'ing Period.*
HMJSSYB:	*Huang Ming jingshi shiyongbian.*
HMZS:	*Huang Ming zhishu.*
Instruction:	*Huang Ming zuxun* (*August Ming Ancestral Instruction*). Cited by article number in appendix 1.
Placard:	*Jiaomin bangwen* (*Placard of People's Instructions*). Cited by article number in appendix 3.
MCKGWX:	*Ming chao kaiguo wenxian.*
MHY:	*Ming huiyao.*
MS:	*Mingshi.*
MSLHW:	*Ming Taizu shilu.*
ZSTX:	(*Yuzhi*) *Zishi tongxun.*
ZWDCD:	*Zhongwen dacidian.* Cited by entry number.

REFERENCES

Anderson, Benedict. [1983] 1991. *Imagined Communities: Reflections on the Origin and Spread of Nationalism*. Revised edition. London: Verso.
Anderson, Perry. 1974. *Lineages of the Absolutist State*. London: Verso.
Andrew, Anita M. 1991."Zhu Yuanzhang and the *Great Warnings* (*Yuzhi da gao*): Autocracy and Rural Reform in the Early Ming." Ph.D. diss., University of Minnesota.
Atwell, William S. 1975."From Education to Politics: The Fu She." In *The Unfolding of Neo-Confucianism*, ed. Wm. Theodore de Bary, 333–67. New York: Columbia University Press.
——. 1988. "The T'ai-sh'ang, T'ien-ch'i, and Ch'ung-chen reigns, 1620–1644." In *The Cambridge History of China*, Vol. 7, *The Ming Dynasty, 1368–1644, Part I*, 585–640. Cambridge: Cambridge University Press.
Biot, Edouard, trans. 1851. *Le Tcheou-li ou Rites des Tcheou*. 3 vols. Paris: Impremerie Nationale.
Blackstone, William. 1979. *Commentaries on the Laws of England*. Facsimilie of the first edition of 1765–1769, 4 vols. Chicago: University of Chicago Press.
Bodde, Derk, and Morris, Clarence. 1973. *Law in Imperial China: Exemplified by 190 Ch'ing Dynasty Cases* (translated from the *Hsing-an hui-lan*). Philadelphia: Univ. of Pennsylvannia Press paperback.
Chan, Hok-lam. 1968. "Liu Chi (1311–75) and his Models: The Image Building of a Chinese Imperial Adviser." *Oriens Extremus* 15.1: 34–55.
——. 1974. "Die Prophezeiung des Liu Chi (1311–1375), Ihre Enstehung und iher Umwandlung im heutigen China." *Saeculum* 25.4: 338–366.
——. 1977. "Xu Yikui xingsi bianwu jian lun Ming chu wenziyu shiliao" (The case of Xu Yikui's alleged execution: a critical appraisal of the sources on `literary persecution' during the early Ming period). *Journal of Oriental Studies* 15.1: 77–84.
Chan, Hok-lam, and de Bary, Wm. Theodore, eds. 1982. *Yuan Thought: Chinese Thought and Religion Under the Mongols*. New York: Columbia Univ. Press.
Chang, George Jerlang, trans. 1978. "The Placard of People's Instructions (Chiao-min bang-wen)." *Ming Studies* 7: 63–72.
Chao, Paul. 1983. *Chinese Kinship*. London: Kegan Paul International.
Ch'en, Paul Heng-chao. 1979. *Chinese Legal Tradition under the Mongols: The Code of 1291 as Reconstructed*. Studies in East Asian Law, Harvard University. Princeton: Princeton Univ. Press.
Ch'ien Mu, trans. Hsueh, Chün-tu et al. 1982. *Traditional Government in Imperial China, A Critical Analysis*. Hong Kong: The Chinese University Press.
Ch'ü, T'ung-tsu. 1961. *Law and Society in Traditional China*. Paris: Mouton.

——. 1962. *Local Government in China under the Ch'ing.* Cambridge, Mass.: Harvard University Press.
——. [1947] 1967. *Zhongguo falü yu Zhongguo shehui.* Hong Kong: Lungmen shudian.
Ciyuan. 1979–83. Revised edition, 4 vols. Beijing: Shangwu yinshuguan.
Couvreuer, S., trans. 1927. *Chou King* [*Shujing*]. Sien Hsien: Catholic Mission edition.
Da Ming ling (*Great Ming Commandment*). HMZS (Taibei edition), vol. 1, 7–117.
Da Ming Lü (*Great Ming Code*). HMZS (Taibei edition), vol. 4, 1605–2206.
Danjo Hiroshi. 1982a. "Gimon Teishi to Genmatsu no shakai" (The righteous Zheng clan and late Yuan society). *Toyo gakuho* 63: 67–103.
——. 1982b. "Gen-Min kotai no rinen to genjitsu—Gimon Teishi o tegari to shite" (Ideology and reality in the Yuan-Ming transition: the experience of the Righteous Zheng clan). *Shirin* 65.2: 177–204.
Dardess, John W. 1970. "The Transformations of Messianic Revolt and the Founding of the Ming Dynasty." *Journal of Asian Studies* 29.3: 539–558.
——. 1983. *Confucianism and Autocracy: Professional Elites in the Founding of the Ming Dynasty.* Berkeley: University of California Press.
De Bary, Wm. Theodore, ed. 1970a. *Self and Society in Ming Thought.* New York: Columbia University Press.
——. 1970b. "Individualism and Humanitarianism in Late Ming Thought." In *Self and Society in Ming Thought,* ed. Wm. Theodore de Bary, 145–247. New York: Columbia University Press.
——. 1981. *Neo-Confucian Orthodoxy and the Learning of the Mind-and-Heart.* New York: Columbia University Press.
——. 1982. "Introduction." In *Yuan Thought: Chinese Thought and Religion Under the Mongols,* ed. Hok-lam Chan, 1–25. New York: Columbia University Press.
——. 1991. *The Trouble with Confucianism.* Cambridge: Harvard University Press.
—— and Chaffee, John W., eds. 1989. *Neo-Confucian Education: The Formative Stage.* Berkeley: University of California Press.
De Groot, J.J.M. 1894. *The Religious System of China.* Vol. 2, Book I, "Disposal of the Dead." Leyden: E.J. Brill.
Dictionary of Ming Biography. 1976. 2 vols. Ed. L. Carrington Goodrich. New York: Columbia University Press.
Dreyer, Edward L. 1982. *Early Ming China: A Political History 1355-1435.* Stanford: Stanford University Press.
Ebrey, Patricia Buckley. 1986. "The Early Stages in the Development of Descent Group Organization." In *Kinship Organization in Later Imperial*

China, 1000–1940, ed. Patricia Buckley Ebrey and James L. Watson, 16–61. Berkeley: University of California Press.

——, trans. and intro. 1991. *Chu Hsi's Family Rituals: A Twelfth-Century Chinese Manual for the Performance of Cappings, Weddings, Funerals and Ancestral Rites*. Princeton: Princeton University Press.

Ebrey, Patricia Buckley and Watson, James L., eds. 1986. *Kinship Organization in Late Imperial China, 1000–1940*. Berkeley: University of California Press.

Eminent Chinese of the Ch'ing Period. 1943–44. 2 vols. Ed. Arthur W. Hummel. Washington, D.C.: U.S. Government Printing Office.

Fairbank, John K., ed. 1968. *The Chinese World Order*. Cambridge: Harvard University Press.

Fairbank, John K.; Reischauer, Edwin O.; and Craig, Albert M.. 1965. *East Asia: The Modern Transformation*. Boston: Houghton Mifflin.

Farmer, Edward L. 1976. *Early Ming Government: The Evolution of Dual Capitals*. Cambridge, Mass: Harvard East Asian Research Center.

——. 1982. "Ming wangchao chuqi (1350–1425) di zhengti fazhan" (Constitutional developments in the early Ming Dynasty, 1350–1425). In *Ming-Qing shi guoji xueshu taolunhui lunwenji* (Collected papers of the international symposium on Ming-Qing history), 16–44. Tianjin: Renmin chubanshe.

——. 1985a. "Civilization as a Unit of World History: Eurasia and Europe's Place in It." *History Teacher* 18.3: 345–63.

——. 1985b."The Status of the Person in Early Ming Law." *Journal of Chinese Studies* 2.1: 73–80.

——. 1987. "Social Order in Early Ming China: Some Norms Codified in the Hung-wu Period." In *Law and the State in Traditional East Asia*, ed. Brian McKnight, 1–36. Honolulu: University of Hawaii Press.

——. 1988. "The Prescriptive State: Social Legislation in the Early Ming Dynasty." In *Proceedings of the 2nd International Conference on Sinology*, Section on Ming, Ch'ing, and Modern History. Taibei: Academia Sinica.

——. 1990. "Social Regulations of the First Ming Emperor: Orthodoxy as a Function of Authority." In *Orthodoxy in Late Imperial China*, ed. Kwang-Ching Liu, 103–25. Berkeley: University of California Press.

——. 1993. "The Great Ming Commandment (*Ta Ming Ling*): An Inquiry into Early-Ming Social Legislation." *Asia Major* 4.1: 181-99.

Feng Han-yi. 1948. *The Chinese Kinship System*. Cambridge, Mass.: Harvard University Press.

Fisher, Carney T. 1990. *The Chosen One: Succession and Adoption in the Court of Ming Shizong*. Sydney: Allen Unwin.

Frank, Arthur W. III, et al, eds. 1986. *The Encyclopedic Dictionary of Sociology*, 3rd ed. Guilford, Conn.: Dushkin Publishing Group.

Franke, Wolfgang. 1968. *An Introduction to the Sources of Ming History.* Kuala Lumpur: University of Malaya Press.

Gates, Hill and Weller, Robert. P. 1987. "Hegemony and Chinese Folk Ideologies: An Introduction" *Modern China* 13.1: 3-16.

Grimm, Tilemann. 1985. "State and Power in Juxtapostion: An Assessment of Ming Despotism." In *The Scope of State Power in China*, ed. Stuart R. Schram, 27–50. London: School of Oriental and African Studies, University of London.

Hazelton, Keith. 1984. *A Synchronic Chinese-Western Daily Calendar 1341–1661.* Minneapolis: Ming Studies.

Hsiao, Kung-chuan. 1960. *Rural China: Imperial Control in the Nineteenth Century.* Seattle: University of Washington Press.

Hsu Daolin. 1953. *Zhongguo fazhi shi lunlue* (A brief account of the history of Chinese legal institutions). Taibei: Zhongzheng shuju.

Hsüeh, Chün-tu, ed. 1971. *Revolutionary Leaders of Modern China.* New York: Oxford University Press.

Huang Ming jingshi shiyongbian. [1604] 1967. 5 vols. Comp. by Feng Yingjing. Taibei: Chengwen chubanshe.

Huang Ming zhishu (a). 1966-67. 2 vols. Edited by Zhang Lu. Tokyo: Koten kenkyukai.

Huang Ming zhishu (b). 1969. 6 vols. Edited by Zhang Lu. Taibei: Chengwen chubanshe.

Huang Ming zuxun (*August Ming Ancestral Instruction*). In MCKGWX 3: 1579–1671.

Huang Zhangjian. 1961. "Lun Zuxunlu banxing niandai bing lun Ming chu fengjian zhuwang zhidu" (On the period when the Imperial Ming *Ancestral Instruction* was published and on the system of pricely enfeoffment in the early Ming). In *Zhongyang yanjiuyuan lishi yuyan yanjiusuo jikan* 32: 119–37.

——. 1977. *Ming-Qing shi yanjiu conggao.* Taibei: Taiwan shangwu yinshuguan.

Huang Qinglian. 1977. *Yuan dai huji zhidu yanjiu* (The household system of the Yuan dynasty). History and Chinese Literature series No. 45. Taibei: Taiwan University.

Hucker, Charles O. 1978. *The Ming Dynasty: Its Origins and Evolving Institutions.* Michigan Papers in Chinese Studies, No. 34. Ann Arbor: Center for Chinese Studies, University of Michigan.

——. 1985. *A Dictionary of Official Titles in Imperial China.* Stanford: Stanford University Press.

Hulsewé, A.F.P. 1961. "Forward." In *Law and Society in Traditional China* by Ch'ü T'ung-tsu, 1–3. Paris: Mouton.

——. 1987. "Law as One of the Foundations of State Power in Early Imperial China." In *Foundations and Limits of State Power in China*, ed. Stuart R. Schram, 11–32. London: School of Oriental and African Studies, University of London.

Jiaomin bangwen (*Placard of people's instructions*). In HMZS, Tokyo edition, Vol. 1, 467–476.

Johnson, Wallace, trans. 1979. *The T'ang Code: Volume I, General Principles*. Princeton: Princeton University Press.

Kamenka, Eugene and Tay, Alice Erh-Soon, eds. 1980. *Law and Social Control*. New York: St. Martin's Press.

Kamenka, Eugene and Tay, Alice Erh-Soon. 1980. "Social Traditions, Legal Traditions." In *Law and Social Control*, ed. Kamenka and Tay, 3–26.

Langlois, John D., Jr. 1974. "Chin-hua Confucianism under the Mongols (1279–1368)." Ph.D. diss., Princeton University.

——, ed. 1981a. *China Under Mongol Rule*. Princeton: Princeton University Press.

——. 1981b. "Political Thought in Chin-hua under Mongol Rule." In *China Under Mongol Rule*, ed. Langlois, 137–85.

——. 1988. "The Hung-wu Reign, 1368–1398." In *The Cambridge History of China*, vol. 7, *The Ming Dynasty, 1368–1644, Part I*, 107–81. Cambridge: Cambridge University Press.

Langlois, John D. Jr., and Sun K'o-k'uan. 1983. "Three Teaching Syncretism and the Thought of Ming T'ai-tsu." *Harvard Journal of Asiatic Studies* 43.1: 97–139.

Legge, James, trans. 1960 [1893]. *The Chinese Classics*. 5 vols. Oxford: Clarendon Press; reprinted Hong Kong.

Li Guangbi. 1957. *Mingchao shilue* (Survey of Ming history). Wuhan: Hubei renmin chubanshe.

Lin Tai-yung. 1979. "Ming T'ai-tsu and his Administration of Justice." Ph.D. diss., University of Minnesota.

Lincoln, Bruce. 1989. *Discourse and the Construction of Society: Comparative Studies of Myth, Ritual, and Classification*. New York: Oxford University Press.

Littrup, Leif. 1981. *Subbureaucratic Government in China in Ming Times: A Study of Shandong Province in the Sixteenth Century*. Oslo: Universitetsforlaget.

Liu, Kwang-Ching, ed. 1990. *Orthodoxy in Late Imperial China*. Berkeley: University of California Press.

Ma Huan. 1970 [1433]. *Ying-yai sheng-lan: The Overall Survey of Ocean's Shores*. Trans. J.V.G. Mills. Cambridge: Hakluyt Society.

MacCormack, Geoffry. 1990. *Traditional Chinese Penal Law*. Edinburgh: Edinburgh University Press.

Massey, Thomas P. 1983. "Chu Yuan-chang and the Hu-Lan Cases of the Early Ming Dynasty." Ph.D. diss., University of Michigan.

Mathews, R. H. 1960 [1931]. *Mathews' Chinese-English Dictionary*. Revised American edition [1944]. Cambridge, Mass.: Harvard University Press.

McKnight, Brian E., ed. 1987. *Law and the State in Traditional East Asia: Six Studies on the Sources of East Asian Law*. Honolulu: University of Hawaii Press.

Meskill, John. 1982. *Academies in Ming China: A Historical Essay*. Association for Asian Studies Monograph No. 39. Tucson: University of Arizona Press.

Ming chao kaiguo wenxian (Documents from the Ming founding). 1966. 4 vols. Taibei: Xuesheng shuju.

Ming Huiyao (Handbook of Ming government). 1956. 2 vols. Beijing: Zhonghua shuju.

Mingshi (Ming history). 1974. 28 vols. Beijing: Zhonghua shuju.

Ming Taizu shilu (Ming veritable record of the Hungwu period). 1961. 8 vols. Taibei: Zhongyang yanjiuyuan lishi yuyan yanjiusuo.

Mote, Frederick W. 1961. "The Growth of Chinese despotism: A critique of Wittfogel's theory of Oriental Despotism as applied to China." In *Oriens Extremus* 8.1 :1–41.

——. 1962. *The Poet Kao Ch'i, 1336-1374*. Princeton: Princeton University Press.

——. "The Limits of Intellectual History?" [Review article on Wm. Theodore de Bary, The Liberal Tradition in China]. In *Ming Studies* 19: 17–25.

——. 1988a. "Introduction." In *Cambridge History of China*. Vol. 7, *The Ming Dynasty, 1368–1644, Part I*, edited by Frederick W. Mote and Denis Twitchett, 1-10. Cambridge: Cambridge University Press.

——. 1988b. "The Rise of the Ming Dynasty." In *Cambridge History of China*. Vol. 7, *The Ming Dynasty, 1368–1644, Part I*, ed. Frederick W. Mote and Denis Twitchett, 11–57. Cambridge: Cambridge University Press.

Mote, Frederick W. and Twitchett, Denis, eds. 1988. *The Cambridge History of China*. Vol. 7, *The Ming Dynasty, 1368–1644, Part I*. Cambridge: Cambridge University Press.

Na Chih-liang and Kohler, William. 1970. *The Emperor's Procession: Two Scrolls of the Ming Dynasty*. Taibei: National Palace Museum.

Niida Noboru. 1964. *Chugoku hoseishi kenkyu* (A study of Chinese legal history). Tokyo: Tokyo University Press.

Noguchi Tetsuro. 1981. *Minshi keihoshi sakuin* (Index to the Essay on Law of Ming History). Tokyo: Kokusho kankokai.

Raeff, Marc. 1983. *The Well-ordered Police State: Social and Institutional Change through Law in the Germanies and Russia, 1600–1800*. New Haven: Yale University Press.

Rapp, John and Andrew, Anita. 1991. "Despotism and China's Peasant Emperors: Ming Taizu and Chairman Mao." Unpublished paper.

Reischauer, Edwin O. and Fairbank, John K.. 1960. *East Asia: The Great Tradition*. Boston: Houghton Mifflin.

Sangren, Steven P. 1984. "Great Tradition and Little Traditions Reconsidered." *Journal of Chinese Studies* 1.1: 1–24.

——. 1987a. "Orthodoxy, Heterodoxy, and the Structure of Value in Chinese Rituals." *Modern China* 13.1: 63–89.

——. 1987b. *History and Magical Power in a Chinese Community*. Stanford: Stanford University Press.

Schurmann, Franz. 1968. *Ideology and Organization in Communist China*. 2d ed., enlarged. Berkeley: University of California Press.

Shen Jiaben. [1929] 1964. *Shen Jiyi xiansheng yishu* (Bequeathed writings of Mr. Shen Jiyi [Shen Jiaben]), first series. 2 vols. Reprinted Taipbei: Wenhai chubanshe.

Staunton, George Thomas, trans. [1810]1966. *Ta Tsing Leu Lee: Being the Fundamental Laws, and a Selection From the Supplementary Statutes of the Penal Code of China*. London: T. Cadell and W. Davies; reprinted Taipei: Ch'eng-wen Publishing Co.

Tao Xisheng and Shen Renyuan. 1967 [1977] *Ming-qing zhengzhi zhidu* (The political system of the Ming and Qing dynasties). 3d ed. Taibei: Commercial Press.

Taylor, Romeyn. 1969. "Yuan Origins of the Wei-So System." In *Chinese Government in Ming Times*, ed. Charles O. Hucker, 23–40. New York: Columbia University Press.

——., trans. 1975. *Basic Annals of Ming T'ai-tsu*. San Francisco: Chinese Materials Center, Inc.

——. 1976. "Ming T'ai-tsu and the Nobility of Merit." *Ming Studies* 2: 57–69.

——. 1977. "Ming T'ai-tsu and the Gods of the Walls and Moats." *Ming Studies* 4: 31–49.

——. 1983. "An Imperial Endorsement of Syncretism: Ming T'ai-tsu's Essay on the Three Teachings: Translation and Commentary." *Ming Studies*, 16: 31–38.

——. 1989. "Chinese Hierarchy in Comparative Perspective." *Journal of Asian Studies* 48.3: 490–511.

Teng Ssu-yu. 1936. "Ming *Da gao* yu Ming chu zhi zhengzhi shehui." *Yanjing xuebao* 20, reprinted in MCKGWX, 1–26.

——. 1967. "Ming T'ai-tsu's Destructive and Constructive Work." *Chinese Culture* 8.3: 14–38.

Vandermeersch, Léon. 1985. "An Enquiry into the Chinese Conception of the Law." In *The Scope of State Power in China*, ed. Stuart R. Schram, 3–25. London: School of Oriental and African Studies, University of London.

Van der Sprenkel, Sybille. 1962. *Legal Institutions in Manchu China: A Sociological Analysis*. London: University of London, Athlone Press.

Watson, Burton, trans. 1988. *The Tso Chuan: Selections from China's Oldest Narrative History*. New York: Columbia University Press.

Watson, James L. and Rawski, Evelyn S., eds. 1988. *Death Ritual in Late Imperial and Modern China*. Berkeley: University of California Press.

Weggel, Oskar. 1980. *Chinesische Rechtgeschichte*. Leiden-Koln: E. J. Brill.

Wolf, Arthur P. and Huang Chien-shan. 1980. *Marriage and Adoption in China, 1845–1945*. Stanford: Stanford University Press.

Wu Han. 1936. "Yuan diguo zhi bengkui yu Ming zhi jianguo" (The collapse of the Yuan empire and the founding of the Ming). In *Qinghua xuebao* 11.1: 359–422.

——. 1948. *Zhu Yuanzhang zhuan*. Hong Kong: Zhuanji wenxue she.

——. [1965] 1979. *Zhu Yuanzhang zhuan*. Beijing: Xinhua shudian.

Yanai, Wataru. 1963. *Yuan dai Meng Han Semu daiyu kao* (Study of the treatment of Mongols, Han Chinese, and Semu in the Yuan dynasty). Trans. Chen Jie and Chen Qingquan. Taibei: Taiwan shangwu yinshuguan.

Yang Lien-sheng. 1969. "Ming Local Administration." In *Chinese Government in Ming Times*, ed. Charles O. Hucker, 1–21. New York: Columbia University Press.

Yang Yifan. 1988. *Ming Da gao yanjiu* (Study of the Ming *Grand Pronouncement*). Nanjing: Jiangsu renmin chubanshe.

——. 1992. Hongwu falü dianji kaozheng (Study of legal codifications of the Hongwu period). Beijing: Falü chubanshe.

Yen Chih-t'ui. 1968. *Family Instructions for the Yen Clan* (*Yen-shih chia-hsun*). Translated with introduction by Teng Ssu-yu. Leiden: E. J. Brill.

Yuzhi da gao (*Grand Pronouncement*). In HMZS (a) 1: 34–62.

Yuzhi da gao sanbian (*Grand Pronouncement Part Three*). In HMZX(a) 1: 108–153.

Yuzhi da gao xubian (*Supplementary Grand Pronouncement*). In HMZS (a) 1: 63–106.

Zhongwen dazidian (The encyclopedic dictionary of the Chinese language). [1973] 1980. 10 vols. 5th ed., revised. Taipei: Zhongguo wenhua xueyuan.

Zi shi tongxun (Instructions to guide the age). In HMZS(b) 3: 1449–84.

GLOSSARY

Note: This list excludes common place names, repetitious official titles, lists of names to be used in princely lines, and the like. Capitalization has been restricted to proper names and titles of documents. English equivalents in parentheses link the terms to the text but should not be considered to be translations in all cases.

ancha si (provincial surveillance office) 按察司
anlong (ceremonial saddle) 鞍龍

ba yi (eight deliberations) 八議
Baihua *guo* (country name) 白花國
baihu suo (company) 百戶所
baize (flag type) 白澤
ban (clapper) 板
banbang (notice board) 板榜
bandu (reader-companion) 伴讀
banjian (dress sword) 班劍
bao (recompense) 報
bei (stele) 碑
Beiping 北平
bianfu (ordinary clothing) 便服
Bianliang 汴梁
bicijuzui 彼此俱罪
bing 兵
binglü (military law) 兵律
bingma si (warden's office) 兵馬司
bingwei (military guards) 兵衛
bingzang 併贓
bingzhang ju (palace armory) 兵仗局
biyou (person junior in generation or age) 卑幼
biyou sishan yongcai (unauthorized use of property by younger or subordinate members of the family) 卑幼私擅用財
bo (earl) 伯
Boni *guo* (Brunei) 浡泥國
bu wang (arrest and flight) 捕亡
buwangfa (bribe-taking without making an unjust decision) 不枉法

buyingwei (that which ought not to be done) 不應爲

cangku (granaries and treasuries) 倉庫
Cao 曹
chaishi renyuan (official personnel on detached service) 差使人員
changrendao (embezzlement of money and grain by those not having responsibility) 常人盜
changshang (death in late teens) 長殤
changsui fengyu (attendent) 長隨奉御
chaofu (court robes) 朝服
Chaoxian *guo* (Korea) 朝鮮國
chen (minister) 臣
Chen Jie 陳捷
Chen jie lu 臣戒錄
Chen Qingquan 陳清泉
Chen Youliang 陳友諒
chengfeng si (office of steward) 乘奉司
chengxiang (grand councilor) 丞相
Chengzu 成祖
chi (edict)
chi (light stick) 笞
chi (idiocy, stupidity) 癡
chishou (observance) 持守
chongjun (military exile) 充軍
chou (an enumerator, the second of the twelve branches) 丑
chuang (pennant) 幢
chuanjiaofan (command streamer) 傳教旛
chuchan yaosha ren (animals biting and killing people) 畜產咬殺人
Chugoku hoseishi kenkyu 中國法制史研究
chumingbuxu 除名不敘
churu ren zui 出入人罪
chushiguan (imperial emissary) 出使官
cimu (concubine acting as foster mother) 慈母
Ciyuan 辭源
cong (B, lower level of rank; retainer) 從
congzhonglun 從重論
Cunxin lu 存心錄

Dadu 大都
da dudu fu (chief military commission) 大都督府
Da gao (Grand pronouncement) 大誥
Da gao wuchen (Grand pronouncement for military officers) 大誥武臣
dagong (mourning grade, greater coarseness for nine months) 大功
dagu (big drum) 大鼓

Daizong 代宗
dali si (court of judicial review) 大理寺
da liyi 大禮議
Da Liuqiu *guo* (Greater Ryukyus) 大琉球國
Da Ming ling (Great Ming Commandment, *Commandment*) 大明令
Da Ming lü (Great Ming Code, *Code*) 大明律
Da Ming lügao 大明律誥
Danjo Hiroshi 檀上寬
danma (ceremonial horse) 誕馬
dao (truth, the way) 道
dao (sword) 刀
Daodejing 道德經
daoli (correct doctrine) 道理
daotong (orthodox tradition) 道統
daoxue (learning of the way) 道學
dashi (commissioner) 大使
dasitan (great sacrificial altar) 大祀壇
daxiong huangdi bixia (your majesty big brother emperor) 大兄黃帝陛下
Daxue (Great learning) 大學
Da Yuan tongzhi (Comprehensive institutions of the great Yuan) 大元通制
dazhang gongzhu (princess supreme) 大長公主
da zhenren (great perfected one) 大眞人
dengzhang (looped staff) 鐙杖
di (flute) 笛
ding (enumerator, fourth of ten stems) 丁
dianbao suo (seals office) 典寶所
dianbing ju (weapons service) 典兵局
dianbu (archivist) 典簿
dianfu ju (apparel service) 典服局
dianfu suo (apparel office) 典服所
dianli (clerk) 典吏
dianshan ju (food service) 典膳局
dianshan suo (foods office) 典膳所
diansheng ju (equipage service) 典乘局
dianxi ju (seal service) 典璽局
dianyao ju (medicine service) 典藥局
dianyi suo (ceremonies office) 典儀所
dianyue (manager of music) 典樂
dianzhang (manager of ceremonial regalia) 典仗
disun (senior grandson) 嫡孫
dizi (eldest son of the wife) 嫡子
dizhi (earthly branches) 地支

donggong (eastern palace, residence of heir apparent) 東宮
douou (assault and battery) 鬥毆
dou song (assaults and accusations) 鬥訟
duan yu (judgement and imprisonment) 斷獄
dubo (gambling) 賭博
dukehua (flower decoration on gowns) 獨科花
dun (shield) 盾

fa (law) 法
falü (law) 法律
fan 凡
fangfu yuanshou (square base and round top) 方趺圓首
Fang Guozhen 方國珍
fangsan (square umbrella) 方傘
Fang Xiaoru 方孝孺
fanjian (sexual violations) 犯姦
fei (cutting off feet) 腓
fengci suo (sacrificial office) 奉祠所
fengguo jiangjun (supporter-general of the state) 奉國將軍
fengguo zhongwei (supporter-commandant of the state) 奉國中尉
fengxian guan (guardians of customs and laws) 風憲官
Feng Yingjing 馮應京
fu (ax) 斧
fu (vice, deputy) 副
fugu (retraditionalization) 復古
fuguo jiangjun (bulwark-general of the state) 輔國將軍
fuguo zhongwei (bulwark commandant of the state) 輔國中尉
fu huang bixia (your majesty father emperor) 父皇陛下
fuma (imperial princess's consort) 駙馬
fuma duwei (commandant-escort) 駙馬都尉
fu qianhu (assistant commander) 副千戶
fushi (deputy commissioner) 副使
fuwutoushui 赴務投稅
fuyi huangce (yellow registers of labor service) 賦役黃册
fuzi (whisk) 拂子

gaozhifan (stopping streamer) 告止旛
ganggu (small drum) 鼓
ganmingfanyi (violating the principles of family hierarchy) 干名犯意
Gaoli (Korea) 高麗
ge (regulation) 格
gechang (spear) 戈氅
Gemingjun 革命軍

Gen-Min kotai no rinen to genjitsu—Gimon Teishi tegari to shite 元--明交替の理念と實--義門鄭氏を手掛りとして
gewu (investigation of things) 格物
Gimon Teishi to Genmatsu no shakai 義門鄭氏と元末の社會
gong (bow) 弓
gong (duke) 公
gong (works; craftsman) 工
gongbing (constable) 弓兵
gongli (merit and profit, utilitarian) 功利
gong lü (laws on public works) 工律
gongren (respectful lady) 恭人
gongshi (standards of official behavior) 公式
gong wei (imperial palaces and guards) 宮衛
gongyong (provisions) 供用
gongzheng suo (construction office) 工正所
gongzhu (imperial princess) 公主
gongzui (public crime) 公罪
gu (insect poison) 蠱
guan (string of cash) 貫
guanglu si (court of imperial entertainments) 光祿寺
guanjin (frontier guard posts) 關禁
guduo (round end staff) 骨朵
gui (ghost) 鬼
guifu chishou (tortoise base and hornless dragon top) 龜趺螭首
guofu 國父
guo furen (consort of state) 國夫人
guogong (duke of state) 國公
Guo Huan 郭桓
guoxue (national university) 國學
Guo Ying 郭英
Guoyu 國語
guozi jian (directorate of education) 國子監
Guo Zixing 郭子興

Han 韓
Han Liner 韓林兒
Han Shantong 韓山童
haojie (hero, military adventurer) 豪傑
hefang (river conservancy) 河防
hegu hemai (mutually beneficial hiring or purchase) 和顧和買
hongchuoxie 紅綽屑
Hongwu 洪武
Hongwu falü dianji kaozheng 洪武法律典籍考正
hongxiaojinsan (decorated gilt umbrella) 紅銷金傘

hongxiusan (red embroidered umbrella) 紅繡傘
hou (marquis) 侯
Hsu Daolin 徐道鄰
hu (revenue, household) 戶
Huai *you buyi* 淮右布衣
huajiao (decorated horn) 畫角
huakuanggu (decorated drum) 花匡鼓
huang (great, august, imperial) 皇
huangfei (imperial consort) 皇妃
Huang Ming jingshi shiyongbian 皇明經世實用編
Huang Ming zhishu 皇明制書
Huang Ming zuxun (*August Ming Ancestral Instruction*, *Instruction*) 皇明祖訓
Huang Qinglian 黃清連
huang taisun (imperial grandson-heir) 皇太孫
Huang Zhangjian 皇彰健
Huaxinghui (Society to Revive China) 華興會
hui (standard) 麾
Hu Han 胡翰
huhun (household and marriage) 戶婚
hu lü (civil law) 戶律
hun (soul) 魂
hunyin (marriage) 婚姻
Huren (Mongols) 胡人
Hu Weiyong 胡惟庸
hu yi (family and corvee service) 戶役

ji (two-pointed lance) 戟
jia (first of ten stems; tithing unit) 甲
jian (arrow) 箭
jiancha yushi (investigating censor) 監察御史
jiang (artisan) 匠
jiangren (soup steward) 漿人
jiangyinfan (red streamer) 絳引旛
jianjiao guan (inspector) 檢校官
jianshoudao (embezzlement of government money and grain by those responsible) 監守盜
Jianwen 建文
jiao (doctrine, teaching) 教
jiao (strangulation) 絞
jiaoguan (education office) 教官
jiaohua (enculturation) 教化
Jiaomin bangwen (*Placard of People's Instructions*, *Placard*) 教民榜文
jiaoshou (instructor) 教授

jiaota (foot rest) 腳踏
jiaoyi (ceremonial chair) 交椅
jiao zi (instruction of children) 教子
jiashou (tithing chief) 甲首
jiashuo (long lance) 夾
jiazi (first pair of cyclical characters) 甲子
jichang (tasseled lance) 戟氅
jie (stele) 碣
jie (time beater) 節
jigang (net ropes) 紀綱
jigang bu zhen (net ropes not shaken) 紀綱不振
jigang fadu (net ropes of the law) 紀綱法度
Jigu dingzhi 稽古定制
jimu (stepmother) 繼母
jin churu (precautions on coming and going) 謹出入
Jing cheng lu 精誠錄
Jing Dehui 景德輝
jingji (patrolman) 警跡
jingli si (registry) 經利司
Jingjiang 靖江
jinguqi (bell flag) 金鼓旗
Jinhua 金華
Jinling 金陵
jinmao ju (caps and kerchief service) 巾帽局
jintiao (restrictions) 禁條
jinyiwei (embroidered uniform guard) 錦衣衛
jinzheng (bell) 金鉦
jinzi (jailer) 禁子
jishan (moral mentor) 紀善
jishan suo (moral mentor's office) 紀善所
jishi fengyu (secretary) 紀事奉御
jisi (state sacrifices) 祭祀
jiucumian ju (condiments service) 酒醋麵局
jiu ku (public stables and granaries) 廄庫
jiumu (horses and cattle) 廄牧
jiuren (wine steward) 酒人
jiuyi guan (censor in charge of deportment) 糾儀關
Jizhi lu 稽制錄
juan (section of a book) 卷
jucheng (deputy chief) 局丞
jue (noble rank) 爵
jufu (court robes) 具服
julang (chief) 局郎
juling 拘鈐

jun (military) 軍
jun bo (commandery earl) 郡伯
Junfa dinglu (statutes on military law) 軍法定律
junfen shuili (equally dividing irrigation water) 均分水利
jun furen (commandery mistress) 郡夫人
jun hou (commandery marquis) 郡侯
junhu (military household) 軍戶
jungong (commandery duke) 郡公
junjun (commandery mistress) 郡君
junwang (commandery prince) 君王
junzheng (administration of armed forces) 軍政
junzhu (princess) 郡主
juqian 拘錢

Kaixi 開熙
kecheng (taxes and tariffs) 課程
Kong Keren 孔克仁
kongyin an (case of prestamped documents) 空印案
Kongzi *miao* (Confucian temple) 孔子廟
Kökö Temur 擴廓帖木兒
ku (storehouse) 庫

Lan Yu 藍玉
laoren (elders) 老人
li (measure of distance, village community) 里
li (natural moral principles) 理
li (personnel, functionary) 吏
li (precedents) 例
li (rites, ritual) 禮
liangyi suo (medical office) 良醫所
Li Chenggui 李成桂
lichun (spring begins) 立春
lifang (personnel department) 吏方
ligua (vertical melon staff) 立瓜
Li Guangbi 李光壁
Liji (Book of rites) 禮記
lijia 里甲
li lü (administrative law) 吏律
li lü (ritual law) 禮律
ling (ordinance, *Commandment*) 令
lingchi (death by slicing) 凌遲
lingli (error for lingshi, clerk, below) 令吏
lingjiedushi (concurrent supply commission) 領節度使
lingqi (command flag) 令旗

lingquanchashi (concurrent surveillance commissioner) 領勸察使
lingshi (clerk) 令使
liqiu (autumn begins) 立秋
Li Renren 李仁人
Li Shanchang 李善長
liu (life exile) 流
liuchu jianshi hejia deng (domestic animals trampling or eating crops) 六畜賤食禾稼等
Liu Futong 劉福通
Liu Ji 劉吉
Li Wenzhong 李文忠
lixianguan 禮賢館
lixue (school of principle) 理學
liyi (ceremony) 禮儀
Liyi dingshi (Fixed regualtions on ceremonial) 禮儀定式
lizhang (community head) 里長
Lizhi jiyao 禮制集要
Longfeng 龍鳳
longting (dragon pavilion) 龍亭
Lunyu (Analects of Confucius) 論語
lunzi (wheel) 輪子
Lun *Zuxunlu* banxing niandai bing lun Ming chu fengjian zhuwang zhidu 論祖訓錄頒行年代並論明初封建諸王制度
luo (gong) 鑼
lü (statute, the Ming Code, *Code*) 律

mali (abusive language) 罵詈
mawu (ceremonial stool) 馬杌
men zheng (gate keeper) 門正
mengun (red stick) 悶棍
Mengzi (Mencius) 孟子
Mengzi jiewen (abridged version of Mencius) 孟子節文
mianfu (ceremonial robes) 冕服
min (commoner, the people) 民
Min 岷
min fu (the people's good fortune) 民福
min huo (the people's calamity) 民禍
Mingchao kaiguo wenxian 明朝開國文獻
Mingchao shilue 明史略
Ming Dagao yanjiu 明大誥研究
Ming huiyao 明會要
ming li (general principles) 名理
Ming-Qing shi yanjiu conggao 明清史研究叢稿

Ming-Qing shi guoji xueshu taolunhui lunwenji 明清史國際學術討論會論文集
Ming-Qing zhengzhi zhidu 明清政治制度
Ming Sheng 明昇
Mingshi 明史
Ming Taizu shilu 明太祖實錄
Ming wangchao chuqi (1350–1425) di zhengti fazhan 明王朝初期的政體發展
mingyi (right principles) 名義
Ming Wang (Prince of Radiance) 明王
Ming Yuzhen 明玉珍
Minshi keihoshi sakuin 明史刑法索引
minyong (on the people) 民用
mou (measure of land) 畝
mu hou dianxia (your majesty mother empress) 母 殿下
Mu Ying 沐英

nan (baron) 男
neichengyun ku (palace storehouse) 內承運庫
neifu gongyong ku (palace supply storehouse) 內府供用庫
neiguan (eunuchs) 內官
neiguan jian (directorate of palace eunuchs) 內官監
neiguan jianguan (eunuch supervisory agency) 內官監官
neiling (palace regulations) 內令
neishi (household agent) 內使
nei zhiran ju (palace weaving and dyeing service) 內織染局
neng shi (able scholar) 能士
Niida Noboru 仁井田陞
ning 寧
nong (farmer) 農
Noguchi Tetsuro 野口鐵郎

pailou (honorary arch) 牌樓
peixiang 配享
Penheng *guo* (Pahang) 湓亨國
pin (rank) 品
po (soul) 魄
Pujiang 浦江

qi (wife) 妻
qianhu suo (battalion) 千戶所
Qianqing 乾清
qianshi (assistant commander) 僉事
qianzhai (money lending) 錢債

qi duwei (commander of cavalry) 騎都尉
qie (concubine} 妾
qiedao (theft) 竊盜
qihui qiwu jiase deng (discarding or destroying utensils or crops) 棄毀器物稼穡等
Qincha 欽察
qinci (respect this; phrase at end of edict) 欽此
Qing 慶
qing (human feelings) 情
qing (unit of land) 頃
qingci (tattooing) 黥刺
qingdao (road clearer) 清道
qinwang (imperial prince) 親王
qugai (curved parasol) 曲蓋
ranren (dye steward) 染人
renming (homicide) 人命
renqing (human feeling) 人情
Renzu 仁祖
ru (Confucian scholar) 儒
rumu (wet nurse) 乳母
sanda (flower) 散搭
Sanfoji *guo* (Srivijaya) 三佛齊國
san gong (three dukes) 三公
sanfu bamu 三父八母
San huangmiao (Temple of the Three Sages) 三皇廟
Sanmin zhuyi (Three People's Principles) 三民主意
san zongsun (fourth degree nephew, ffbssss) 三從孫
Semu 色目
shang (merchant) 商
shang (death in youth) 殤
shangbao jian (directorate of palace seals) 尚寶監
shanggong (exalted duke) 上公
shanggongju (general palace service) 尚宮局
shang hujun (senior military protector) 上護軍
shang qi duwei (commander of cavalry) 上騎都尉
shang qingche duwei (senior commander of light chariots) 上輕車都尉
shangshan jian (directorate for palace delicacies) 尚膳監
shangyi jian (directorate of imperial apparel) 尚衣監
shang zhuguo (supreme pillar of state) 上柱國
shanshi tianyuan guaguo deng (eating fruits of gardens and orchards without permission) 擅食田園瓜果等
shan xing (unauthorized levies) 擅興
sheji (gods of soil and grain) 社稷
shen (spirit, god) 神

shengdao (way of the sages) 聖道
shengong jian (directorate of grounds) 神宮監
shen guozheng (prudence in affairs of state) 慎國政
Shengxue xinfa (The system of the mind-and-heart in the learning of the sages) 聖學心法
shengyuan (student) 生圓
Shen Jiaben 沈家本
Shen Jiyi xiansheng yishu 沈寄簃先生遺書
shenli suo (disciplinary office) 審理所
shenming ting (exhibition pavilion) 申明亭
shenqi (divine instrument) 神器
Shen Renyuan 沈任遠
shenxing si (punishment reviewing office) 審刑司
shexue (community school) 社學
shi (ordinances) 式
shi (picul) 石
shi (scholar) 士
shichan (public markets) 市廛
shichen 時辰
Shichen zonglu 世臣總錄
shidafu 士大夫
Shidian xianshi Kongzi yizhu 釋奠先師孔子儀注
shi e (ten abominations) 十惡
shihuo (fire) 失火
shi wu xieshu (witches and heterodoxy) 師巫邪術
Shizong 世宗
Shizu 世祖
shouling guan (staff supervisor) 首領官
shouzang (bribery and squeeze) 受贓
shucha (forked spear) 殳叉
shuiguan (water jug) 水罐
shuipen (water pan) 水盆
Shujing (Book of documents) 書經
shuli (clerk) 書吏
shumu (father's concubine) 庶母
Shundi 順帝
shuo (long lance)
shuo (first day of lunar month) 朔
Shuo yuan 說苑
shu xing (redemption of punishment) 贖刑
shuzhuang renli (accusation writing clerk) 書狀人吏
shuzi (son born of concubine) 庶子
si (Buddhist monastery) 寺
si (death) 死

si (registry) 司
si fu (deputy supervisor) 司副
si fuguan 四輔官
si gongshi (household agent for bows and arrows) 司弓矢
sili (staff foreman) 司吏
sili jian (directorate of ceremonial) 司禮監
sima (mourning grade, coarse hemp for three months) 緦麻
sinong si (agricultural propagation office) 司農司
sishe jian (directorate of equippage) 司設監
Si shu (Four Books) 四書
si yao (household agent for medicine) 司藥
siyao ku (palace key storehouse) 司鑰庫
siyuan ju (gardening service) 司苑局
siyu guan (warder) 司獄官
sizai gengniu (illegal killing of plowing oxen) 私宰耕牛
sizheng (director) 司正
sizui (private crime) 私罪
Song Lian 宋濂
Sumendala (Samudra) 蘇門答剌
suo (battalion) 所
su song (accusations and suits) 訴訟

taiji (supreme ultimate) 太極
taijian (director) 太監
Taisui (star god) 太歲
Taizong 太宗
Taizu 太祖
Tang He 湯和
Tao An 陶安
Tao Xisheng 陶希聖
tiangan (heavenly stems) 天干
tianli (heavenly principle) 天理
Tianwan 天完
tianxia (all under heaven) 天下
tianshi (Celestial Master) 天師
tiantu (land) 田土
tianzhai (landed property) 田宅
tiaoge (articles) 條格
tiaoli (ruling) 條例
tidiao zhengguan (principal supervising official) 提調正官
tiehuang (yellow notice) 貼黃
tieshu (writer) 貼書
tilao guan (jailer) 提牢官
Tingzhou 汀州

Toghto 托克托
tongzhi (vice commander) 同知
touguan (Qiang horn) 頭管
tu (penal servitude) 徒
tuiguan (judge) 推官
tuohu (covered pot) 唾壺
tuoyu (covered vessel) 唾盂

wang (prince) 王
wangfa (making unjust decisions in exchange for bribes) 枉法
Wang Guangyang 汪廣洋
Wang Mang 王莽
wang sun (grandson of prince) 王孫
Wang Yangming 王陽明
Wang Yi 王禕
wang zi (son of prince) 王子
wei jin (imperial guard and prohibitions) 衛禁
wei zhenfusi (guard prison) 衛鎮撫司
Wei Zhongxian 魏忠賢
wen 文
wenyin (travel document) 文引
wogua (horizontal melon staff) 臥瓜
wu (enumerator, fifth of the ten stems) 戊
Wu 吳
Wuding 武定
Wu Han 吳
Wujing sishu xingli daquan (Great compendia of the Five Classics, Four Books, and Human Nature and Principle) 五經四書大全
Wumen (Meridian Gate) 午門
wuqi wei (commandant of militant cavalry) 武騎尉
wu xing (five punishments) 五刑
wuzhang (wooden staff) 梧杖
Wuzong 武宗
wuzuo (coroner) 仵作
xian 咸
xianghe (incense box) 香盒
xiangjie (resonant beater) 響節
xiangjun (township mistress) 鄉君
xianglu (incense burner) 香爐
xiang yinjiu li (community wine-drinking ceremony) 鄉飲酒禮
xianjun (district mistress) 縣君
Xianluo *guo* (Siam) 暹羅國
xiannan (district baron) 縣男
xiannu (ceremonial crossbow) 攙弩

xiansi (provincial surveillance commission) 憲司
xianwang (ancient rulers) 先王
xianzhu (district princess) 縣主
xianzi (district viscount) 縣子
xiaogong (mourning grade, lesser coarseness for five months) 小功
Xiao He 蕭何
Xiaoling shengong jian (Xiaoling directorate of grounds) 孝陵神宮監
Xiao Liuqiu *guo* (Lesser Ryukyus) 小琉球國
Xiao Ming Wang 小明王
Xiao Ming Zhu 小明主
xiaoren (inferior person) 小人
xiashang (death in childhood) 下殤
xiedu shenming (dishonoring the spirits) 褻瀆神明
Xin 信
xinfan (insignia streamers) 信旛
xing (punishment, justice) 刑
Xinggong lu 省躬錄
xing lü (penal law) 刑律
xingren (messenger) 行人
xingzhi ke (rotations section) 行止科
Xingzhonghui (Revive China Society) 興中會
xinxue (school of mind) 心學
Xiping 西平
xiren (vinegar steward) 醯人
xixin si (office of fuel) 惜薪司
Xiyang *guo* (Western Ocean Country) 西洋國
xizhu (music stopper) 戲竹
xuanli (error for xuanshi, below) 宣吏
xuanshi (courier) 宣使
Xu Da 徐達
Xu Shouhui 徐壽輝
xundao (teacher) 訓導

Yan 燕
Yanai Wataru 箭内亙
yang (order, the male principle) 陽
Yang Yifan 楊一凡
yange (castration) 閹割
yangmu (adoptive mother) 養目
Yang Xian 楊憲
yan jisi (proper sacrifice) 嚴祭司
yan yun si (salt distribution commission) 鹽運司
Ye Chen 葉琛
yi (aunt, mother's sister) 姨

yi (cutting off nose) 劓
Yi (dynasty in Korea) 李
yi (physician) 醫
yibin (ceremonial companion) 儀賓
yidao (ceremonial sword) 儀刀
yihuang (tasseled halberd) 儀鍠
yin (disorder, the female principle) 陰
yin (protection privilege) 蔭
yingshan (construction) 營繕
Yingzong 英宗
ying zao (public construction) 營造
yinli sheren (household receptionist) 引禮舍人
yinshou jian (directorate for credentials) 印綬監
yinyang (geomancer) 陰陽
Yi Pang-won 李芳遠
yiren (manifest lady) 宜人
Yi Song-gye (see Li Chenggui)
yiwei si (cermonial guard) 儀衛司
yixiang (relocation) 移鄉
yizhi (ceremonial regulations) 儀制
Yongjian lu 永鑑錄
Yongle 永樂
Yongle dadian (Great Yongle encyclopedia) 永樂大典
youyi (postal services and transport) 郵驛
you zhangshi (right administrator) 右長史
yu (ignorance) 愚
yuan (academy) 院
yuan (clerk) 掾
Yuan dai huji zhidu yanjiu 元代戶計制度研究
Yuan dai Meng Han Semu daiyu kao 元代蒙漢色目待遇考
yuandian (clerk) 掾典
Yuan dianzhang (Yuan regulations) 元典章
Yuan diguo zhi bengkui yu Ming zhi jianguo 元帝國之崩潰與明之建國
yuanli (clerk) 掾吏
Yuan shi (Yuan history) 元史
yuanshi (administrative aid) 掾史
yulu (jade carriage) 玉輅
yuma jian (directorate of imperial horses) 御馬監
yumin (ignorant people) 愚民
yunqi wei (commandant of the fleet-as-clouds cavalry) 雲騎尉
yushi tai (tribunal of censors) 御史臺
Yu Xin 郁新
Yuzhi dagao (Grand Pronouncement) 御制大誥

Yuzhi dagao sanbian 御制大誥三編
Yuzhi dagao xubian 御制大誥續編
Yuzhi zishi tongxun (Comprehensive imperial instruction to aid the world) 御制資世通訓
yuzu (guard) 獄卒
zafan (miscellaneous offenses) 雜犯
zaizongsun (third degree nephew, fbss) 再從孫
za lü (miscellaneous articles) 雜律
zang (illgotten goods) 贓
zangzui (crime involving ill-gotten goods) 贓罪
zei dao (violence and robbery) 賊盜
zhan (decapitation) 斬
Zhancheng *guo* (Champa) 城國
zhancui (grade of mourning, unhemmed sackcloth for three years) 斬衰
zhang (heavy stick) 杖
zhang (measurement of distance) 丈
Zhang Chang 張昶
zhang gongzhu (grand princess) 長宮主
zhanggu (double drum) 杖鼓
Zhang Juzheng 張居正
Zhang Lu 張鹵
zhangshang (death in late teens) 長殤
Zhang Shicheng 張士誠
zhangshi si (administrator's office) 長史司
Zhang Tang 張湯
Zhang Yi 張益
Zhangzhou 漳州
zhangzi (senior son) 長子
Zhan Tong 詹同
zhaomu 昭穆
Zhaowa *guo* (Java) 爪洼國
zha wei (deception and counterfeit) 詐僞
Zhen (Saturn) 鎮
zhenfu (judge) 鎮撫
zheng (A, upper level of rank) 正
zheng (director, steward; principal official) 正官
Zheng He 鄭和
zhengong ju (sewing service) 針工局
zheng qianhu (battalion commander) 正千戶
zhenguo jiangjun (defender-general of the state) 鎮國將軍
zhenguo zhongwei (defender-commandant of the state) 鎮國中尉
zhengzhan (disputes over ownership) 爭
Zhenla *guo* (Cambodia) 眞蠟國
zhenjie (warnings) 箴戒

zhenren (chosen one) 眞人
zhenru (authentic scholar) 眞儒
zhidian jian (directorate for palace maintenance) 直殿監
zhifu geshanjin 指腹割衫襟
zhihou (usher) 祗侯
zhihui shi si (guard command) 指揮使司
zhishi (administrative clerk) 知事
zhiyin (seal keeper) 知印
Zhizhi 至治
zhizhi (rules of office, administrative regulations) 職制
Zhongguo falü yu Zhongguo shehui 中國法律與中國社會
Zhongguo fazhi shi lunlüe 中國法制史論略
zhonggu si (office of music) 鐘鼓司
zhongshang (death in early teens) 中殤
zhongshanzhuang 中山裝
zhongshi si (supervisory office) 中使司
zhongshu sheng (secretariat) 中書省
zhongsun (non-senior grandson) 衆孫
Zhongwen dacidian 中文大辭典
Zhongyong (Doctrine of the mean) 中庸
zhongzi (non-senior son) 衆子
Zhou li (Rites of Zhou) 周禮
Zhu Biao 朱標
Zhu Chun 朱椿
Zhu Di 朱棣
Zhu Shouqian 朱守謙
Zhusi zhizhang 諸司職掌
Zhu Xi 朱熹
Zhu Yuanzhang 朱元璋
Zhu Yuanzhang zhuan 朱元璋傳
Zhu Yunwen 朱允炆
Zhuzi jiali 朱子家禮
zi (elder sister) 姊
zi (viscount) 子
zicui (degree of mourning, hemmed sackcloth for three years) 齋衰
Zishi tongxun (Instructions to aid the world) 資世通訓
zisun weifan jiaoling (son or grandson violating instructions) 子孫違反教領
zong (lineage) 宗
zongmiao (ancestral temple) 宗廟
zongsun (second degree nephew, bss) 從孫
zouchai (agent) 奏差
zufu huangdi bixia (your majesty grandfather emperor) 祖父黃帝陛下

zumu huanghou dianxia (your majesty grandmother empress) 祖母黃殿下
zunsao huanghou dianxia (your majesty honorable elder sister-in-law empress) 尊嫂皇 殿下
zunzhang (person senior in generation or age) 尊長
zuoerguan (assistant magistrate) 佐貳官
zuo jiancheng (left supervisor) 左監丞
zuo shaojian (left vice director) 左少監
zuozang (receiving illgotten goods) 坐贓
zuo zhangshi (left administrator) 左長史
Zuozhuan 左傳
Zuxunlu 祖訓錄

INDEX

This index applies only to Chapters one through seven. Chinese terms occurring through the text, including the appendices, are listed with characters in the glossary.

SINICA LEIDENSIA

11. ZÜRCHER, E. *The Buddhist Conquest of China.* The Spread and Adaptation of Buddhism in Early Medieval China 1. Text. 2. Notes, Bibliography, Indexes. Reprint of the 1st (1959) ed.,. with additions and corrections. 1972. ISBN 90 04 03478 1
12/2. ACKER, W.R.B. (tr.). *Some T'ang and Pre-T'ang Texts on Chinese Painting.* With Annotations. Vol. II. Chang Yen-Yüan. *Li tai ming hua chi,* Chapters IV-X 1. Translation and Annotations. 2. Chinese text. 1974. ISBN 90 04 03938 4
13. IDEMA, W.L. (ed.). *Chinese Vernacular Fiction.* The Formative Period. 1974. ISBN 90 04 03974 0
15. IDEMA, W.L. (ed.). *Leyden Studies in Sinology.* Papers Presented at the Conference Held in Celebration of the Fiftieth Anniversary of the Sinological Institute of Leyden University, December 8-12, 1980. 1981. ISBN9004 06529 6
16. IDEMA, W.L. *The Dramatic Œvre of Chu Yu-Tun (1379-1439).* 1985. ISBN 90 04 07291 8
17. HULSEWÉ, A.F.P. *Remnants of Ch'in Law.* An Annotated Translation of the Ch'in Legal and Administrative Rules of the 3rd Century B.C. Discovered in Yün-meng Prefecture, Hu-pei Province, in 1975. 1985. ISBN 90 04 07103 2
18. HEER, PH. DE. *The Care-Taker Emperor.* Aspects of the Imperial Institute in Fifteenth-Century China As Reflected in the Political History of the Reign of Chu Chi'i-yü. 1986. ISBN 90 04 07898 3
19. STANDAERT, N. *Yang Tingyun, Confucian and Christian in Late Ming China.* His Life and Thought. 1987. ISBN 90 04 08127 5
20. ZURNDORFER, H.T. *Change and Continuity in Chinese Local History.* The Development of Hui-Chou Prefecture 800 to 1800. 1989. ISBN 90 04 08842 3
21. MANSVELT BECK, B.J. *The Treatises of Later Han.* Their Author, Sources, Contents and Place in Chinese Historiography. 1990. ISBN 90 04 08895 4
22. VERMEER, E.B. (ed.). *Development and Decline of Fukien Province in the 17th and 18th Centuries.* 1990. ISBN 90 04 09171 8
23. RUITENBEEK, K. *Carpentry and Building in Late Imperial China.* A Study of the Fifteenth-Century Carpenter's Manual *Lu Ban jing.* 1993. ISBN 90 04 09258 7
24. IDEMA, W.L. (ed.); ZÜRCHER, E. (ed.). *Thought and Law in Qin and Han China.* Studies Dedicated to Anthony Hulsewé on the Occasion of His Eightieth Birthday. 1990. ISBN 90 04 09269 2
26. HAAR, B.J. TER. *The White Lotus Teachings in Chinese Religious History.* 1992. ISBN 90 04 09414 8
27. YOSHIDA, T. *Salt Production Techniques in Ancient China.* The *Aobo Tu.* Translated and revised by H.U. VOGEL. 1993. ISBN 90 04 09657 4
28. HUANG CHUN-CHIEH (ed.); ZÜRCHER, E. (ed.). *Norms and the State in China.* 1993. ISBN 90 04 09665 5
29. BLUSSÉ, L. (ed.); ZURNDORFER, H.T. (ed.). *Conflict and Accommodation in Early Modern East Asia.* Essays in Honour of Erik Zürcher. 1993. ISBN 90 04 09775 9
30. MING-WOOD LIU, *Madhyamaka Thought in China.* 1994. ISBN 90 04 09984 0
31. EDWARDS, L.P. *Men and Women in Qing China.* Gender in *the Red Chamber Dream.* 1994. ISBN 90 04 10123 3

32. EIFRING, H. *Clause Combination in Chinese.* 1995. ISBN 90 04 10146 2
33. HUANG CHUN-CHIEH (ed.); ZÜRCHER, E. (ed.). *Time and Space in Chinese Culture.* 1995. ISBN 90 04 10287 6
34. FARMER, E.L. *Zhu Yuanzhang and Early Ming Legislation.* The Reordering of Chinese Society following the Era of Mongol Rule. 1995. ISBN 90 04 10391 0